Planning for Protraction
A Historically Informed Approach to Great-power War and Sino-US Competition

Iskander Rehman

Planning for Protraction
A Historically Informed Approach to Great-power War and Sino-US Competition

Iskander Rehman

IISS The International Institute for Strategic Studies

The International Institute for Strategic Studies
Arundel House | 6 Temple Place | London | WC2R 2PG | UK

First published November 2023 by **Routledge**
4 Park Square, Milton Park, Abingdon, Oxon, OX14 4RN

for **The International Institute for Strategic Studies**
Arundel House, 6 Temple Place, London, WC2R 2PG, UK
www.iiss.org

Simultaneously published in the USA and Canada by **Routledge**
52 Vanderbilt Avenue, New York, NY 10017

Routledge is an imprint of Taylor & Francis, an Informa Business

© 2023 The International Institute for Strategic Studies

DIRECTOR-GENERAL AND CHIEF EXECUTIVE Dr Bastian Giegerich
SERIES EDITOR Dr Benjamin Rhode
ASSOCIATE EDITOR Alice Aveson
EDITORIAL Gregory Brooks, Christopher Harder, Graham Ivory, Kevin Jewell, Jill Lally, Grainne Lucey-Tremblay, Michael Marsden, Adam Walters
PRODUCTION Alessandra Beluffi, Ravi Gopar, Jade Panganiban, James Parker, Kelly Verity
COVER PICTURE John Northcote Nash/Alamy Stock Photo

The International Institute for Strategic Studies is an independent centre for research, information and debate on the problems of conflict, however caused, that have, or potentially have, an important military content. The Council and Staff of the Institute are international and its membership is drawn from almost 100 countries. The Institute is independent and it alone decides what activities to conduct. It owes no allegiance to any government, any group of governments or any political or other organisation. The IISS stresses rigorous research with a forward-looking policy orientation and places particular emphasis on bringing new perspectives to the strategic debate.

The Institute's publications are designed to meet the needs of a wider audience than its own membership and are available on subscription, by mail order and in good bookshops. Further details at www.iiss.org.

British Library Cataloguing in Publication Data
A catalogue record for this book is available from the British Library

Library of Congress Cataloging in Publication Data

ADELPHI series
ISSN 1944-5571

ADELPHI AP496–497
ISBN 978-1-032-73477-4

Contents

AUTHOR

Iskander Rehman is an Ax:son Johnson Institute for Statecraft and Diplomacy Postdoctoral Fellow at the Henry A. Kissinger Center for Global Affairs, Johns Hopkins School of Advanced International Studies. He is also the Senior Fellow for Strategic Studies at the American Foreign Policy Council (AFPC), which he joined in July 2020. His work focuses on applied history, grand strategy and US defence strategy in Asia. Dr Rehman is also the founder of the Rochambeau Dialogue, a Track 1.5 Franco-US defence dialogue held every year in Newport, Rhode Island.

Prior to joining the AFPC, Dr Rehman was the Senior Fellow for International Relations at the Pell Center for International Relations and Public Policy, Salve Regina University, in Newport, Rhode Island. Over the course of his career, he has held fellowships at a number of think tanks, including the Brookings Institution, the Center for Strategic and Budgetary Assessments, the Carnegie Endowment for International Peace and the German Marshall Fund of the United States. Dr Rehman has also lived and worked in India, holding visiting fellowships at the Observer Research Foundation and at the Manohar Parrikar Institute for Defense Studies and Analyses, both in New Delhi. He has published a number of think-tank monographs, book chapters and articles in journals such as *Survival*, the *Washington Quarterly*, the *Naval War College Review*, *Asian Security*, *India Review* and *Texas National Security Review*. He is a contributing editor and regular writer for War on the Rocks, and his work has featured or been cited in the *Guardian*, the *American Interest*, the *Financial Times*, *Engelsberg Ideas*, *The Economist*, the *Indian Express*, *Le Monde*, the *Diplomat*, the *National Interest* and *BBC World*, amongst others. Dr Rehman holds a PhD, with distinction, from the Institute of Political Studies (Sciences Po) in Paris.

ACKNOWLEDGEMENTS

For Doctor Alim John Rehman

Research for this book was made possible, in part, through the support of the Office of Net Assessment, Office of the US Secretary of Defense, US Department of Defense. I am grateful for its permission to publish elements of the earlier unpublished study from which this book evolved.

CHAPTER ONE

Planning for protraction

US defence planning and the China challenge

For much of the US defence commentariat, it has become evident that the early twenty-first century constitutes something of an interstitial age – one marked by the advent of disruptive technologies, the rise of aggressive authoritarian challengers and the twilight of the unipolar era. Both the Trump-era 2017 National Security Strategy (NSS) and the 2018 National Defense Strategy (NDS) had stressed the need to refocus on 'inter-state strategic competition' after almost two decades of costly nation-building and counter-terrorism efforts.[1] The Biden administration's recently published NSS and NDS place a similar emphasis on great-power rivalry, all while accentuating to a greater degree the importance of deft alliance management, and a robust and innovative industrial policy.[2] Meanwhile, a series of administrations have tasked the US armed forces with reprioritising their ability to prevail in a high-intensity conflict against a peer or near-peer adversary, and with devising innovative operational concepts that can mitigate, or overcome, the challenges to their ability to achieve rapid battlefield dominance in contested regions around the globe. Several recent events, however, from the severe supply-chain and workforce disruptions experienced during the COVID-19 pandemic to the war in Ukraine, with its prodigious consumption of munitions, have heightened concerns in US defence circles over the nation's state of preparedness for future wars.[3]

Russia's brutal invasion of a neighbouring sovereign country may currently dominate the headlines, as well as the daily agendas of US national-security managers, but Beijing's military expansionism, calcifying authoritarianism and bellicose regional behaviour are cause for even deeper concern. From its militarisation of disputed islets in the South China Sea to its unabashed use of economic coercion against countries ranging from South Korea to Australia and Mongolia, China has become ever more assertive in its near abroad.[4]

Meanwhile, Beijing's long-standing model of authoritarian governance – centred on collective decision-making and an orderly succession process – has precipitously crumbled.[5] President Xi Jinping's shift toward a strongman style of rule has been accompanied by an evolution of Chinese discourse and internal politics, all of which points to a more combative, jingoistic and embattled regime.[6] Washington's concerns over the People's Republic of China's (PRC) trajectory have been compounded by certain disquieting signals that its urge to forcibly reshape the regional order – most notably with regard to the long-festering issue of Taiwan – has been steadily growing, and may now be reaching boiling point.[7] Ever-growing numbers of People's Liberation Army Air Force (PLAAF) combat aircraft routinely violate Taiwan's air defence identification zone, and in August 2022, the PLA staged three days of intense live-fire drills around and over Taiwan, seemingly to signal its displeasure at former US House of Representatives speaker Nancy Pelosi's visit to Taipei the same month.

More generally, the exponential shift of the cross-strait military balance in Beijing's favour appears to have led to a dangerous degree of Chinese self-confidence. One analyst argues that while 'Chinese leaders used to view a military campaign to take the island as a fantasy, now they consider it a real possibility'.[8] Beijing's temptation to use force – whether over Taiwan or another regional territorial dispute – may also be exacerbated by its leadership's desire to seize what it deems to be a critical window of opportunity in the evolution of global geopolitics.[9] Indeed, China, for all its public expressions of triumphalism, may well have reached the apex of its ascendant trajectory, before a combination of severe challenges – socio-economic, demographic and environmental – conspire to arrest its march toward regional hegemony, as this study will explore in greater depth.[10] Like many other anxiety-ridden revisionist powers throughout history, Beijing may consider a preventive war to be a risk worth taking.[11]

These grim regional atmospherics have engendered a new-found sense of urgency within Washington's sprawling national-security establishment. Indeed, as the foreboding tone of the current administration's NSS indicates, there is now a clear bipartisan consensus that the PRC constitutes the United States' most formidable long-term competitor – or, to employ current US Department of Defense (DOD) jargon, its prime 'pacing threat'.[12] As the White House-issued NSS notes:

> Russia and the PRC pose different challenges. Russia poses an immediate threat to the free and open international system, recklessly flouting the basic laws of the international order today, as its brutal war of aggression against Ukraine has shown. The PRC, by contrast, is the only competitor with both the intent to reshape the international order and, increasingly,

the economic, diplomatic, military, and technological power to advance that objective.[13]

At the same time, there is a growing recognition that some of the key assumptions that have undergirded US force planning and defence doctrine throughout much of the post-Cold War era – most notably the notion that technology-fuelled advances in combat velocity will automatically lead to great-power wars that are shorter, sharper and more localised – may no longer prove valid.[14] Indeed, an increasing number of knowledgeable observers have begun to warn that, to the contrary, armed conflict with a Eurasian behemoth as large, wealthy and militarily redoubtable as China could morph into something very different: a protracted struggle that also evolves into a gruelling war of attrition, spanning multiple theatres and drawing on all dimensions of national power.[15] As former DOD planner Jim Mitre has noted, in any future great-power war, the US military 'will have to endure loss, will have to compete for domain advantages, and will have to confront greater uncertainty regarding the pace and scope of conflict', adding that the 2018 NDS he helped write 'presumes greater attention to protracted conflicts with great powers and mobilization of personnel and materiel needs beyond the Active Component'.[16] Similarly, one of the Pentagon's more recently developed war-fighting concepts, the so-called 'Expanded Maneuver Concept', draws attention to the issue of contested logistics, thus tacitly acknowledging the potential for a more drawn-out and geographically extended conflict – a war 'contested in all domains and spread across a large and potentially non-contiguous area', which would severely stress the United States' ability to rapidly reinforce, sustain and resupply forward-deployed assets in Asia.[17]

The enduring allure of short, sharp wars

And yet, despite this growing realisation of the potential for protraction, US and Chinese military doctrines still place an overwhelming emphasis on 'blinding campaigns', on rapidly seizing the initiative, and on combat celerity in an era marked by the diffusion of precision strike and an increased dependence on exquisite, multilayered C4ISR networks.[18] Indeed, as one close observer of the Sino-US security dynamic notes, 'Chinese and American operational preferences are remarkably similar – both put a premium on striking first and controlling the initiative'.[19] (And this despite the fact that the PRC has its own rich tradition of thinking on protracted warfare, defence-in-depth and people's war.)[20] Since the end of the Cold War, America's war-fighting philosophy – from the network-centric warfare of the 1990s and early 2000s to the rich smorgasbord of multi-domain operational concepts under development today – has sought to exploit the power of data and information technologies to burn through the fog and friction of war, all while maintaining the ability to pre-emptively neutralise a lesser adversary's defensive capabilities.[21] The DOD's current grand umbrella concept – the Joint All-Domain Command and Control (JADC2) strategy – thus repeatedly refers to the need to 'accelerate decision-making', to 'act inside an adversary's decision cycle' and to 'operate faster relative to adversary abilities'.[22] As US Naval War College professor Nina Kollars mordantly observes:

> the physical battlespace is being reimagined into a networked informatic system of systems: a kind of multi-dimensioned, semi-automated lethal information processor. It is a peculiarly narrow perspective. Future warfighting systems centred on information technology, in theory, achieve victory by equating

the complexity of warfare with the complexity of data processing … Battlefield dominance becomes synonymous with algorithmic dominance. It is a dream of war at information speed.[23]

This focus on speed, and on the associated ability to bludgeon one's way into a dazed opponent's OODA (observe–orient–decide–act) loop, thus unlocking an irreversible military momentum, is very much shared by Chinese defence planners.[24] Indeed, the PLA's concept of 'system destruction warfare' emphasises the need to rapidly and systematically dismantle the adversary's information networks, which it equates to nerve centres, noting, for example, in the 2013 Science of Military Strategy, that:

in the military field, computer-centred network systems serve as the nerve centres of modern military forces and military activity, and interlink the various operational strengths, as well as military activity of different types and in different spaces, into an organic integrated whole, which is a decisive factor and basic condition in the transformation of the form-state of war into informationized war.[25]

Interestingly, China's concept of system destruction warfare appears closely tied to its perceptions of escalation management, or 'war control'.[26] Indeed, Chinese military writings suggest that by rapidly taking the initiative and hamstringing the enemy's system-of-systems through both kinetic and non-kinetic means, the PLA can prevail in a 'localized war under informationized conditions' without incurring the human and military costs of a more protracted and expansive campaign of attrition.[27] As the sinologists John Costello and Peter Mattis have shrewdly observed, these technology-driven concepts have been neatly bolted onto earlier, Maoist tenets of asymmetric warfare, with Mao Zedong having famously written about the need to 'seal up the enemy's eyes and ears ... and make them blind and deaf ... confusing the minds of their commanders and turning them into madmen, using this to achieve our own victory'.[28]

It is impossible, however, for the military historian, when parsing such statements, not to be reminded of even earlier advocacies of targeted paralysis over widespread attrition – and of neatly choreographed and time-bound sequences of operation over messy, protracted bouts of bloodletting. Indeed, Washington and Beijing's shared focus on 'blinding' or 'paralysing' campaigns – complete with their colourful visualisations of the adversary as a biological entity complete with a brain and nervous system – is strongly reminiscent of the writings of prominent British advocates of manoeuvre warfare during the interwar years.[29] For veterans of the trench warfare of the First World War such as Basil Liddell Hart and J.F.C. Fuller, the 'dislocation' or 'paralysis' of the adversary was to be prioritised over its physical destruction. Not only were such swiftly and surgically conducted campaigns deemed more cost-effective in terms of men and materiel – they were also framed as conducive to war termination.

The devastating psychological impact of a crippling assault on the command-and-control apparatus of a bewildered foe, it was posited, would help precipitate the latter's surrender. Thus Liddell Hart argued that 'a strategist should think in terms of paralyzing, not of killing', whether that was by terrifying an individual enemy soldier into becoming an agent of panic, psychologically paralysing an opposing commander, or applying 'psychological pressure on the government of a country [which] may suffice to cancel all the resources at its command so that the sword drops from a paralyzed hand'.[30]

Whereas for Fuller and Liddell Hart mechanised deep thrusts constituted the prime vectors of enemy dislocation, twenty-first-century planners visualise such a role being fulfilled via intricately assembled reconnaissance-strike complexes, with close-knit networks of sensors and platforms standing ready to disgorge tightly focused pulses of military power at a moment's notice. What happens, though, when two such battle networks' interlocking fields of fire are arrayed against each other, like two nervously twitching duellists facing off in an ice-rimed field in a Tolstoy novel?[31]

Amid a high-stakes military crisis, each party would find itself under extreme pressure to seize the first-mover advantage by initiating a pre-emptive assault on its opponent's C4ISR architecture. Operating under a shared 'cult of the offensive', and riven with similar 'use it or lose it' anxieties, China and the US could thus find themselves almost instantaneously catapulted into the throes of a 'mutual blinding' campaign.[32] The question – and one that remains insufficiently addressed – is what happens the next day, once both battered, sensorially impaired pugilists groggily face off in a newly casualty-stricken and communications-degraded environment?

Thinking beyond the first salvo

As two US military strategists caustically note, 'in operational planning, there is a stark contrast between stunning an enemy into submission and killing him'.[33] Moreover, it has been shown that pre-emptive or surprise attacks have a way of hardening an opponent's resolve and of impeding, rather than encouraging, war termination. One of the most well-known examples remains the infamous Japanese attack on Pearl Harbor in December 1941, after which 'the American people reeled with a mind-staggering mixture of surprise, awe, mystification, grief, humiliation, and above all, cataclysmic fury'.[34] Japanese planners were fully aware of the material superiority of the US, but chose to gamble on its reluctance to underwrite and sustain a protracted war thousands of miles from its shores, especially once the residually isolationist great power had experienced such a devastating first strike on its power-projection capabilities.[35] However, rather than strong-arming a chastened US into negotiating a compromise settlement with Japan in Asia, as some Japanese planners had foolishly projected, the Pearl Harbor attack united America's people in a grim determination to annihilate the regime in Tokyo.

And yet, due to the operational premium placed on seizing the initiative, there is a high probability that, in times of extreme tension, one party in the Sino-US rivalry would seek to employ the element of surprise to pre-emptively kneecap their opponent, thus potentially fostering the psychological and political conditions for further escalation and protraction. Firstly, authoritarian regimes appear, in general, to demonstrate a greater proclivity toward resorting to pre-emption and surprise in conflict, in part due to their more cramped and vertical internal decision-making arrangements.[36] And secondly, the PLA, whose thinking on matters of escalation appears singularly underdeveloped, has its own uniquely rich history of seeking to leverage the effects of surprise in conflict, as it did during the Korean War, the 1962 Sino-Indian War and the 1979 Sino-Vietnamese War.[37] In the context of a contemporary Taiwan invasion scenario, Beijing's desire to pre-empt and/or deny the arrival of US follow-on forces to the theatre of operations would act as a particularly powerful incentive for the Chinese to strike first, to strike fast and to strike hard.[38] Furthermore, one of the lessons that China may have drawn from Russia's early failures in Ukraine – and notably Moscow's failure to immediately neutralise President Volodymyr Zelenskyy and his close entourage – is the need to act as brutally and swiftly as possible to decapitate Taiwan's leadership and dismember

Image 1: **US War Production Board poster following the Japanese attack on Pearl Harbor, 1942**

(Smith Collection/Gado/Getty Images)

its institutions, so as to impede the emergence of an organised and internationally popular resistance movement on the island. Indeed, such concerns could act as yet another potent accelerant on Chinese thinking in times of crisis.[39]

Judging from historical experience, any pre-emptive attack on US military platforms, installations and sovereign territory (should the PLA target bases in locations such as Guam) would immediately fuel the American people's desire for punitive, larger-scale retaliation, leaving Washington little choice but to escalate both vertically and horizontally. In sum, some of the measures, strategies and operational concepts designed to avoid or forestall the prospect of a protracted war could – somewhat perversely – help advance that very outcome. Neither the political nor the operational dimensions of the Sino-US security dynamic render a short, sharp war very likely.

While the opening phases of a high-intensity conflict are critical, they are rarely determinative. Temporarily crippled opponents can recuperate, reknit the sinews of their strength and wade back into the arena to reprise hostilities. Indeed, little in the history of great-power war would suggest that such momentous conflicts can be resolved in the aftermath of a first volley, however surgical, devastating or demoralising. There are inherent risks to overly focusing on the blistering choreography of the opening salvo. Indeed, as Antulio Echevarria presciently observed at the turn of the century, the new American way of war, with its intense emphasis on speed and precision firepower, can occasionally appear excessively geared toward fighting 'wars as if they were battles', and thus risks confusing 'the winning of campaigns or small-scale actions with the winning of wars'.[40] An equal, if not greater, degree of attention should therefore be placed on the study of the less operationally absorbing – but more deliberate – tempo of protracted warfare, and on prevailing at the end of a drain-ing marathon rather than an intense opening sprint.

Naturally, in the event of any Sino-US military conflagra-tion, much would depend on the stakes and circumstances of the conflict in question, on the core calculations of each country's respective leaderships, and on the extent of each belligerent's gains or losses incurred during the war's initial mutual blinding phase.[41] The US should certainly fret over the possibility of a Chinese fait accompli – that is, a military action so sudden, seamlessly executed and overwhelming in its sheer force that it is rendered irreversible, thus ending the conflict in its opening stages – but it would be imprudent, given the history of great-power wars, to sideline the far greater poten-tial for protraction.[42] In all likelihood, intra-war pressures would lead to an expansion not only in the scale and scope of the confrontation, but also in its duration.

Throughout history, short-war thinking has all too often run aground on the jagged shoals of political reality, with states repeatedly underestimating the amount of pain and devastation their determined adversaries could absorb prior to even contem-plating surrender.[43] After much expenditure of blood and treasure, war termination is rendered all the more elusive by the desire to honour sunk costs, and by the resultant escalation of commitments serving to justify earlier military investments and sacrifices.[44] As Fred Iklé has noted, 'the greater the enemy's effort and costs in fighting for a war, the more will he become commit-ted to his own conditions for peace, thus rendering the prospect of any mutually acceptable resolution all the more difficult'.[45] Protraction also tends to breed brutality, whether through delib-erate or inadvertent escalation, as increasingly frustrated and vengeful antagonists progressively jettison their self-imposed operational restrictions and moral reservations, ratcheting up levels of aggression before eventually engaging in total warfare.

As medievalists have shown, the frustrations borne out of drawn-out conflicts, and sieges in particular, would frequently result in horrific norm-shattering acts of violence, even by the ruthless standards of the time. One particularly ignominious example is the sack, in the early stages of the Cathar (or Albigensian) Crusades, of the fortified southern French town of Béziers – a 'calculated act of terror' during which it was estimated that up to 20,000 civilians were put to the sword within only a few hours. Another is Henry V's slaughter of unarmed prisoners at the Battle of Agincourt in 1415.[46]

Infamously, on 22 April 1915, the German armed forces, in violation of the Hague Convention of 1899, introduced poison gas to the Western Front, deploying more than 170 tonnes of chlorine gas from thousands of cylinders positioned along a four-mile stretch of trenches. French and British outrage led to their developing and employing their own chemical arsenal.[47] During the Second World War, despite some countries' prior moral qualms, all parties engaged in unrestricted submarine warfare and mass aerial bombardment of civilian targets.[48] More recently, during the eight years of the Iran–Iraq War – the most protracted inter-state war of the twentieth century – both parties descended into increasingly gruesome levels of savagery, with Iraq employing chemical weapons on a mass scale, and Iran dispatching thousands of child soldiers to clear minefields and storm Iraqi machine-gun nests.[49] Such escalating spirals of brutality – particularly if they are seen to have been triggered by a major violation of pre-existing cultural norms – naturally also only fuel protraction, by rendering a mutually acceptable settlement all the more elusive, thus spawning something of a vicious circle. In short, the longer a conflict lasts, the harder it is to bring it to a mutually satisfactory and decisive close.

Image 2: **Iranian child soldier Hassan Jangju, 1980**

(Alfred Yaghobzadeh)

Attrition as the historical norm

For all these reasons, prolonged campaigns of debilitating attrition have been the norm rather than the exception throughout the history of great-power war, with a bitter resolution only achieved once the exsanguinated loser collapsed under the weight of its own moral, financial and physical exhaustion, often succumbing at the same time to internal unrest or political upheaval.[50] As Cathal Nolan notes in his magisterial recent history of Western warfare:

> Exhaustion of morale and materiel rather than finality through battles marks the endgames of many wars. Even of most wars. Almost always of wars among the major powers in any era. This was especially true for the largest states struggling for military and political primacy in the modern era, for the Great Powers that seemed best able to sustain the

enormous efforts and cost of the biggest wars fought to exhaustion all the same.[51]

Even then, a peace bloodily acquired may prove to be only ephemeral. Whether during the Hundred Years War, the Punic Wars, or the Franco-German wars of the late nineteenth to mid-twentieth centuries, great powers have consistently refused to embrace a lasting peace in the absence of a final resolution – either crushingly imposed or grudgingly accepted – of the war's core underlying causes. Truces can be employed tactically or serve as a means of partial recuperation, allowing haggard competitors the time to catch a ragged breath and quietly sharpen their dulled blades. As the great late French medievalist Philippe Contamine remarks in his landmark study of the Hundred Years War, temporary peace arrangements between England and France could paradoxically elongate, rather than shorten, their hostilities, as they

> provided an opportunity for the protagonists to regain their breath. Partial or general truces, whether tacitly accepted or legally formalized, were part of the great respiratory rhythm of war, they allowed for its prolongation. ... The diminution of the quantity of troops, the economic enfeeblement of both parties, the reduction in fiscal revenue – none of this sufficed to put a durable halt to the war – it would continue to be waged, come what may, but simply via more modest means and manpower.[52]

The fact that so many bipolar military confrontations have been such drawn-out, spasmodic affairs has rendered their precise periodisation somewhat challenging. Indeed, when should a staggered series of conflicts be categorised as one larger war?[53] For example, should the long period stretching from the Franco-Prussian War of 1870–71 to the end of the Second World War be considered as one long Franco-German war? Or could one range back even further, at the risk of descending into casuistry? After all, if Otto von Bismarck insisted on holding the proclamation of the German Reich in the mirrored halls of Versailles, with its walls festooned with paintings of seventeenth-century French campaigns across the Rhine, it was out of revenge for what he perceived as generations, if not centuries, of French military arrogance and predations on German soil, from Louis XIV to the battle of Jena.[54] Meanwhile, the 116 years of brutal, yet intermittent, conflict that raged between the kingdoms of France and England from 1337 to 1453 only acquired its famed, unifying moniker of the 'Hundred Years War' in the nineteenth century.[55] Furthermore, within a competitive dyad, one rival may have a wildly divergent perception of the temporal span of the conflict than the other. For instance, did the Cold War ever truly end for Vladimir Putin and his ideological bedfellows among the *siloviki*, many of whom formerly served alongside him in the KGB?[56]

Historiographical quibbling aside, these debates serve to highlight a broader issue in the history of peer-to-peer military rivalry: the difficulty of bringing such confrontations, once initiated, to a decisive close. Indeed, as the great Greek historian Polybius wryly observed on the causes of the revived Romano-Carthaginian hostilities in the lead-up to the Second Punic War: if the tumorous roots of a bipolar rivalry are not forcibly extirpated, conflict will almost inevitably metastasise once more. Statesmen should 'observe when it is that men come to terms under pressure of circumstances and when owing to their spirit being broken'. 'In the former case', he added, decision-makers may regard their former foes as simply 'reserving themselves for a favourable opportunity and be constantly on their guard', whereas in he latter they could allow themselves to eventually 'trust them as true friends'.[57]

As the Ancients well knew, questions of national 'spirit', morale and resiliency are at the heart of any examination of protracted great-power competition.[58] So are proud societies' collective appetite for retribution following the trauma of defeat, occupation or national humiliation.[59] The very origin of the word 'revanchism', now so habitually employed to characterise the foreign policies of revisionist state actors, was in 1870s France in the aftermath of its crushing defeat in the Franco-Prussian War. Deriving from the French word *revanche* (revenge), it came to designate the widely shared desire for retaliation against Germany, and most notably the French Third Republic's burning ambition to recapture the annexed provinces of Alsace and Lorraine.[60]

Protracted war, non-instrumental factors and the 'forgotten dimensions of strategy'

This points to yet another key issue in the study of protracted warfare: the importance of understanding its ideological drivers, underpinnings and characteristics. Indeed, one of the key reasons why many enduring rivalries exist in the first place is precisely because pre-existing ideational divergences, including non-instrumental motives, frustrate compromise and preclude any meaningful mutual accommodation.[61] For instance, one cannot comprehend England's multigenerational rivalry with France during the Hundred Years War without taking into consideration the potency of England's Angevin revanchism on the one hand and France's sense of royal exceptionalism on the other.[62] Similarly, one cannot come to a proper understanding of Franco-Spanish statecraft during the Italian Wars of 1494–1559 without acknowledging that both powers' competing grand

Image 3: *La Tache Noire (The Black Stain)* **by Albert Bettannier, 1887**

(The Picture Art Collection/Alamy Stock Photo. The 1887 painting *La Tache Noire (The Black Stain)* by Albert Bettannier, showing French schoolboys learning about the territories of Alsace–Lorraine, lost in the aftermath of the Franco-Prussian War, and depicted by a black stain on the schoolmaster's map.)

strategies of primacy were often undergirded by millenarian and messianistic belief systems.[63] The current Sino-US relationship is characterised by a stark ideational divide, and these fault lines will, in all likelihood, expand ever further under the ideologically charged tenure of Xi Jinping. In the event of an actual conflict, these fundamental differences in world view would heighten misunderstandings and suspicion, encourage diplomatic maximalism and render the prospect of rapidly reaching a mutually acceptable peace settlement more challenging.

In addition to grappling with the question of competing ideologies, it is crucial to gain a clearer sense of some of the less immediately tangible aspects of the competition, or of what Michael Howard termed the 'forgotten dimensions of strategy', that is, its societal aspects.[64] What are the wellsprings of strength, resourcefulness and cohesion within each belligerent polity, and, conversely, what are its sources of weakness, stagnation and division? Perhaps most importantly for the purposes of this study, which society seems better poised to weather the effects of a protracted great-power war?

All these questions are in dire need of examination. Indeed, while the higher potential for protraction in a Sino-US conflict is certainly acknowledged in certain quarters of the United States' strategic community, its broader ramifications have yet to receive a sufficient degree of analytical attention.[65] Indeed, whereas during the Cold War, defence intellectuals devoted substantial attention to prevailing in the long 'twilight struggle' against the Soviet Union and to planning across varied time horizons, current thinking on protracted competition – let alone on the issue of protracted warfare – remains somewhat underdeveloped.[66] Indeed, one could argue that signalling to the Soviets the possibility of and risks tied to protraction was formerly cemented into the very foundations of Western conventional deterrence, and that providing for the requisite mobilisation and sustainment base for such a conflict featured at the heart of US grand-strategy documents.[67]

Contemporary security managers, however, are not animated by a similar sense of clarity or purpose. Indeed, much of the US strategic community has yet to move from a clear diagnosis of contemporary geopolitical ills – as encapsulated by much of the fretful commentary on the revival of geopolitical competition or on a 'new Cold War' with China – to actual prescriptive guidance as to how Washington and its allies should revise and/or tailor its grand strategy accordingly.[68]

This should not necessarily come as a surprise. Defence planning can be singularly challenging in times of relative uncertainty, and grand strategic adaptation – a complex process that hinges not only upon successful material rebalancing efforts but also on broader societal and intellectual shifts – is never instantaneous.[69] This *Adelphi* book seeks to aid in this collective process of mental adjustment by providing an empirically grounded study of protracted great-power war. By engaging in an exercise of applied history, the report will aim to tease out certain shared principles, or common explanatory factors, of past great-power actors' successes or failures in protracted warfare – with an eye to applying these various insights to the current Sino-US military competition.

For centuries, a solid grounding in history has been considered essential to the planning and prosecution of military strategy. Not only does the study of warfare across space and time greatly enrich the inherently bounded experience of any one country or military organisation; it also helps refine individual security managers' ability to process information, manage complexity, and detect patterns of cause and effect.[70] From Julius Caesar, who famously obsessed over every aspect of Alexander the Great's Eurasia-sweeping campaigns, to General George Patton, who lugged a personal library of hundreds of custom-bound works of ancient history across the battlefields of the Second World War, a deep immersion in past rivalries, conflicts and battles has traditionally been perceived as contributing to the development of what Carl von Clausewitz called the *coup d'oeil* – the 'flexibility of mind' that allows the military planner, in the face of adversity and uncertainty, to adapt and reshape 'events on their own terms'.[71] Perhaps most importantly, it helps inculcate in the harried, self-important decision-maker a welcome degree of humility and perspective – along with an understanding that the more fundamental aspects of great-power politics have not changed all that much, or at least not as much as one may initially have been led to believe. And then, of course, there is history's more classically didactic function: the desire to learn directly from the past, draw instructive parallels or, at a minimum, not blindly stumble through the same errors as one's predecessors. For Polybius, there were thus 'two ways by which all men can reform themselves, the one through their own mischances, the other through those of others, and of these the former is the more impressive, but the latter less hurtful'.[72] Making a similar point, albeit with his own characteristic bluntness, former US secretary of defense (and retired Marine general) Jim Mattis recently quipped that all military officers should study history, if only because 'learning from others' mistakes is far smarter than putting your own lads in body bags'.[73]

In addition to casting light on enduring truths and recurring trends, applied history can help identify certain key discontinuities. The advent of the atomic age constituted one such intellectual revolution in the history of strategy. The ever-deepening integration of next-generation cyber capabilities and artificial intelligence (AI) into military planning may well presage another. For all of these reasons, therefore, it remains vital to take a historically informed approach to the study of contemporary military dynamics, and to extend one's analytical focus, as General Douglas MacArthur once exhorted, not only to those relatively recent, well-known conflicts 'still reeking with the scent of the battle', but also to those 'dust-buried accounts of wars long past', whose study has, sadly, all too often fallen into abeyance within the defence policymaking community.[74] The utility of engaging in such an intellectual exercise is very much acknowledged in Beijing, and by the PLA in particular, whose analysts regularly carry out granular analyses of past conflicts ranging from the period of Sun Tzu and the Warring States to the Pacific campaigns of the Second World War, the 1982 Falklands War and the First Gulf War, to name but a few.[75]

In accordance with the tradition of net assessments, the analysis presented in this book is comprehensive and multi-disciplinary in nature, and focuses on identifying key areas

of asymmetry or competitive advantage.[76] It seeks to eluci-
date both short- and long-term trends in the US–China rivalry
and assumes that this rivalry is interactive rather than static.
Its findings are intended, first and foremost, to form an aid to
judgement, and thus – in line with past exercises in net assessment – to be more diagnostic than openly prescriptive.[77]

The remainder of this book is divided into two major chapters. Chapter Two provides a historically informed analysis of
protracted warfare, its core drivers and characteristics, and an
examination of the following components or patterns of behaviour that appear to have consistently had the most impact on a
great-power competitor's long-term strategic performance:

1. Military effectiveness and adaptability
2. Socio-economic power and resiliency
3. Grand strategy and diplomatic dexterity

While for purposes of clarity and readability the collected
insights fall under the aegis of this tripartite structure, it is
important to note that – due to the all-encompassing, whole-
of-government character of any protracted great-power war
– these domains or lines of effort naturally bleed into each
other and form complementary rather than competing levels
of analysis.

Chapter Three will draw on this same triadic framework to
provide a detailed and structured assessment of the contemporary Sino-US rivalry, with the aim of providing a detailed
diagnosis of how both parties are currently positioned to
compete and/or prevail in the event of a protracted war. The
analysis will also draw attention to some of the novel and
significant differentiating aspects of a putative Sino-US war,
most notably its nuclear and cyber dimensions. It will be argued
that while strategic planners should naturally be concerned
with the risk of inadvertent nuclear escalation, this risk does

not obviate the need to reflect on the potential dynamics of protracted conflict. Indeed, the very fact that neither great-power competitor appears to perceive the nuclear dimension of their rivalry as constituting a major impediment to the pros-ecution of large-scale and ambitious military strategies would suggest that the potential for a conventional war has not been erased, in and of itself, by their possession of nuclear weapons.

The book will then conclude both by distilling some of its core insights, and by providing some modest suggestions as to avenues for follow-on research and inquiry.

CHAPTER TWO

Great-power success in protracted warfare: key drivers and core components

Military effectiveness and adaptability

Cycles of action and counteraction

Protracted conflicts are extended cycles of action, counter-action and experiential learning. As a result, the ability of a belligerent to adapt rapidly and decisively – whether in terms of training, tactics or overarching military strategy – is critical.[1] While peacetime innovation can certainly help foster an environment more conducive to wartime adaptability, it is essential to note that the two phenomena are distinct. Successful peacetime innovators can be poor wartime adapters, and vice versa.[2] Indeed, one should not necessarily assume that a competitor with little experience in one aspect of warfare is incapable, under the galvanising pressures of combat, of rapidly overcoming its earlier deficiencies.

An instructive case study in this regard is that of the Roman Republic, and its remarkable maritime transformation over the course of the First Punic War (264–41 BCE).[3] At the outset of the conflict, Carthage enjoyed a stark maritime superiority over its Roman adversary. Over centuries, the North African trading state had consolidated its position as the premier naval power of the Western Mediterranean, with its heavily armed flotillas roaming the most busily trafficked sea lanes and waterways at will. The Carthaginian people could boast a long and proud seafaring tradition, and their naval engineers, with their fine-grained knowledge of shipbuilding technology, were second to none. In contrast, Rome had traditionally been a land-bound power, with little expertise or experience in maritime warfare or amphibious operations. In 311 BCE, the Roman Senate had made a first, abortive attempt to form a small navy optimised for coastal defence, before abandoning its somewhat desultory efforts and delegating the development of naval capabilities to Rome's newly acquired southern Italian allies.[4]

There was also a marked technological gap between the antagonists, with the fledgling Roman navy still only floating triremes – an earlier, lighter class of vessels than the Carthaginian fleet's hulking quinqueremes.[5] As tensions rose in the lead-up to the First Punic War, Carthage felt understandably confident in its ability to retain command of the sea, and thus to deter its Roman rival from further meddling in Sicily's convoluted politics. Famously, the Carthaginian general Hanno imperiously warned the Romans to withdraw their forces from the island and not inflame the situation further, for otherwise they 'would not dare to even wash their hands in the sea', for fear of Carthaginian naval retribution.[6] The Greek historian Diodorus Siculus later provided his own memorable rendering (or perhaps reimagining) of the Roman consul Appius Claudius's defiant response, which stressed Rome's ability to engage in intra-war adaptation:

> The Romans, for their part, advised the Carthaginians
> not to teach them to meddle with maritime affairs,
> since the Romans, so they asserted, were pupils who

always outstripped their masters. … So now, should
the Carthaginians compel them to learn naval warfare,
they would soon see that the pupils had become superior to their teachers.[7]

And indeed, when Diodorus Siculus was compiling his
Bibliotheca Historica (Library of History) a full century after the
fall of Carthage, the Roman military had repeatedly displayed
a striking proclivity for selective emulation and experimen-
tation: adopting and adapting, amongst other items, Spanish
short swords (the *gladius*), Celtiberian throwing spears (the
heavy *pilum*), Gallic helmets (the *Coolus*-design helmet) and
Gallic saddles (the four-horned saddle).[8]

At the beginning of the Punic Wars, however, vanishingly
few observers would have been able to express the same degree
of self-confidence as Appius Claudius in Diodorus's narrative,
or predict that within only a few years, Rome's mariners would
decisively wrest control of the Mediterranean from Carthage,
thus vaulting their city-state into the position of uncontested
naval hegemon, a position it would occupy for centuries to
come. In a tone of almost breathless admiration, Polybius
recounted how, even as the conflict seemed to have devolved
into an unbreakable stalemate, the Romans startled their
opponents by reverse-engineering a captured Carthaginian
quinquereme and initiating a massive naval-armaments and
training programme.[9]

Rome's Herculean shipbuilding efforts, however remarkable, could not compensate for its sailors' relative lack of
experience.[10] In addition to emulating Carthaginian galley
design, Roman shipwrights sought to level the playing field
by introducing their own unique innovation: the *corvus*. The
corvus, or raven, was an adjustable spiked plank that could
be lowered by rope onto an enemy ship to skewer it in place.

This was a creative means, in the midst of a tight naval skirmish, of neutralising the manoeuvrability of the Carthaginian vessels, whose crews and captains would be far more skilled at ramming, and of forcing their lightly equipped crews to engage in melee combat against the more heavily armoured Roman boarding parties.[11] Although Romano-Carthaginian enmity endured until the final destruction of Carthage in 146 BCE, Rome's meteoric rise to naval dominance in the early years of the First Punic War laid the foundation for its survival during the darkest days of the Second Punic War, and for its eventual triumph over a century later. Indeed, if Carthage had succeeded in regaining a measure of control over Mediterranean sea lanes, it would hypothetically have been able to provide Hannibal with more of the reinforcements and supplies he so desperately needed during his long years of campaigning on Italian soil, from 218 to 203 BCE.[12] It is not unreasonable to assume that, under such circumstances, the superlatively skilled Carthaginian commander might have succeeded in finally extinguishing the guttering flames of Roman resistance. A Carthage that had retained a strong navy would also have been able to better deter or deny Roman amphibious landings in North Africa, thus preventing its nemesis from repeatedly striking at its political centre of gravity over the course of the three wars.[13]

By seizing and maintaining control of the sea, Rome had denied Carthage the benefits of reciprocal maritime access and resupply. (Hence why Hannibal and the bulk of reinforcements dispatched to aid his efforts in Italy were obliged to travel by land all the way from Carthaginian strongholds in Spain, transiting through southern France and ranging over the Alps.)[14] In short, by engaging in such a costly exercise of large-scale adaptation in the earliest phases of the Punic Wars, Rome had ensured the conditions for its future success. If it had found itself compelled

Image 4: **The Battle of Cape Ecnomus, 256 BCE, engraving from *Naval Battles, Ancient and Modern* by Edward Shippen, 1883**

(Science History Images/Alamy Stock Photo. Colourised engraving depicting the Battle of Cape Ecnomus, from *Naval Battles, Ancient and Modern*, by Edward Shippen, 1883. This climactic fleet engagement of the First Punic War (264–241 BCE), possibly one of the largest naval battles in history, took place off the coast of southern Sicily in 256 BCE, and resulted in a Roman victory over their Carthaginian rivals.)

to do so in the throes of conflict, it was largely because Rome's leadership had not anticipated that a minor dispute over Sicilian proxies would spiral into a large-scale protracted war, especially with Carthage, an erstwhile ally and trading partner.[15] Rome's dilatory attitude toward maritime issues in the years leading up to the First Punic War was thus partially because they had not projected the pressing need to float a blue-water navy. Indeed, this points to one of the fundamental challenges in great-power war: the oft-urgent requirement to successfully adapt to the unexpected or unanticipated, all while operating under extreme pressure and facing an enemy that itself adapts in turn.[16]

In his *Philippics*, Demosthenes famously drew on the metaphor of wrestling when lamenting the fact that his fellow Greeks appeared far too reactive in their military responses to Philip of Macedon's armies. He likened them to a barbarian fighter who simply raised his hands to ward off each anticipated blow rather than attempting to catch his wilier and more adaptive opponent off guard, in essence what modern-day boxing would term 'performing a slip', that is, weaving away from an attack while placing oneself in position to deliver a sharp, and unexpected, riposte.[17] In *On War*, Carl von Clausewitz famously pushed this athletic analogy further, stating that

> if we would conceive as a unit the countless number of duels which make up a war, we shall do so best by supposing to ourselves two wrestlers. Each strives by physical force to compel the other to submit to his will: each endeavours to throw his adversary, and thus render him incapable of further resistance.[18]

Indeed, another key measure of military effectiveness is the ability to demonstrate flexibility over the course of an extended campaign, and to recuperate swiftly from an initial surprise (whether technological, doctrinal or tactical) or defeat, by engaging in a prompt and fundamental revision of tactics, force-structure design or military strategy.[19] For great-power competitors engaged in a protracted war, and especially for those initially facing off against a more conventionally redoubtable opponent, acquiring such a degree of operational suppleness is crucial in order to not be irredeemably weakened in the opening round of conflict. As Michael Howard once sardonically observed when commenting on British military doctrine during the Cold War:

> I am tempted to declare dogmatically that whatever doctrine the Armed Forces are working on now, they have got it wrong. I am also tempted to declare that it does not matter that they have got it wrong. What

matters is their capacity to get it right quickly when the moment arrives.[20]

The evolution of Spanish infantry during the Italian Wars (1494–1559) under Gonzalo Fernández de Córdoba, famously known as El Gran Capitán (The Great Captain), provides another illuminating example of wartime organisational agility and reform.[21] In 1495, when the Spanish and their French rivals first engaged in battle at Seminara, in southern Italy, the Spanish were clearly outclassed. Although both the Iberian troops and their commander were grizzled veterans of the punishing ten-year crusade to conquer the Emirate of Granada, they were unaccustomed to the tactics and troop types deployed by their French adversaries in Italy – a deadly combination of advanced artillery, bristling squares of Swiss pikemen and glittering squadrons of *gensdarmes*, or heavy cavalry.[22]

In the course of the engagement, France's serried ranks of disciplined Swiss mercenaries made short work of the lightly armed Spanish *rodeleros* (sword and buckler men), while Córdoba's wings of *jinetes* (light cavalry) proved to be little more than an irritant, with their clouds of javelins unable to penetrate the French *gensdarmes*' heavily plated armour.[23] In the aftermath of the battle, in a despondent missive to his rulers, Isabella and Ferdinand of Spain, Córdoba confessed that the French had 'wielded a great advantage over his forces' in the form of their well-trained Swiss infantry and formidable force of shock cavalry.[24] Seminara would constitute the only defeat in Córdoba's long and distinguished military career, and the bitter lessons that he would draw from his failure would lead not only to an immediate change in his tactics, but also to a fundamental redesign of Spanish force structure.[25]

Only a few years later, when Córdoba faced off against his French foes once again, the results were very different, with the

Castilian general going on to win a series of crushing victories. While there is little doubt that El Gran Capitán was a tactical genius, fully deserving of his sobriquet, the triumph of Spanish arms was the result, first and foremost, of his complete overhaul of the Spanish infantry. It was now composed of mixed companies or captaincies of cuirass-equipped pikemen fighting *a la suiza* (in the Swiss style), and of the agile, lightly armed *rodeleros*, whose task was now not so much to engage in fruitless frontal assaults, but rather to weave in between the dense thickets of clashing pikemen, creating and exploiting bloody gaps in their formations. Most importantly, the Spanish infantry now incorporated large numbers of arquebusiers (up to 25% by 1500, only five years after the Battle of Seminara). The latter had yet to be introduced in any significant numbers into the French army. Deployed behind hastily fortified trenches and ditches, their volleys could shatter the charges of the fearsome *gensdarmes*, something that famously occurred at the Battle of Cerignola in 1503.[26] Spain's early adoption of the arquebus en masse was critical to its armies' success. Indeed, although early arquebuses were not necessarily more effective than bows or crossbows (they took a long time to reload, and could prove unreliable, especially in poor weather), their use required far less training – something that allowed the Kingdom of Spain to rapidly expand the numbers of arquebusiers in its armed forces.[27] And indeed, this points to another critical aspect of military competition during a protracted war, including the current conflict in Ukraine: simplicity of equipment maintenance and operability can have a virtue all of its own, especially if one is seeking to both rapidly induct freshly trained troops and conduct operations at scale.[28]

Córdoba's newly designed Spanish companies were each subdivided into two *cuadros* (squads) containing roughly one-third of each troop type: pikemen, *rodeleros* and crossbowmen or arquebusiers.[29] These early efforts laid the foundation for the subsequent transformation of the Spanish infantry into Renaissance Europe's most capable 'pike and shot' force. Spain continued to refine and improve upon its infantry force structure during the sixteenth century, increasing the proportion of arquebusiers and, later, musketeers, until they equalled or surpassed the number of men equipped with melee weapons. Sophisticated combined infantry tactics were adopted and perfected through drill and geometry, and by the late 1530s Spain's famed *tercios* were universally considered to be the finest infantry in Europe.[30] And indeed, France's eventual defeat and expulsion from Italy following six bloody decades of conflict can largely be attributed to the inferior quality of its foot soldiers.[31] The French were fully aware of this critical asymmetry. Indeed, throughout the long war with Spain for control of the Italian peninsula, France continuously struggled to develop a well-trained and reliable native infantry force, with successive kings sporadically launching hugely ambitious new force-development plans within France, only to encounter middling success and revert to relying primarily on expensive foreign mercenaries. [32]

Cultural considerations and political constraints

While there were many material factors behind these chronic difficulties, some more intangible elements – cultural, societal or political – played an equally important role.[33] Indeed, it has been suggested, including by some commentators at the time, that the French monarchy was leery of training and arming large numbers of its populace for fear of one day falling victim to a well-organised commoners' revolt. Meanwhile, France's higher nobility (unlike that of Spain, whose aristocrats readily sought officer commissions in the *tercios*) remained wedded to their ancestral tradition of service in the prestigious heavy cavalry units, the *compagnies d'ordonnance,* and reluctant to fight alongside the common infantry.[34] Furthermore, the unique

institutional culture of Spanish infantry units, which was structured around *camarada* (best described as military fraternities or
soldiers' associations), inculcated a form of intra-unit cohesion
or '*esprit de corps* and general motivation' that greatly contributed to the troops' morale and discipline – all critical sources of
competitive advantage in a gruelling war of exhaustion.[35]

These examples provide an important reminder that such
cultural factors can play an important role in either facilitating
or impeding adaptation over the course of a protracted war.[36]
The respective institutional cultures of each competing military
apparatus are naturally of fundamental importance, whether
they spontaneously engender the conditions for tactical initiative, for bottom-up initiatives or shared lessons learned. For
example, during the First World War the German army was
highly effective at engaging in 'horizontal innovation', allowing its troops to adapt, often extremely rapidly and effectively,
in the face of the introduction of new Allied tactics and technologies.[37] More broadly, recent scholarship has demonstrated
the extent to which the war, contrary to conventional wisdom,
was in fact characterised by remarkably rapid cycles of technological and tactical innovation.[38]

Political considerations or constraints can also act as powerful barriers to tactical adaptation, or to the revision of military
strategy, even when the great-power actor in question is aware
of the operational costs and risks in not modifying its approach.
For example, during the first great phase of the Hundred Years
War, it was clearly in France's interests to pursue a *Vegetian*
strategy of battle avoidance and exhaustion against its more
martially accomplished English foes.[39] Indeed, at that precise
juncture in the conflict, the French had yet to devise an effective
counter to England's deadly 'combined arms' combination of
longbowmen and dismounted men-at-arms.[40] And yet, despite
French King Philip VI's own preference for a scorched-earth

approach to territorial defence, one that would exploit France's strategic depth and latent socio-economic resiliency, he found himself strong-armed, after a decade of inconclusive struggle, into confronting the armies of Edward III of England directly – leading to his crushing defeat at Crécy in 1346, when more than 15 successive French cavalry charges were annihilated by volley upon volley of English arrows. Indeed, Philip's prior (and well-advised) refusal to meet Edward in direct combat – although arguably tactically successful – had come to jeopardise his political standing in a society profoundly wedded to traditional notions of chivalric honour, with French nobles defecting to Edward III, or reportedly wearing fox caps at court in mockery of their liege lord's 'fox-like' cowardice.[41] In this instance, seemingly non-material stakes in a crisis (concerns over national honour and royal prestige) had begun to have very real political ramifications, thus forcing Philip VI to pursue a suboptimal military strategy.[42] In this regard, as historians have noted, Edward III's calculated strategy of provocation had proven to be highly successful.[43]

Philip's son and successor, John II, was subjected to similar socio-political pressures in the lead-up to the Battle of Poitiers in 1356. Having intercepted an Anglo-Gascon army led by Prince Edward of Woodstock (more commonly known as the Black Prince), the French monarch initially appeared willing to entertain negotiations with his adversary, only to be bulldozed by hawkish members of his entourage into engaging in a frontal assault of the well-defended English position.

The net result was one of the most cataclysmic defeats in French military history, with the slaughter of thousands of French nobles and, most disastrously, the capture of King John. It was only after this seismic event that the French reverted to their previously successful *Vegetian* strategy, managing to progressively reconquer under the rule of Charles V (Charles

the Wise) nearly all the territories lost by the latter's predecessors.[44] The failures of French military strategy during the first
decades of the Hundred Years War thus provide an invaluable
case study of how political and/or ideological considerations,
including autocratic audience costs, can act as impediments to
successful adaptation in a protracted war.[45]

Another illustrative example is Iran's persistent adherence
to human-wave tactics during the Iran–Iraq War of 1980–88.
The Iranian regime's stubborn persistence in employing
such methods, notes Efraim Karsh, 'despite their obvious
futility and prohibitive costs', was partially motivated by its
desire to strengthen the Pasdaran, or newly created Islamic
Revolutionary Guard Corps (IRGC), which led such assaults,
vis-à-vis the regular Iranian army, which was excluded from
these assaults' operational planning.[46] Millenarian fervour,
and the belief that religious fanaticism, in and of itself, could
provide Iran with a war-winning 'moral advantage', naturally
also played an important role.[47] Similarly, Moscow's current,
and seemingly baffling, willingness to repeatedly throw
what has been grimly described as 'meat waves' of troops at
Ukrainian targets of questionable strategic value can, in fact,
be explained both by autocratic audience costs – Vladimir
Putin's burning need to point to some form of large-scale
victory, however symbolic – and by the Russian regime's
brutish internal politics, as the late Yevgeny Prigozhin, head
of the Wagner mercenary group, sought to burnish his own
stature by leading campaigns that, although horrifically costly,
were framed within Russia as an epic, valiant struggle against
the vilest of foes.[48]

Conversely, the enervating experience of protracted great-
power war can encourage a certain tactical lethargy, or foster
an excessive degree of wariness with regard to reform, innovation or initiative-taking.[49] In some instances, the greater sense

of physical security provided by the 'defensive form' can, as Clausewitz famously remarked, 'act as a ratchet wheel in the machinery of war', bringing it to a temporary, grinding halt.[50] The very importance of the issues at stake, with all the attendant political risks in the event of failure, may incline military commanders and political leaders toward excessive military caution and conservatism.[51]

Wartime decision-making thus involves continuous, laborious efforts at adjudication and risk management, whether with regard to managing domestic audience costs, timing the development of a game-changing technology or formulating a new strategy. Moreover, as Nora Bensahel and David Barno note, 'an organization cannot simply adapt to one changed circumstance and declare victory, because by the time it has done so, the environment will likely have changed again and more adaptation will be required'.[52] For instance, while during much of the first century of the Hundred Years War France failed to adapt to English infantry tactics, and thus was compelled to eventually revert to a *Vegetian* strategy under the rule of Charles V, over the course of the fifteenth century it technologically leapfrogged its opponent by establishing clear superiority in the resourcing, development and production of artillery.[53] The glorious feats of the outnumbered yeoman archers at Crécy and Agincourt may continue to occupy pride of place in England's Shakespearean national mythos, but it was the French kingdom's more coldly methodical mastery of gunpowder, logistics and siegecraft that allowed it to ultimately prevail, with its master gunners pulverising dozens of previously unassailable English fortified positions into oblivion.[54]

Peripheral strategies and centres of gravity

Faced with the pain, sorrow and sheer monotony of a protracted war, security managers can find themselves grappling with

Map 1: **Evolution of territorial holdings during the Hundred Years War**

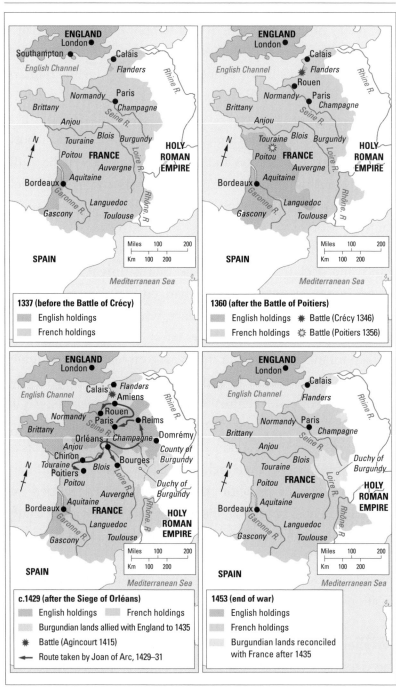

1337 (before the Battle of Crécy)

English holdings

French holdings

1360 (after the Battle of Poitiers)

English holdings   ✳ Battle (Crécy 1346)

French holdings   ❖ Battle (Poitiers 1356)

c.1429 (after the Siege of Orléans)

English holdings   French holdings

Burgundian lands allied with England to 1435

✳ Battle (Agincourt 1415)

← Route taken by Joan of Arc, 1429–31

1453 (end of war)

English holdings

French holdings

Burgundian lands reconciled
with France after 1435

(IISS)

burdensome decisions as to when and where to escalate their efforts. These regional prioritisation decisions are often tortuous – few, if any, great powers throughout history have been able to apportion their forces equally across disparate regions. When Chosŏn Korea, following its invasion by Japanese forces in 1592, appealed to the Ming Emperor Wanli for aid, the latter's advisers were initially reluctant to send large bodies of troops in defence of Imperial China's smaller ally, out of concern that this would open their northern frontier to attacks from Mongol and rebel warlords.[55] Wanli ultimately committed tens of thousands of Chinese troops to the war in Korea, which continued for almost seven years – but only once the security situation along the empire's northern border had been stabilised. And wrenchingly, during the Second World War, Great Britain found itself compelled to reluctantly privilege the European theatre of operations over a more robust defence of its Asian colonial possessions.[56]

Impatience with a bruising stalemate in the primary conflict arena can also result in poorly conceived diversionary or peripheral attacks (the Athenian Sicilian expedition during the Peloponnesian War, or the Franco-British Dardanelles campaign during the First World War come to mind), ill-considered large-scale offensives or overly costly campaigns of attrition.[57] At the same time, a reluctance to explore novel options, to gamble finite resources on the development of exotic new technologies, such as the Manhattan Project during the Second World War, or to take decisive aim at the enemy's centre of gravity, can sometimes prove equally costly – it can increase the likelihood of a war dragging on inconclusively, draining ever more blood and treasure. Famously, the Truman administration justified the development and use of atomic weaponry on the basis of the allegedly grievous costs of further protraction, arguing that with Japan still stubbornly refusing to surrender, an Allied invasion of the main archipelagic territories might have cost tens, if not hundreds of thousands of American servicemembers' lives.[58]

Putting a decisive end to a protracted conflict thus hinges upon a clear identification of the enemy's sources of social, as well as material, support for the war – what John David Lewis describes as its 'essential source of ideological and moral strength, which, if broken, makes it impossible to continue the war'. Moreover, echoing Polybius's aforementioned focus on the importance of said moral factor, 'to break the "will to fight" is to reverse not only the political decision to continue the war by inducing a decision to surrender, but also the commitment of the population to continue (or to restart) the war'.[59]

During the Second Punic War, two of Rome's greatest commanders, Quintus Fabius Maximus and Publius Cornelius Scipio (later more commonly known as Scipio Africanus), famously engaged in a heated debate over the direction of Rome's wartime strategy. Fabius Maximus, also known as Cunctator (the Delayer), wished to perpetuate the strategy of exhaustion that had allowed Rome to survive during the darkest hours of the Hannibalic War, after its terrible defeats in the battles of Trebia, Trasimene and Cannae.[60] For Fabius, as long as Hannibal and his armies remained in Italy, it made sense to concentrate the bulk of Roman military assets and resources close to Rome, where they could engage in home-land defence, targeting Hannibal's allies and supply lines, and patiently whittling away at the invaders' foraging parties and new-found Italian allies. Any attempt to divide Roman armies could jeopardise the capital's own defence, and Fabius strongly urged his fellow general to reconsider his plans to cross the Mediterranean to attack Carthage. In Livy's account (or reconstruction) of these public deliberations, Fabius directs his young and ambitious rival to the precedent of the ill-fated Athenian expedition to Sicily, pointedly emphasising that

> the Athenians, a state distinguished for prudence, leaving a war at home, sent a great fleet into Sicily at the urging of a young man as enterprising and illustrious as you, but by one naval battle they reduced their flourishing republic to a state of humiliation from which she could never recover.[61]

For Scipio, on the other hand, the only means to bring the war to a close was to transfer its costs onto enemy territory by invading North Africa, and to directly threaten the very nucleus of Carthaginian power, thus luring Hannibal, its most capable commander, back to his home shores. He preferred, he noted somewhat provocatively, to 'devastate the territories of another', rather than to see his own 'destroyed by fire and sword', and to 'draw Hannibal after him' rather than 'be kept here [in Italy] by him'.[62]

Scipio's bold gambit ultimately proved more successful than the more static, attritional approach espoused by Fabius. His opening of an African front generated widespread panic in Carthage, which had not experienced the horrors of war on its home soil for several decades, leading to the recall and eventual defeat of Hannibal, as well as to Carthage's surrender.[63] Fabius, despite the previous efficacy of his defensive grand strategy, had failed to appreciate the decisive impact that attacking the enemy's economic and political heartland would have on its war-fighting endurance.[64] Scipio, on the other hand, had correctly identified and targeted the adversary's moral centre, thus putting an end to the war.

This leads to a discussion of the next main component of success in protracted war: a greater ability to weather losses, absorb damage, regenerate strength and continue hostilities, that is, socio-economic power and resiliency.

Socio-economic power and resiliency

Positional strength and natural advantages

In 1632, Cardinal Richelieu, France's chief minister, shared his prognosis of the state of Franco-Spanish competition in a letter to the French royal ambassador in Madrid. Despite the fact that France was still recuperating after decades of civil strife, and Spanish armies hovered menacingly along almost every French border, the saturnine clergyman indulged in a rare moment of optimism, buoyantly predicting that 'nowhere is Spain in a position to resist a concentrated power such as France over a long period, and in the final analysis the outcome of a general war must necessarily be calamitous for our Iberian neighbour'.[65]

For Richelieu there were certain enduring factors, or foundational aspects of French national power, that lent it a distinct advantage over Spain and its more dispersed holdings, ranging from its superior demographic and economic resources to its agricultural self-sufficiency and central geographical position. Time was thus France's most precious commodity in its protracted competition with its Iberian rival. Provided the battered kingdom could finally unify under a shared vision and regenerate its considerable military strength, all while weakening the Habsburgs – with their twin dynasties in Vienna and Madrid – through a league of well-funded and capable proxies, its final victory seemed preordained. Granted, detailed accounts of Richelieu's tumultuous tenure as chief minister have highlighted the extent to which these seemingly straightforward tasks were, in fact, often to prove almost insuperably challenging, requiring a Herculean administrative and intellectual effort on the part of one of history's most consummate practitioners of statecraft.[66] Richelieu himself often traversed periods of extreme despondency and pessimism, most notably when a Habsburg invasion force suddenly blazed a path through France's northern plains and threatened Paris in 1636.[67] Nevertheless, the cardinal ultimately proved correct in his assessment of both powers' respective core strengths and weaknesses, and in his confidence that France's greater degree of socio-economic resiliency would eventually enable it to prevail in a protracted great-power war.

Certain pre-existing material factors do, indeed, allow for a rough estimation of a country's ability both to amass power and to endure the pain and devastation of a protracted war: a nation's demographic 'reservoir' and profile; its levels of industrial and agricultural self-sufficiency; and the nature of its geography – whether, for instance, it possesses strategic depth allowing it to trade space for time, easy maritime access or an internal topography favourable to its defence.[68] All these are relatively self-evident and easily measurable sources of competitive advantage. In its most classical sense, geopolitics serves to highlight 'that securing political predominance is not merely a question of having power in the sense of availability of natural resources, the acquisition of wealth or a capacity for projecting force', as Geoffrey Sloan notes, 'but it is also dependent on the (physical) configuration of the field within which that power is exercised'.[69]

In this regard, the United States has historically benefited from an overwhelming geopolitical advantage over its main competitors, with the relative isolation of the American mainland from traditional Eurasian loci of great-power confrontation providing the majority of its people with an inbuilt degree of protection from the horrors of conventional great-power war. As Nicholas Spykman famously warned on the eve of the Second World War, the blessings of such a privileged geographical position could also form something of an intellectual curse, breeding strategic naivety and complacency.[70] Whether the American mainland's relative sanctuary status from conventional attack will endure is one of the questions tentatively raised in a later section of this study.

Material capabilities and capacity for regeneration

In addition to assessing a belligerent's active strength at the outset of a conflict, one must also consider its latent material capabilities, along with its potential for regeneration, mass production and mobilisation. Famously, the Japanese Admiral Yamamoto Isoroku, the operational architect of the raid on Pearl Harbor, warned his government not to initiate war with the US, pointing to the awesome underlying strength of its industrial base. 'Anyone who has seen the auto factories in Detroit and the oil fields of Texas', he cautioned, 'knows that Japan lacks the national power for a naval race with America. We must not start a war with so little chance of success.'[71] Like the wretched figure of Cassandra in the *Iliad*, Yamamoto was ignored, even though his bleak forecast was entirely accurate.

Over the course of the Second World War, the US engaged in an unprecedented exercise of industrial mobilisation, emerging as the 'great arsenal for democracy', converting humming assembly lines from civilian to military production en masse, hugely expanding its shipyard capacity and greatly outproducing its Axis competitors.[72] A key factor in America's final victory was its ability to preserve a functioning transoceanic logistics network by sustaining a vast merchant fleet even in the face of heavy losses. Even then, it was only in 1943 that US cargo-ship production began to outpace losses at sea, largely due to successful, albeit back-breaking, efforts to enhance speed of delivery and production capacity.[73]

Meanwhile, neither Japan nor Nazi Germany was able to secure access to sufficient levels of resources or mass-produce enough ordnance and weaponry to win the *Materialschlacht* (battle of materiel) that has always played such an important role in shaping the outcomes of protracted conflicts. For instance, by 1942, the Soviet Union was already achieving war-production ratios over Germany 'of over 3:1 in small arms and artillery, 4:1 in tanks, and 2:1 in combat aircraft'.[74] Thus, notes the historian Adam Tooze,

> an understanding of the economic fundamentals also serves to sharpen the profound irrationality of Hitler's project. ... Hitler's regime after 1933 undertook a truly remarkable campaign of economic mobilization. The armaments program of the Third Reich was the largest transfer of resources ever undertaken by a capitalist state in peacetime. Nevertheless, Hitler was powerless to alter the underlying balance of economic and military force. The German economy was simply not strong enough to create the military force necessary to overwhelm all its European neighbours, including both Britain and the Soviet Union, let alone the United States.[75]

One Wehrmacht captive in Normandy, surveying the gargantuan logistical footprint of the Allied forces as he was driven through recaptured French villages, bitterly confided to his American captors that he understood the true reasons for his unit's defeat: 'You simply piled up the supplies and let them fall on us.'[76]

Troop-mobilisation rates and levels are also critical components of competitiveness in a protracted war. Rome's peer competitors – who relied on professionalised and/or mercenary armies – were continuously astonished by the hardy republic's ability to replenish its forces through the mass drafting of Roman and allied citizens almost 'as if from a fountain gushing indoors, easily and speedily filled up again', in the purported words of Pyrrhus of Epirus, one of the early Roman Republic's most formidable foes.[77] Even after the most terrible defeats, such as the Battle of Cannae in 216 BCE, during which Rome and its allies may have lost up to 50,000 men, the Romans, refusing to come to terms, managed to raise another 14 legions – at least 75,000 additional troops.[78]

During periods of acute national peril, whether during the Punic Wars or later conflicts, Rome was also known to lower recruitment standards, releasing prisoners or even manumitting slaves in order to cobble together additional units or provide much-needed rowers for its expanding fleet.[79] Polybius famously argued that the superiority of the Roman military system – its tradition of shared national service and its organisational prowess with regard to full-scale mobilisation – was one of the determining factors in its eventual victory in the Punic Wars, providing it with an edge in morale as well as in deployable manpower. 'Even if they happen to be worsted at the outset, the Romans redeem defeat by final success, while it is the contrary with the Carthaginians', stated Polybius. 'For the Romans, fighting as they are for their country and their children, never can abate their fury but continue to throw their whole hearts into the struggle until they get the better of their enemies.'[80]

Polybius may have attempted too schematic a dichotomy. Punic citizens were also known to serve, sometimes with extreme valour and determination, in Carthaginian armies, and many of Rome's troops would have been composed of *socii* from allied Italian city-states.[81] Moreover, as discussed earlier, by the time of the Second Punic War, Rome had already overtaken Carthage at sea. Nevertheless, there is little doubt that Rome's unique system of military mobilisation provided it with powerful regenerative abilities.

Similarly, during the Second World War, Hitler clearly underestimated the Soviet Union's ability to recover, whether in terms of industrial capacity or manpower, from the devastating initial blitzkrieg of *Operation Barbarossa*.[82] Indeed, despite incurring severe demographic and territorial losses, the USSR's strategic depth, when combined with a well-executed strategy of industrial evacuation and relocation, allowed it to rapidly reconstitute its productive capacity.[83] Thus, 'in 1941 the central functions of the Soviet military-economic apparatus were neither fully stunned nor paralyzed'.[84] Meanwhile, the People's Commissariat of Defence displayed its customary brutal efficiency by mobilising truly staggering levels of manpower to replace its grievous losses, drafting older reservists, convicts, women, ethnic minorities and non-Russians from liberated territories (during the later stages of the war).[85] At the outset of Nazi–Soviet hostilities, the Red Army fielded 303 divisions; by the war's end it had raised another 981.[86]

Saturating moral forces

What about other less materially quantifiable, but arguably even more essential, aspects of national power and socio-economic resiliency? War, Clausewitz memorably observed, is often 'saturated' by great moral forces that leave it with a 'leaven of its own'.[87] A protracted great-power war is above all an extended clash of national wills, and the preservation of military and civilian morale, even in the face of severe loss and deprivation, must be at the heart of any viable theory of victory. During both world wars, national governments directed considerable energy toward the study of public morale, drawing from the nascent fields of psychology and behavioural science in addition to sociology and economics. Their detailed studies, and the work of later generations of military historians, provide valuable insights into how both military and civilian subjects weather the experience of protraction.

For example, for soldiers deployed for long stretches in the trenches along the Western Front in 1914–18, the sheer tedium and sense of powerlessness in the face of prolonged exposure to danger, along with the complete lack of knowledge of when the war might end, was often the prime source of psychological collapse.[88] (Recent reporting would indicate that many Ukrainian soldiers currently serving in sodden, crater-pocked trenches and under relentless artillery barrages are – for all their grim resolve – grappling with a strikingly similar set of mental challenges.)[89]

German soldiers posted along the Western Front longed to take part in the more fast-moving campaigns to the east, even though it might have put them at greater risk. As one German army doctor quipped, while the 'mobile war' along the Eastern Front was a 'muscle war', the exhausting campaign of attrition along the border with France was a 'nerve war'.[90] For military personnel serving during the First World War, the passage of time, in and of itself, came to possess a morally erosive quality. As the conflict dragged on, war-weariness became more pronounced among the general populations and soldiers' dissatisfaction grew more intense. In 1917, in the wake of the disastrous Nivelle offensive during which over 100,000 French troops were killed or wounded in less than a week, large numbers of French soldiers mutinied, leading to 3,400 court martials and over 600 death sentences.[91] And in November 1918, sailors of the German High Seas Fleet famously triggered an uprising, helping to spark the revolution that eventually resulted in the overthrow of the German government.[92] Over the course of the four years of conflict, even formerly robust democracies such as France and Great Britain felt obliged to adopt more coercive and authoritarian behaviour – heightening internal censorship and repression – in order to forestall what they perceived as the imminent threat of a generalised moral collapse.[93]

During the Second World War, with the advent of so-called 'total war' and its mass targeting of civilians, greater efforts were put into studying the resiliency of a nation's broader populace during a protracted war. In a series of studies conducted on British citizens' morale and behaviour during the Blitz, UK government officials and scientists thus concluded that the civilian population often placed a high psychological value on routine and predictability, and that 'people generally find a continued succession of air raids to be less trying than sporadic ones since they become disadapted [sic] during the quiet intervals'.[94]

Big towns also appeared more resilient to bombing than smaller urban communities, as displaced populations could be more easily rehoused. In order to bolster morale, it was

Image 5: **Painting entitled *The Menin Road* by Paul Nash (1889–1946), oil on canvas, 1919**

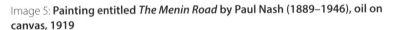

(Ian Dagnall Computing/Alamy Stock Photo. Painting from the Imperial War Museum)

considered absolutely crucial to involve the general public in their own defence as much as possible, in order to inculcate a sense of collective ownership and responsibility for the community's safety.[95] As a series of historical studies have shown, the British government sought continuously to balance safety and national self-confidence. It was thus thought that inappropriate or excessive precautionary measures 'might seek to weaken society's natural bonds and, in turn, create anxious and avoidant measures'.[96] When officials gathered to discuss the construction of a sprawling network of large-scale bunkers deep under central London – which would have conceivably provided far stronger protection than the London Underground or more common household air-raid shelters – they ended up turning down the proposal, and not only due to its exorbitant cost. Indeed, as one study observes, 'planners believed that it might create a shelter mentality and that essential war production would suffer as workers became increasingly reluctant to emerge from positions of safety'. Moreover, 'the system was also rejected on ground of equality, as the Hailey Conference of February 1939 had decided the national morale could only be maintained if the same standards of protection were applied across areas of equivalent risk'.[97]

These historical examples provide a brief, yet valuable, reminder of the trade-offs and challenges inherent to many of the deliberations surrounding civil resiliency during a multi-year conflict, as well as of the overarching importance, in the eyes of the belligerents, of shielding and nurturing the 'moral centre' of their war effort.[98] And indeed, it is precisely due to the huge importance of socio-economic resiliency that strategies of terror (such as strategic bombing) or of economic exhaustion (such as naval blockades) have often been placed at the very heart of protracted war efforts.

In 1917, when a young Winston Churchill was minister of munitions, he had expressed a scepticism over the coercive effectiveness of strategic bombing, writing that

> it is improbable that any terrorization of the civil population which could be achieved by air attack would compel ... surrender. ... We have seen the combative spirit of the people roused, and not quelled, by the German air raids. Nothing that we have learned of the capacity of the German population to endure suffering justifies us in assuming that they could be cowed into submission by such methods, or ... not be rendered more desperately resolved by them.[99]

As prime minister during the Second World War, however, he abandoned his reticence, famously telling Stalin that 'German morale was now a military target' and that the devastation wrought by area bombing could spur the German people into revolt. Churchill's controversial embrace of strategic bombing has been heatedly debated by generations of historians, and there is no clear academic consensus as to the effect the British strategic bombing campaign (as with any other 1939–45 strategic bombing campaign, for that matter) may have had on the societal resiliency of Nazi Germany.[100] As Robert Pape notes in his seminal examination of air power and coercion in war:

> Societies differ in their vulnerability to countercivilian attacks according to such factors as their degree of urbanization, their use of burnable building materials, and the susceptibility of their food supplies to destruction. ... Countercivilian attacks can lower morale, increase absenteeism, and cause some deurbanization as refugees flee vulnerable cities, but these problems

> rarely have serious effects on production or cause
> civilians to put effective pressure on the government
> to surrender. Punishment can generate more public
> anger against the attacker than against the target
> government. ... Economic deprivation does often
> produce personal frustration, but collective violence
> against governments requires populations to doubt
> the moral worth of the political system as a whole, as
> opposed to specific policies, leaders or results.[101]

French civilians' reactions to English *chevauchées* (mounted raids) during the Hundred Years War provide an interesting example of how resourceful and resilient populations can absorb and adapt to strategies of terror and economic devastation. Fast-moving and hard to intercept, *chevauchées* were a key feature of medieval warfare and a recurrent aspect of English military strategy in France. They were more than simple, mindless exercises in destruction: there was a clear strategic, psychological and economic rationale behind them. In addition to demonstrating the patent incapacity of France's nobility to fulfil its feudal duty by protecting the third estate (i.e., France's commoners), an important subsidiary objective consisted in inflicting such grievous and lasting damage – on mills, vines and other local industries – that the targeted French region's ability to contribute to the country's broader defence was durably impaired.[102] The scale of devastation could be almost biblical in its proportions. During his 1355 *chevauchée* across the Languedoc, the Black Prince and his mounted force of Anglo-Gascon raiders thus covered over 675 miles in 68 days, divided into three columns riding abreast, and methodically burned and pillaged everything in a broad band stretching from the Atlantic to the Mediterranean.[103] As one historian notes, 'if the soldiers who rode on this expedition did indeed scour the landscape for a breadth of ten leagues, they would have devastated a total of over eighteen thousand square miles – nearly four miles for every man in the force'.[104] Some astonishingly rigorous accounts by the English crown's financial agents also gleefully detail how France's economic losses during such *chevauchées* led to a corresponding depletion in its fiscal resources and thus in its ability to sustain large-scale military operations.[105]

Over time, however, France's beleaguered peasantry adapted to English *chevauchées*, fortifying their towns and hamlets, building hidden granaries and storehouses, strengthening town militias, and erecting early-warning networks of beacons and watchtowers.[106] While these preventive hardening measures could not stop whooping Anglo-Gascon raiders from devastating French fields and vineyards, they did greatly alleviate their capacity for lasting damage, while depriving them of the immediate resources they needed to continue to pursue such extended raiding campaigns. Thus, by the fifteenth century, English *chevauchées* had become both far less frequent and much less effective.

History would suggest that strategies of economic exhaustion, devastation and harassment encounter the most success when they are sustained efforts that directly affect the enemy military's supply lines and resource base. Counter-civilian strategies only occasionally seem to bear fruit, as they often seem to only harden the resolve of the target populations in question.[107] Consider, for example, the unflagging determination and resilience of the contemporary Ukrainian civilian populace, which polls indicate remain stronger than ever, even as they are subjected to a steady escalation in Russia's willingness to commit atrocities and war crimes.[108]

The British naval blockade of Germany during the First World War, on the other hand, was strategically significant largely because it acted as a steadily tightening noose, reaching beyond the civilian populace to progressively asphyxiate the German army itself, along with its ability to reprovision itself, thus precipitating its moral collapse and defeat.[109] By contrast, English *chevauchées* during the Hundred Years War, or the various aerial bombing campaigns during the Second World War, may have caused widespread misery among the wretched civilian populations subjected to their wrath, but they did not succeed in fatally weakening the socio-economic resiliency or military capability of their great-power targets.

Brutalisation and the risks of stasis

Finally, how might the experience of protracted warfare affect a great-power competitor's long-term internal stability? As Thucydides continuously reminds us throughout his *History of the Peloponnesian War*, drawn-out conflicts have a tendency to breed 'stasis' in the classical sense, that is, internal factionalism and disarray.[110] While the exhilaration of victory and the memory of shared sacrifices might act as a stimulant to national unity or consolidation, the general brutalisation of society, especially if paired with the trauma of defeat, can also gravely accentuate centrifugal pressures.[111] Whether surrender leads to territorial loss, diplomatic subjugation or merely a suite of humiliating concessions, its effects can often be likened to an invisible but devastating bow wave – profoundly reshaping the nation's collective psyche and, in so doing, its internal politics. The release of these pent-up pressures has thus led to regime collapse (Germany after its defeat in the First World War) or revolution (La Commune de Paris after France's defeat in the Franco-Prussian War), or it has accentuated the slide toward civil war (the Wars of the Roses in England after its defeat in the Hundred Years War, and the Wars of Religion in France in the wake of its ejection from Italy in 1559).[112]

Civil–military relations, in particular, have a tendency to become especially fraught, leading to armed uprisings by disgruntled military personnel (the revolt of the mercenaries during the so-called Truceless War pursuant to Carthage's defeat in the First Punic War) or coup attempts (the Generals' putsch following the French Fifth Republic's withdrawal from Algeria).[113] The bitterness of defeat can form the dank loam within which populist, extremist or conspiratorial movements flourish, further sapping a reeling nation's energy from within. In his magisterial study of the societal effects of military defeat, the German cultural historian Wolfgang Schivelbusch observes that for the losers of a protracted conflict, the creation of a new narrative or mythology justifying their defeat is more than a 'mere neurotic fiction of the imagination', and, by providing a shield against a 'reality unbearable to the psyche', it 'can be compared to the coagulation of blood and the formation of scabs necessary for wounds to heal'.[114] The most infamous such narrative, of course, remains the German *Dolchstoss im Rücken* (stab in the back) legend following the First World War, but one could equally point to the noxious effects of the mythology of the lost cause in America's post-Confederate South or the toxic, post-Battle of Sedan climate of suspicion and intolerance in France during the Dreyfus affair.[115]

In short, the drummed-up ideological fervour, total military mobilisation and societal brutalisation inherent to protracted warfare can occasionally extract a heavy price, particularly if the great power in question is on the losing side. Tectonic shifts in the balance of power can also lead to much wider convulsions and transformations in the international system, triggering 'waves of domestic reforms that sweep across borders and deeply alter the paths of state development'.[116] Consider, for example, the lasting impact of the Russian Revolution of 1917 on European – and global – geopolitics.

Grand strategy and diplomatic dexterity

Success in protracted war also hinges upon the soundness of a belligerent's grand strategy, on the dexterity of its diplomacy and on the adroitness of its more covert efforts to undermine the foundations of its rival's strength. Contemporary analytical efforts often segment categories of conflict into neat taxonomies, from economic coercion to grey-zone 'salami-slicing' tactics to proxy wars, or depict them as 'levels' of violence on a sliding scale toward high-intensity warfare. History would suggest, however, that when protracted great-power wars do erupt, their intensity is such that they are waged across the spectrum of conflict, as the sparring antagonists seek to weaken their opponent by any means possible. Meanwhile, temporary pauses in general hostilities have often provided the opportunity for more subterranean or indirect expressions of violence.

Proxy wars

Throughout history, whenever a protracted conflict has reached something of an operational stalemate or proved too onerous to maintain, it has frequently been channelled, or redirected, toward secondary theatres in the form of confrontation by proxy. Thus, during the Hundred Years War, whenever there was a formal peace treaty, or a lull in conventional inter-state violence, vicious proxy wars were fought between French- and English-backed armies in theatres ranging from Wales to Spain, Scotland and Brittany.[117] English and French involvement in the Spanish War of the Two Peters, which raged from 1356 to 1375, is one such example. If both parties' main bodies of military forces are already deployed within the primary zone of peer-to-peer conflict, it can be more cost-effective to employ proxies or surrogates in the more remote, peripheral theatre of operations.[118] This was the case, for instance, during the eighteenth-century French and

Indian War, in which the colonies of British America fought against those of New France, with each drawing on alliances with groupings of indigenous American tribes. (It is important to note that the use of the term 'proxies' does not imply that Europeans' native allies were hapless pawns in this confrontation. On the contrary, they were often remarkably shrewd and proactive actors within the turbulent political maelstrom of colonial America.)[119]

The North American confrontation, despite having been the point of origin for the Seven Years War, remained in many ways a peripheral 'offshoot', or sub-conflict, of what was a larger and more global protracted struggle.[120] France's loss of the Ohio Valley and subsequent defeat in North America can thus be tied to broader issues pertaining to French force adjudication and theatre prioritisation. 'The French command decided to invest its men and material resources in the European theatre, leaving its officers in North America with dwindling stores of food, munitions, and gifts to supply their indigenous allies', notes the historian Paul Kelton. Moreover, 'smallpox compounded the problem. Late in 1757 and into 1758, an epidemic devastated France's Native allies, leading to a substantial drop-off in indigenous support for the remainder of the war'.[121] Meanwhile, Britain's Cherokee allies, who were superlative combatants and expert at undermining France's own network of native partners, played a pivotal role in France's defeat.[122]

Two-level games and the spectrum of conflict

Other tactics that might be considered relatively modern – such as the sophisticated use of lawfare, or of economic statecraft and coercion – have all been widely practised, and sometimes to great effect, since antiquity.[123] In the fraught decades leading up to the Hundred Years War, French officials deployed their expertise in the arcane intricacies of feudal law to continuously undermine Plantagenet (English) authority over their continental territories, 'clogging up administrative processes', 'interfering with fiscal activities' and burying English officials under a deluge of legal cases.[124] The targeted use of economic coercion in the event of a protracted war is also nothing new, as evidenced, once again, by the rich and varied history of the Hundred Years War.[125] When Franco-English conflict finally erupted in 1337, Edward III sought to undermine France's diplomatic position in the Low Countries by exploiting England's quasi-monopoly in the production of high-quality wool.[126] By implementing a harsh wool embargo that reduced much of the urban citizenry of the Low Countries to a state of dire poverty (in cities such as Ghent, close to 60% of the population worked in the textile industry), and then selectively offering advantageous trade terms and wool staples to different duchies and principalities, the English monarch successfully fractured France's alliance with the powerful state of Flanders while co-opting other smaller polities into an English-led coalition. In effect, aggressive economic statecraft has been widely employed throughout history, whether in the form of punitive trade policies, industrial espionage or aggressive dumping tactics.[127] Contemporary policy practitioners must therefore realise that, from the Megarian Decree to Bismarck's weaponisation of trade tariffs, none of these tactics are new and that, most importantly, during a protracted war, all instruments of national power have traditionally been called upon in order to weaken the societal, economic and diplomatic foundations of the adversary's war-fighting potential.[128] During the Second World War, Nazi Germany even tried to cripple Britain's economy by flooding it with millions of expertly made counterfeit banknotes.[129]

After all, great-power competition has always been a multi-level game, and in times of protracted competition, belligerents will seek to exploit their adversary's internal weaknesses and exacerbate any pre-existing fissiparous tendencies.[130] During France's sixteenth-century Wars of Religion, Philip II of Spain sought to maintain his European rival in a state of continuous disequilibrium and civil strife by secretly providing limited military aid and subsidies to the rebellious Catholic League led by the Guises.[131] His goal being to weaken the French monarchy rather than see its resurgence under another form, he only openly committed large numbers of Spanish forces once it appeared that Henry of Navarre might succeed in seizing the throne and reconsolidating French power (which he ultimately succeeded in doing, despite Spain's best efforts). The French, for their part, regularly meddled in Imperial Spain's fractious internal politics, covertly and openly supporting secessionist movements by the Moriscos, Portuguese and Catalonians. This strategy was to prove ultimately far more successful than Spain's efforts to permanently break up France, leading to a French-supported Catalonian revolt that raged for over 12 years, draining much Spanish blood and treasure, and to the permanent secession of Portugal.[132]

Alliances, swing states and cordons sanitaires

Being able to draw on a robust alliance system is also critical for success in any protracted war. In some cases, allies can lend invaluable military capabilities – not only in terms of added mass, but also in terms of quality or niche specialisation. During the Punic Wars, the Hundred Years War and the Franco-Spanish conflicts of the early modern era, each principal antagonist sought to fill key gaps in its force design with allies. Over the course of the Punic Wars, Rome's Italian allies, or *socii*, provided the infantry-dominated Roman legions with much-needed cavalry and sailors. During the Hundred Years War, Edward III initially sought to compensate for his numerical inferiority in elite men-at-arms via the fielding of a large number of allied Low Country shock cavalry. Meanwhile, the French monarchy was in many ways saved from extinction by its Scottish and Castilian allies following the Battle of Agincourt, providing it with the necessary manpower to protect its positions south of the Loire and rebuild its strength.[133] This points to another recurrent facet of protracted warfare: a fresh influx of allies has often been the decisive factor that breaks a weary stalemate between seemingly evenly matched adversaries. Without America's commitment of large numbers of combat troops in 1917, the First World War might have ground on for many more years.[134]

Allied or partner nations can also provide vital positional advantage, whether in the form of forward-basing access or transit rights, or – if situated to the other side of the belligerent's target state – they can exert a welcome diversionary pressure on its flank. For example, during the later stages of the Cold War, the Soviet Union was compelled to station at least 25% of its troops along its border with China – troops that it could not necessarily reposition in the event of a protracted war with the US for fear of an opportunistic Chinese attack.[135] During the sixteenth century, France established a controversial alliance with the Ottoman Empire for somewhat similar purposes – to siphon Spanish and Habsburg military resources away from France's borders.[136] This diversionary strategy was pursued with an even greater degree of success under Richelieu, who succeeded in positioning France as a counterweight to Habsburg hegemony through a network of alliances with foreign powers.

According to the Renaissance-era statesman Philippe de Commines, each state in the international system had to contend with a 'thorn in its side' that its great-power adversary could exploit.[137] For France it was England, for England it was Scotland, for Spain it was Portugal. Interestingly, rather than viewing this state of affairs as being conducive to conflict, he suggested that it contributed to a general state of equilibrium by forestalling the establishment of hegemony.[138] And indeed, for two powers locked in a bitter, seemingly unending struggle, acquiring the support of powerful third parties, or 'swing states', rapidly becomes a diplomatic priority. A swing state can be loosely defined as a nominally neutral or non-aligned state with the latent capacity to lend decisive, and in some cases game-changing, power to any counterbalancing coalition.[139] In early sixteenth-century Europe, for example, that state was Tudor England, which was assiduously courted by both France and Habsburg Spain, and whose conniving ruler, Henry VIII, ably played both sides to advance his own aims and maximise England's degree of autonomy.[140] And indeed, second-tier powers, provided they play their cards right, can occasionally derive rich dividends from the ungainly wrestling of two leading states in the international system. A prime example is Thomas Jefferson's adroit manipulation of Franco-English rivalry during the Napoleonic Wars.[141] By cultivating French fears that the US might form an *entente* with Britain, America's third president succeeded, during the negotiation of the so-called Louisiana Purchase, in more than doubling the young nation's territory, and at very low cost.

In the absence, or failure, of acquiring new allies, establishing a buffer zone or a shatter belt of neutral states can provide a measure of physical security along certain putative axes of aggression.[142] As one of Vladimir Putin's former chief advisers stated, with characteristic cynicism, in the year before the all-out invasion of Ukraine, when attempting to explain the rationale behind Russia's continued violation of its neighbour's sovereignty:

> Two bones need soft tissue between them. Ukraine is right between Russia and the West, and the geopolitical gravity of both will sever Ukraine. Until we

reach that outcome, the fight for Ukraine will never cease. It may die down, it may flare up, but it will continue, inevitably.[143]

However unsavoury such blunt defences of the virtues of spheres of influence, buffer zones or cordons sanitaires may seem, they reflect long-standing practices among competing parties ensnared within protracted wars or competitions. The Roman Principate and the Parthian Empire each acted in much the same way in a broad area stretching from Armenia to Anatolia, engaging in political interference or limited military interventions to restrict the number of potential avenues of attack from their sole peer competitor.[144] In the lead-up to a renewed bout of Romano-Parthian conflict, each protagonist would endeavour to temporarily seize control of the sovereignty of a medial buffer state. In effect, both great powers were engaging in a mixture of regional diplomacy, influence operations and coercion as a means of pre-emptively shaping their future battlespace.

Accurately assessing the solidity of countervailing alliance structures is therefore crucial in a protracted war. Hannibal invaded Italy with the hope and expectation that Rome's subordinate allies would either voluntarily defect or be pummelled into submission. Although certain large cities, such as Capua, did cross over to the Carthaginian side following the Battle of Cannae, Hannibal largely underestimated the strength of Rome's ties with most of its allies, and especially within the Latin 'core' girdling Rome in central Italy.[145] Those few partners that did temporarily defect did so for their own exceedingly complex and parochial reasons, and in a manner that ultimately burdened rather than assisted the Carthaginian invaders. In his superb examination of Roman–Carthaginian competition in Italy during the Second Punic War, historian

Michael Fronda provides a compelling explanation of how the reactivation of pre-existing local rivalries undermined Hannibal's grand strategy.[146] Indeed, whereas Roman hegemony had exerted a dampening effect on regional tensions, Carthage's sudden appearance as a rival powerbroker on the peninsula only served to reawaken slumbering antagonisms, with each community making the decision 'whether or not to rebel (against Rome) based on the unique history of relations with its neighbours and the specific ways in which the larger events of the war affected these local rivalries'.[147] Moreover, once Hannibal had entered into formalised alliance structures with cities such as Capua, he was forced to provide for their defence against waves of vengeful Roman raids – therefore assigning large numbers of his elite veterans to a more static form of territorial defence, at a far remove from the highly mobile warfare in which they had traditionally excelled. As a result, 'instead of being a firm basis for his grand design', notes one classicist, Hannibal's dispersed congeries of Italian allies 'became a chain that started to hobble him'.[148]

The failure of Hannibalic grand strategy in Italy provides a series of valuable reminders of the challenges inherent to coalition management, along with the perennial difficulties tied to playing an 'away game' in a resident power's backyard. Finally, it highlights that while alliances can serve as force multipliers, state belligerents must also take pains to carefully evaluate the opportunity costs, as well as the benefits, tied to the establishment of a new alliance or security commitment amid a protracted war.

This chapter has ranged widely across time and space in its empirical examination of past great-power wars. How, now, can the many insights gleaned thus far help us fine-tune our understanding of the dynamics of contemporary US–China competition, and – more importantly – of each party's strengths and weaknesses in the grim event of a protracted Sino-US conflict?

CHAPTER THREE

China, the US and protracted war: a comparative evaluation

The preceding chapter of this book endeavoured to distil a series of shared insights drawn from the rich history of protracted war, highlighting the enduring importance of military adaptability, socio-economic resiliency and diplomatic dexterity in a drawn-out conflict. Before engaging in a tentative diagnosis of how China and the United States might currently be positioned to perform in each of these three core areas, it is worth considering how a Sino-US conflict might differ in some respects from all the conflicts previously mentioned, notably in its nuclear and cyber dimensions.

Some novel elements

The nuclear dimension
The first key distinction lies in the nuclear dimension of the Sino-US rivalry. While the analytical community can draw on the experience of certain limited wars fought under a nuclear shadow – such as the 1969 Sino-Soviet border war, or the 1999 Kargil War between India and Pakistan – there has not yet been a protracted, high-intensity war between two nuclear-armed

opponents.[1] It remains difficult to ascertain whether both countries' possession of nuclear weapons, in and of itself, reduces the possibility of a protracted conventional war or, somewhat perversely, renders it more likely. Indeed, arguments can, and have, been advanced in each direction. Some have argued that protracted great-power wars are a relic of the pre-atomic age, and that any US–China conflict would likely be short, sharp and limited, precisely due to fears of nuclear escalation.[2] As Sinologists Fiona S. Cunningham and M. Taylor Fravel have shown, many Chinese military planners and experts appear to think along these lines, operating under the belief that the nuclear shadow would have a powerful cooling effect on the scope and scale of military campaigns, stopping limited conventional conflicts from spiralling into more general wars.[3] Leading military figures such as General Fu Quanyou, who served as the People's Liberation Army (PLA) Chief of General Staff from 1995 to 2002, are thus on record as confidently stating that all future great-power wars would be limited and local, pointing to the example of the Cold War:

> The US and Soviet superpowers both had strong nuclear capabilities able to destroy one another a number of times, so they did not dare to clash with each other directly, war capabilities above a certain point change into war-limiting capabilities.[4]

Although there are some tentative signs that the Chinese political leadership's thinking with regard to protraction may be undergoing a subtle shift, the PLA's overriding doctrinal focus remains on prevailing in 'informationised local wars' – that is, wars that are both temporally limited and geographically circumscribed – which it sees as being the predominant form of conflict in the twenty-first century.[5] Somewhat revealingly, one of the key training manuals for the former Second Artillery Corps – now known as the PLA Rocket Force (PLARF) – suggested that the effect of their merely engaging in overt nuclear signalling (i.e., by putting Chinese intercontinental ballistic missiles on alert) would 'create a great shock in the enemy psyche' and 'dissuade the continuation of the strong enemy's conventional attacks against our major strategic targets'.[6]

Many US analysts are not quite so sanguine about the stability of nuclear deterrence in the event of a Sino-US conflict. Some have pointed to the risks of inadvertent escalation tied to entanglement – due to either the alleged collocation of conventional and nuclear delivery systems, or the possibility of incidental US attacks against Chinese C4ISR capabilities being misinterpreted as attempts to degrade China's nuclear retaliatory capabilities in preparation for a first strike.[7] These anxieties were echoed in the 2019 US Department of Defense's (DOD) report on Chinese military power (but interestingly not in its later iterations, including the most recent report in 2022):

> China's commingling of some of its conventional and nuclear missile forces, and ambiguities in China's NFU [no first use] conditions, could complicate deterrence and escalation management during a conflict. Potential adversary attacks against Chinese conventional missile force-associated C2 [command and control] centers could inadvertently degrade Chinese nuclear C2 and generate nuclear use-or-lose pressures among China's leadership. Once a conflict has begun, China's dispersal of mobile missile systems to hide sites could further complicate the task of distinguishing between nuclear and conventional forces … China's leadership calculus for responding to conventional attacks on nuclear forces remains a key unknown.[8]

For MIT professor Caitlin Talmadge, the issue of commingling is not as much of a risk as China's seeming difficulty to fully conceptualise how its current, crisply delineated notions of intra-war deterrence might founder in the face of reality. 'A US conventional campaign would indeed pose a large, though not total, threat to China's nuclear arsenal. More important than the purely military-technical implications of the US campaign, however', she argues, 'is what China is likely to believe the campaign signals about US intentions in a world where conventional deterrence has failed'.[9]

Over the past decade, these concerns over the risks of inadvertent nuclear escalation have led some analysts to advance alternative operational concepts that forgo large-scale US strikes on the Chinese mainland in favour of 'maritime denial', 'offshore control' or meticulously planned strike campaigns that scrupulously avoid any targets that might be either enmeshed with China's strategic deterrent or shielding senior members of its political leadership.[10] While the desire to calibrate military action to avert escalation is laudable, such finely tailored approaches seem unlikely to survive the fog and friction of a high-intensity great-power war. Interestingly, these alternative strategies are also all conducive to further protraction, either by advocating for distant blockades – which, by their very nature, can take months, if not years, to exert any decisive coercive effect – or by their refusal to take a stake to the heart of China's reconnaissance-strike complex, along with their willingness to accord the Chinese mainland relative sanctuary status, thus allowing Beijing's war-fighting potential to endure.[11]

One could also argue that over the next few decades, the growing density and sophistication of anti-access systems will lead to an increasingly defence-dominant environment – one in which neither the US nor China will view power projection across an Asian maritime 'no-man's land' as cost-effective or viable.[12] Indeed, as the defence analyst Christian Brose notes:

> a great-power war by these technologically advanced competitors [China and the US] would likely be governed by the brutal, unforgiving logic of World War I: forces could stand a decent chance of surviving and fighting effectively, but the moment they step off from their points of departure and try to advance against their opponents, they would likely enter a new 'no man's land' that is teeming with ubiquitous sensors, intelligent machines, and advanced weapons, operating from the ocean floor to outer space, that are capable of closing the kill chain at scales and speeds that attacking forces would struggle to survive. And like World War I, conflicts between peer competitors fighting with most, if not all, of the same weapons would likely erode into stalemate.[13]

If such a stalemate was reached, each conflict party might begin to place a greater reliance on more indirect and protracted approaches to military competition, channelling their military resources into less contested peripheral theatres, or choosing to wage wars of a thousand cuts via proxy.[14]

In the short to medium term, however, it does not appear realistic to assume that the US would deter itself from conducting strikes on the Chinese mainland for fear of nuclear escalation, especially if Chinese land-based precision-strike systems initiated the first salvo. After all, the US military would have little choice: if it wished to maintain access within the first island chain, it would have to attempt to roll back, or at least seriously degrade, the People's Republic of China's (PRC) seaward-facing reconnaissance-strike complex, to include its

Map 2: **Indo-Pacific featuring the island chains**

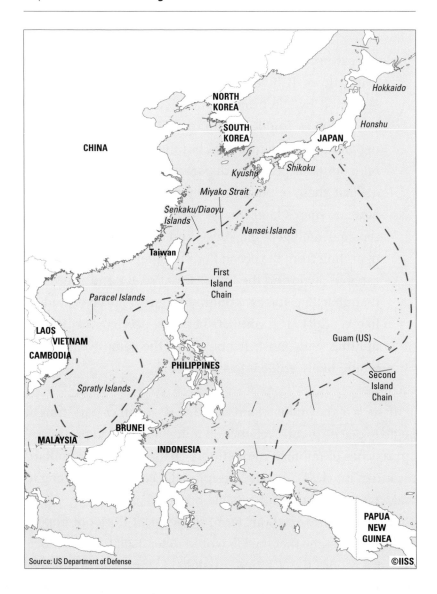

Source: US Department of Defense   ©IISS

integrated air-defence networks, air-basing infrastructure and
mobile missile-delivery systems, in addition to its space assets.[15]
And indeed, a recent study incorporating detailed surveys of
US national-security managers revealed that, when the latter
are questioned on this thorny issue, the collective tenor of

their responses strongly suggests that the relationship between nuclear weapons and conventional escalation does not either 'rule out' or 'guarantee' US strikes against the Chinese mainland, and that such a decision would largely hinge on the origins and early evolution of the conflict.[16] For example, if the PLA were to pre-emptively target US bases in either sovereign (Guam) or allied territory (the Kadena air base in Japan), the willingness of US defence advisers to 'recommend mainland strikes' as a retaliatory measure would be greatly strengthened.[17]

This stark reality explains why – barring the note of caution enunciated in the aforementioned 2019 DOD report – there is little indication in recent American operational discourse that there is any move away from the NIA-D3 (networked, integrated, attack-in-depth to disrupt, destroy and defeat) approach to dismantling A2/AD (anti-access/area denial) networks – a concept first enunciated in the Air–Sea Battle Concept in 2013 and then subsequently reiterated, or sedimented, across several administrations in a bewildering array of follow-on concepts, including the Joint Concept for Entry Operations (JCEO); the Joint Concept for Access and Maneuver in the Global Commons (JAM-GC); the Joint All-Domain Operations (JADO) and Joint Forcible Entry Operations (JFEO); the Joint Warfighting Concept (JWC), now nearing its third iteration as 'JWC 3.0'; the US Army in Multi-Domain Operations (MDO) 2028 Concept; the Navy's Distributed Maritime Operations (DMO) concept; and the US Marine Corps Planning Guidance and evolving Expeditionary Advanced Base Operations (EABO) concept.[18] Similarly, the Trump administration's 2018 National Defense Strategy (NDS) announced the need to 'be able to strike diverse targets inside adversary air and missile defense networks to destroy mobile power-projection platforms', while the Biden administration's 2022 NDS, sounding an only marginally more cautious note, called for the US joint force to 'mitigate adversary anti-access/

area denial capability' by developing 'concepts and capabilities that improve our ability to reliably hold at risk those military forces and assets that are essential to adversary success while managing escalation'.[19]

There are also indications that some of the broader concerns regarding the risks of entanglement – particularly with regard to China's supposed collocation of conventional and nuclear assets – may have been somewhat overstated. As one recent detailed analysis of Chinese-language and open-source materials pertaining to PLA force posture observed:

> Geographic entanglement within China's missile forces appears moderate and generated not by the peacetime co-location of conventional and nuclear units but, rather, the possibility of mobile missiles operating near one another in a crisis or conflict. ... Concerns about co-location of home garrisons and launch brigades do not appear substantiated. Open-source analyses have concluded that each brigade for which information is available is garrisoned in a separate location. Further ... there appears to be clustering of conventional and nuclear brigades, with conventional brigades largely located near the southeastern coast and nuclear brigades located toward the centre of the country, reflect-ing different mission sets and operational concerns. Further, the home garrisons of launch brigades are generally at least 100 kilometres apart, suggesting that strikes against the garrisoned units or facilities of a launch brigade are unlikely to implicate the garrisoned units or facilities of another launch brigade.[20]

This is not to say that strategic planners should not be preoccupied, as in any conflict between atomic powers, with the risk of inadvertent nuclear escalation in the wake of a mutual blinding campaign. Indeed, the same author notes, somewhat unreassuringly, that, if anything, Chinese thinking pertaining to these risks is underdeveloped and that 'Chinese writings are notable for their lack of attention to the potential risks of entanglement'.[21] The DOD's 2022 report to Congress on the Chinese military also ominously observes that, unlike many of their Western counterparts, PLA strategists 'view warfare as a science, discounting the possibility of inadvertent escalation and the effects of the "fog of war"'.[22] Certain recent evolutions in Chinese missile-delivery systems and associated training regimens provide additional causes for concern. For example, Beijing's most advanced and accurate theatre-range delivery system, the DF-26 intermediate-range ballistic missile (IRBM), is a dual-use, or 'hot-swappable' system – meaning that it can be rapidly refitted with a nuclear warhead in the event of heightened tensions.[23] Knowledgeable observers have also pointed to the fact that DF-26 brigades now appear to drill for both conventional and nuclear operations, in a troubling departure from earlier, more rigidly compartmentalised, PLARF training regimens.[24] This suggests that previously clear-cut distinctions between conventional- and nuclear-armed missile units could swiftly erode in the early phases of a conflict, particularly if the PLA opts to implement more distributed warhead-handling practices.[25]

In short, and all things considered, neither great-power competitor seems to view the nuclear dimension of their rivalry as being somehow antithetical to the prosecution of large-scale and ambitious military strategies. This grim reality strongly indicates that the potential for a conventional war has not been neutralised, in and of itself, by the joint possession of nuclear weapons. Once a war has begun, however, fears of escalation may paradoxically foster its prolongation. Indeed, once the first 'systems-destruction' and NIA-D3 strikes have been executed, concerns may grow on both sides over the robustness of the conventional–nuclear firebreak.[26] This, in turn, may lead to a temporary deceleration of the rhythm and intensity of armed confrontation, or to a growing reticence by each party to commit the full range of their military capabilities. Consider, for example, the shadow that the fear of Russian tactical nuclear-weapon use has cast on US decision-making during the current war in Ukraine – even though US forces are not directly fighting their Russian counterparts. Indeed, the White House's concerns over the possibility of nuclear escalation have affected its rate of delivery of certain key weapons systems to Ukraine, and rendered it more reluctant to openly support some of Kyiv's more maximalist war aims, such as retaking Crimea.[27] In short, nuclear weapons are unlikely to prevent the initiation of a Sino-US war, but they may very well, through the practice of mutual restraint, contribute to its protraction.

Another question worth pondering is what Beijing's alarming recent build-up of its nuclear arsenal means for general crisis stability, as well as for potential intra-war dynamics.[28] As the most recent US Nuclear Posture Review (NPR) noted, after several decades of fielding a relatively modest nuclear deterrent, the PRC is now racing to deepen and diversify its atomic stockpile, and appears well on track to possess 'at least 1,000 deliverable warheads by the end of the decade'.[29] China's access to a broader gamut of nuclear options, suggests the NPR, might embolden it 'to adopt a broader range of strategies to achieve its objectives, to include nuclear coercion and limited nuclear first use'.[30] Beijing's thinking on the coercive utility of nuclear weapons also appears to have been reinforced by its analysis of the impact of Russia's recent nuclear threats, which many Chinese analysts believe have played a major role in deterring more direct NATO intervention in Ukraine.[31]

Such an evolution in the PRC's thinking on deterrence, particularly if it is accompanied by a formal departure from its stated NFU policy, a move toward a launch-on-warning posture or intensified research on low-yield nuclear weapons, would certainly be cause for concern. When combined with the barrenness of Chinese strategic thought on escalation, this evolution has the potential to further erode the conventional–nuclear firebreak, but will also, inevitably, spur a revitalised nuclear-arms race with the US. Indeed, if confronted with a PRC more willing to engage in provocative acts of nuclear-tinged brinkmanship and signalling, the US will no doubt respond by moving away from arms control and nuclear-risk reduction to focus more resolutely on expanding the flexibility of its own sub-strategic arsenal and posture. As demonstrated by the controversy over the recent cancellation by the Biden adminis-tration of the Sea-Launched Cruise Missile–Nuclear (SLCM–N) programme – the development of which was approved by the Trump administration – these questions are already at the heart of heated debates in Washington, as concerns grow over the robustness of America's conventional deterrent, and more specifically over the combat viability and survivability of its forward-postured military assets in Asia.[32] A PRC more inclined to throw its (growing) nuclear weight around in its near abroad is also more likely to incite nervous neighbouring countries, such as Japan and South Korea, to reconsider their current attitudes toward nuclear-sharing arrangements, and perhaps even toward nuclear-weapons development.[33] Indeed, Washington has already found itself compelled, under the aegis of the 2023 Washington Declaration, to greatly enhance its degree of cooperation with Seoul on deterrence-related matters, dispatching, for the first time since the 1980s, a nuclear ballistic-missile submarine to the South Korean port of Busan, and, more importantly, establishing a new joint planning group on nuclear issues – the Nuclear Consultative Group (NCG).[34] While the Washington Declaration was largely designed to provide additional reassurance to South Korea in the face of Pyongyang's nuclear build-up and continued bellicosity, the concurrent rapid expansion of Beijing's strategic arsenal can only act as an additional stressor on the perceived viability of US extended deterrence in the region.[35]

At the same time, and somewhat paradoxically, note Evan Montgomery and Toshi Yoshihara from the Center for Strategic and Budgetary Assessments, China's possession of a more secure nuclear arsenal could also 'free Washington's hands' somewhat, by alleviating its long-standing concerns over the escalatory potential of a rolling strike campaign directed against Chinese submarine bases, air-defence networks and coastal missile launchers. Indeed, concerns that, under such conditions, US joint fires might also irredeemably degrade China's nuclear second-strike capability would no longer prove as valid. Thus, they note, the 'more secure China's arsenal is, the less worried the United States should be, and the fewer restraints it might accept, if Beijing were to begin a war'.[36]

The cyber dimension

In addition to the nuclear dimension, another key difference between a putative Sino-US war and past protracted conflicts is the cyber aspect of the competition. Indeed, both military powers strongly emphasise the importance of prevailing in the cyber domain as well as in the electromagnetic spectrum, especially in the opening phases of a major conflict.[37] China, which has relentlessly pursued an industrial-scale cyber campaign of US-technology theft in the past two decades, is now clearly identified as the United States' most redoubtable adversary in the digital battlespace.[38]

While internet connectivity is very much a function of physical infrastructure – from hulking data-storage banks, to fragile satellite constellations, to hundreds of thousands of miles of undersea cables – within the cyber domain itself traditional geographical boundaries have largely been erased, providing nation-states with exquisite cyber arsenals with a powerful global reach. Cyber payloads can thus be used not only to attack military systems and platforms, but also to repeatedly strike at an enemy homeland, society and economy in ways that would have been inconceivable in past protracted wars. Furthermore, there is the challenge of traceability and deniability, which, although certainly not impossible in the cyber domain, somewhat complicates deterrence, signalling and escalation management, and perhaps even raises the possibility of opportunistic third-party interference.[39]

At the same time, cyber, and, to a lesser extent, electronic warfare remain among the hardest military competencies to rigorously benchmark and assess, especially when relying wholly on open-source information and/or intelligence.[40] This analytical elusiveness is attributable to a number of factors, ranging from the aforementioned challenges of traceability to the 'invisible' and fluid nature of cyber confrontation, along with its inherently scopious, cross-domain dimensions. Moreover, great-power competitors are understandably reluctant to advertise or demonstrate their most potent cyber capabilities in times of peace, even though they engage in aggressive cyber probing or 'sparring' on a daily basis.[41] The risk of cascading collateral effects once a major cyber weapon is unleashed must also be considered – something first made evident in 2010 when the Stuxnet worm spread well beyond its original Iranian target to infect computer systems around the world.[42]

Chinese strategists openly acknowledge the United States' formidable competencies and what they deem to be

Washington's continued superiority in cyber warfare, along with their own baked-in vulnerabilities due to Beijing's continued (albeit diminishing) reliance on foreign technology across key aspects of its cyber architecture.[43] Yet these same thinkers also appear to relay a strong confidence in their belief that the PLA's Strategic Support Force, working in concert with PLA-linked civilian hackers, could engage in cyber warfare to secure an early asymmetric advantage against their more networked foe, temporarily 'paralysing' the US military by carefully targeting various select nodes and 'strategic weak points', all while simultaneously engaging in 'information and infrastructure warfare' against vital civilian infrastructure on US and allied/partner territory.[44] And indeed the most recent annual threat assessment from the Office of the US Director of National Intelligence cautioned that Beijing is 'certainly capable' of launching such large-scale cyber attacks on American soil, before referencing Chinese state hackers' ability to potentially disrupt 'critical infrastructure services within the United States, including against oil and gas pipelines and rail systems'.[45]

Putting aside the challenging issue of ascertaining whether the PRC would, in the event of a crisis, truly be willing and able to pre-emptively launch such a ferocious cyber campaign, one can question whether the PLA's current conviction that a more interlinked and networked US military is asymmetrically vulnerable to digitalised assault remains relevant. Indeed, under the aegis of its own Multi-Domain Precision Warfare (MDPW) concept, which the PLA has framed as a counter to US efforts under the Joint All-Domain Command and Control (JADC2), Beijing is also striving to more tightly align and fuse its command-and-control networks, from space to cyberspace.[46] As these efforts continue apace, it should become increasingly apparent that, contrary to what some Chinese defence intellectuals may believe, both great powers are in fact condemned to

live for the foreseeable future in a state of mutual cyber vulnerability – in effect, in a shared digital glasshouse.

Last but not least, if Beijing were to conduct devastating
cyber attacks against critical infrastructure on US soil, American
security managers would inevitably perceive this as a grievous form of aggression, especially if these attacks resulted in
widespread economic disruption and/or civilian casualties.[47]
After all, NATO officials have already stated that under certain
conditions, a particularly damaging set of 'cumulative cyber
activities' against an Alliance member – aimed at its healthcare
facilities or energy grid, for example – might be considered an
armed attack, and one that meets the threshold for triggering
Article V.[48] There is little reason to believe, therefore, that, when
operating under a similar set of circumstances, US leadership
would not construe a Chinese-directed information and infrastructure warfare campaign against its populace as a serious
form of horizontal and vertical escalation, which would, in
turn, fuel conflict protraction.

The revived role of non-state and para-state actors

As Chapter Two showed, there is nothing inherently new about
the employment of non-state or para-state actors in protracted
warfare. From the privateer Francis Drake's 'singeing of the
king of Spain's beard' to the hundreds of foreign mercenaries
who plied their grisly trade in the Angolan civil wars of the late
twentieth century, protracted conflicts have always embraced
unorthodox methods of mobilisation alongside more conventional forms of troop levies.[49] Large and powerful para-state
entities – from the East India Company, to Chinese Communist
Party (CCP)-controlled enterprises, to the Wagner Group – have
also historically played a key, if often somewhat ambiguous,
role in servicing the foreign and military policies of their countries of origin.

Despite the historical commonplaceness of these forms of private–public interaction, twenty-first-century American military planners are no longer accustomed to conceptualising great-power competition, orders of battle or protracted warfare along such irregular lines. In the event of a protracted war with China, however, they would have to consider other, more unconventional, forms of Chinese military strength and power projection. Thousands of Chinese private-security contractors, most often composed of ex-PLA and People's Armed Police (PAP) personnel, are currently deployed across geopolitical theatres such as Africa and, increasingly, Central Asia.[50] What role would these widely dispersed, well-trained parastate actors play in the event of a Sino-US war? Mention was also made earlier of the large number of Chinese hackers who would be called upon to supplement the Chinese government's cyber-warfare efforts in the event of a conflict with the US.

There are other examples of potential civil–military cooperation, or what Beijing has come to term 'civil–military fusion'. For example, it is worth considering what logistical role China's gargantuan civilian shipping and aviation sectors might play in the event of a conflict in the PRC's near abroad, whether over Taiwan or disputed islets in the South and East China seas. For example, China's growing fleet of civilian roll-on/roll-off ferries is more than three times larger, in aggregate tonnage, than the People's Liberation Army Navy's (PLAN) entire fleet of amphibious assault ships, and overshadows in its displacement all the US Navy's amphibious assault vessels combined.[51] These behemoth-sized vessels now regularly take part in mass amphibious invasion drills, and PLA-affiliated experts have carefully catalogued the number of large and medium-sized civilian cargo aircraft that could be requisitioned for 'strategic projection' under China's National Defence Mobilization Law and National Defence Transportation Law.[52]

Finally, as the remainder of this study will show, the role of private-sector innovation, logistics and manufacturing – along with latent societal education and talent more broadly – would all prove critical in the event of a back-breaking war of attrition. For example, Starlink, a private US company, has played a game-changing role in Ukraine, with its small, easily transportable satellite dishes and associated terminals proving crucial to the war effort.[53] Furthermore, Ukraine's unusually dynamic domestic tech sector, with its vibrant start-up culture and hundreds of thousands of highly skilled software developers, has given it something of an asymmetric advantage over its larger Russian rival, providing it with the means to more rapidly absorb and develop innovative military technologies.[54] One could also point to the vital role played in Ukraine by cheap, widely available commercial drones, both for reconnaissance purposes and, when retrofitted with explosives, for kinetic actions.[55]

In short, protraction can breed innovation and engender creativity, just as much as it can foster stasis and desperation. Ascertaining which way this pendulum might swing requires one to be both historically minded and aware of the speed of contemporary developments, all while striving to continuously engage in a more comprehensive view of the foundations of national power.

Military effectiveness and adaptability

In a protracted Sino-US war, which actor would be likely to hold a clear edge in terms of military effectiveness and adaptability?

Training, combat experience and command philosophy

On first examination, it would appear self-evident that the US joint force, by virtue of its unparalleled combat experience, full-spectrum suite of capabilities and highly trained personnel, would hold a decisive advantage. As is often noted, Beijing has not fought a large-scale conflict since its mediocre performance during the Sino-Vietnamese war of 1979. In addition, its relative lack of proximity with the world's most advanced and experienced Western militaries has deprived the PLA of the opportunity to sharpen its war-fighting capabilities through sophisticated joint training. Indeed, the only experienced and technologically advanced military with which China currently engages in training for high-intensity warfare is Russia's, the general combat proficiency of which has now been severely called into question.[56]

Meanwhile, US troops regularly take part in highly realistic multinational war-fighting exercises with a wide variety of international partners, providing them with the opportunity, in some cases, to gain experiential learning from their smaller allies' expertise in niche areas.[57] Indeed, studies have shown that large-scale, high-end multinational training exercises can greatly accelerate the diffusion of valuable war-fighting skills.[58] Recent revelations over Beijing's intense efforts to recruit recently retired Western air-force pilots to serve as trainers only reinforce the fact that there remains a qualitative gap in terms of capabilities and training between PLA personnel and their more combat-experienced European and American counterparts.[59]

Furthermore, the increased politicisation of the PLA under the leadership of Xi Jinping – most notably the renewed emphasis on ideological indoctrination, and the empowerment of political commissars – may come to undermine the professionalism of its officer corps, or dilute their capacity for personal initiative, and hence adaptability in combat.[60] Ever since the Bolsheviks, drawing inspiration from the French Revolution's system of *commissaires politiques*, instituted their own system of political officers, communist states ranging from North Korea to the PRC have experimented with the commissar system, as a means of both coup-proofing and enforcing ideological conformity.[61] The

Soviet Union's attitude toward the empowerment of commissars was especially erratic. At certain periods in its history – during the Stalinist military purges of the late 1930s, for example – commissars were elevated to a rank co-equal to that of their unit commanders.[62] At other times, when emphasis was laid on military efficiency and unitary command over ideological purism, they were downgraded to the rank of deputies.

In China, commissars have been part of the PLA since the early days of the CCP in the 1920s. For much of the PRC's history, there existed a tacit form of compromise whereby even though on paper the commissar and unit commander were co-equal in rank, it was understood that in times of actual conflict, the commander would be largely responsible for operational decision-making. This no longer necessarily holds true in Xi's China. The traditional notion that commissars should focus primarily on peacetime, quality-of-life and organisational issues while their 'conventional' military counterparts concentrate more exclusively on war fighting has increasingly been dismissed by state propaganda as outdated, with PLA political officers regularly exhorted to involve themselves more in military decision-making.[63] Meanwhile, whereas the Soviet Navy eventually opted to retain a single-command structure with a political commissar serving under the commanding officer, it appears that Chinese commissars are now viewed as co-equal in rank to PLAN commanders.[64] This somewhat cumbersome dual-command structure could naturally act as an impediment to rapid decision-making in the event of a conflict.[65]

Xi's efforts to exert further political control on the PLA have been partially motivated by the discovery of increasingly systemic corruption and cronyism across its ranks, and concomitant concerns over its growing ideological laxity and lack of discipline. In the summer of 2023, General Li Yuchao, the commander of the PLARF, along with its political commissar, General Xu Zhongbo, were suddenly removed – with no form of public explanation accompanying this high-level purge within China's prime nuclear service.[66] One can only imagine how recent revelations over the debilitating levels of theft and graft within the Russian military system – with much of the latter's previously vaunted modernisation drive now being dismissed as mere *pokazukha* (window dressing) – have exacerbated Xi's concerns over the depth of the internal rot within China's own sprawling security apparatus.[67] As some respected Sinologists have observed, these concerns are tightly interwoven with more deep-rooted fears over long-term regime stability, and of the party either succumbing to the subtly erosive effects of Western ideology, or being ideationally outflanked by hardline nationalists, some of whom may emanate from the ranks of the PLA itself.[68] If one subscribes to Samuel Huntington's argument that long-term military effectiveness is best attained through 'objective' civilian control – that is, politicians remaining in control but at a remove from the day-to-day operations of a fully professionalised and depoliticised military – China's current civil–military compact would appear to be to its disadvantage.[69]

As a growing body of defence planners and strategists have observed, a high-intensity Sino-US conflict would require soldiers from both countries to fight in and through a communications-denied or degraded environment. This would necessitate a level of operational, unit-level autonomy with which the US military may be far more comfortable – and toward which it has directed much thought in recent years. Indeed, the challenge in this context, note a number of American defence strategists, is how to resolve the stubborn tension between the need to inculcate principles of mission command and autonomous execution with the increasingly networked and centralised reality of military command-and-control systems.[70] As one US military officer urges, fighting under such constraints must be both embedded at the heart of US command philosophy and routinised within its training practices, through a revitalised emphasis on critical thinking, rapid adaptation and independent initiative in a multi-domain environment where information flows are both more complex and contested.[71] Increasingly, this has also required the painstaking reacquisition of long-atrophied, pre-digital skills. For example, since 2015, celestial-navigation theory has been reinserted into the US Naval Academy's curriculum, and young naval officers are now required to familiarise themselves with the use of sextants, compasses, paper maps and nineteenth-century navigational encyclopaedias.[72]

In essence, militaries training to 'fight dark' within a more chaotic, scrambled and static-filled environment will need to be able to move toward implementing a 'starfish strategy'. This nomenclature was first popularised in the world of private enterprise, with business strategists arguing that organisations with a more decentralised decision-making process are more liable to self-regenerate in the event of major damage – just as a starfish's capacity for neural regeneration allows it to grow a new limb in the event of amputation.[73] On the other hand, organisations with a more rigid command structure – such as the PLA – are less likely to survive crippling blows to their anatomy. In short, the US joint force's experience and command culture should give it a decisive edge in terms of wartime adaptability, especially within the degraded battlespaces of a future Sino-US war. As former US DOD strategist Christopher Dougherty has noted, the highly centralised armed forces of China and Russia may struggle to match this comparative advantage, which US military planners should further cultivate. 'Instead of striving for information dominance, the DoD should seek "degradation dominance" ... This notion attacks their [Chinese and Russian] theory of victory', argues Dougherty, 'by demonstrating the ability to operate effectively enough with degraded systems in contested environments, while imposing proportional degradation on Chinese and Russian systems, thereby causing them to lose confidence in their ability to gain an insuperable advantage in the techno-cognitive confrontation'.[74]

There is growing evidence that the Chinese leadership is acutely aware of, and concerned about, these pre-existing asymmetries, whether in terms of combat experience, realistic training opportunities or the general quality of their officer corps. Several of the numbered formulas so ubiquitous in PRC government communications have thus been introduced as a means of better highlighting these perceived deficiencies, from the 'Five Weaknesses' (Ability to Adapt to Circumstances; Ability to Manage and Coordinate; Ability to Command Operations; Ability to Operate Sophisticated Equipment; Ability to Organise High-Quality Training) to the 'Five Inabilities' (Inability to Analyse a Situation; Inability to Understand the Higher Echelon's Intent; Inability to Make a Decision on a Course of Action; Inability to Deploy Forces; Inability to Handle Unexpected Situations) to the 'Four Winds' undermining societal cohesion and discipline (formalism, bureaucratism, hedonism and extravagance).[75]

Xi has repeatedly drawn attention to the need to 'prepare to fight and win modern wars' by boosting the scientific and technological expertise of PLA officers, improving combat readiness and joint command, and enhancing realistic joint training in order to be able to prevail in a 'system of systems confrontation'.[76] In addition to constructing and upgrading its physical network of training bases across varied terrains (mountainous, jungle, desert, etc.), there is evidence that the PLA is investing heavily in advanced technologies – from simulations and synthetic training to big data and artificial intelligence (AI) – in order to improve the realism, sophistication and efficiency of their training and compensate for some of the lack of 'quality talent throughout the force'.[77] There is also a heightened emphasis on war-gaming in Chinese professional education, with a PLA National Defence University professor recently observing that war games with '30 different strategic scenarios', along with both 'theoretical and practical scenario-based training', now form part of a revised curriculum to enable PLA officers to 'better judge certain situations, understand the intentions of higher authorities, make the correct operational decisions, deploy troops, and deal with unexpected circumstances'.[78] Whether these efforts can help compensate for a lack of sophisticated international training opportunities, and for the absence of any recent combat experience, remains open to question.[79] Indeed, Chinese military writings frequently refer to the dangers of 'peace disease', 'peacetime habits' and 'peacetime practices', reflected in a lack of battle-readiness and the persistence of corruption and cronyism.[80]

There are also concerns in Beijing that the increased technological sophistication of China's platforms may have outpaced the technical knowledge and training of many of their operators, and that the sweeping 2016 military reforms, which led to the folding of China's military regions into five new joint theatre commands, may have been too abrupt, fostering widespread bureaucratic 'growing pains', with suddenly reassigned military officers struggling with the new exigencies tied to joint training and operations.[81]

Finally, one detects a certain amount of wishful thinking in the PLA's recent emphasis on the 'intelligentisation of warfare', and in its heady predictions that through the mastery of AI, human–machine teaming, quantum computing and automation it will be able to leapfrog its more sluggish adversaries by hugely accelerating its decision-making process and dominating the 'cognitive confrontation'.[82] Indeed, the notion that technological wizardry alone can overcome such deep-rooted challenges in training, unit cohesion and command philosophy seems implausible.

Long-range power projection

The PLA's capacity for sustained, long-range power projection is another area in which it would currently find itself at a distinct disadvantage in the event of a protracted war. This could emerge as a particularly salient area of weakness should the US, either alone or in combination with its allies, decide to enact a distant blockade or engage in opportunistic attacks against extra-regional Chinese military assets and overseas bases. As numerous close China-watchers have highlighted, the PLA only has a limited ability to conduct complex joint operations beyond the second island chain. To date, all the PLA's overseas operations or exercises have been conducted in highly permissive environments, and few can be truly characterised as joint. And despite its increasingly active anti-piracy and peacekeeping operations, the depth and quality of the PLA's engagement with foreign partners is often stymied by its personnel's limited linguistic and cultural expertise.[83] Indeed, in some cases, foreign militaries have been compelled to provide Mandarin-language training to their own troops in order to communicate with their Chinese counterparts, due to the latter's lack of English-language skills.[84]

PLA planners are all too aware of their country's state of geographical vulnerability, given China's continued – and growing – dependence on imported commodities ranging from oil to vital foodstuffs such as grain, pork and soybeans.[85]

Unlike the US or the Soviet Union during the Cold War, China does not currently benefit from a sprawling network of overseas bases and logistical hubs, or from reliable and capable allies positioned along its exterior lines that could help secure its sea lines of communication (SLOC) in the event of conflict, or assist in what the PLAN describes as 'joint breakthrough operations' or 'counterstrike naval manoeuvre operations'.[86]

In addition, the PLAN has only limited experience in at-sea replenishment and resupply. PLAN Flotillas operating in more remote locales such as the South Pacific or Western Indian Ocean would also be deprived of the protective umbrella provided by China's land-based aircraft and shore-based integrated air-defence systems (IADs), rendering them vulnerable to enemy prosecution, especially given the PLAN's still limited (albeit improving) anti-submarine-warfare (ASW) and anti-air capabilities.[87] In recent years, Beijing's overseas military deployments have relied on a sprawling – and growing – network of close to 100 Chinese-owned or -operated port terminals around the world. According to one recent analysis, Chinese state-owned enterprises own or operate 'two-thirds of the 96 ports', thus facilitating 'deeper integration of PLA operations into commercial facilities'.[88]

While this may be a relatively canny and cost-effective means of projecting power and sustaining a globe-girdling presence in times of peace, it would soon prove politically vitreous in the event of war. In the absence of formal alliance arrangements, and regardless of the ownership of the port terminals in question, few host nations outside the first island chain would prove willing to incur the lasting enmity of the US by allowing PLA forces to use their sovereign territory for combat operations. Three noteworthy exceptions, explored in a later section, might be Iran, North Korea and Russia – all of which have demonstrated a troubling willingness to cooperate militarily in Ukraine, with operatives from the Islamic Revolutionary Guard Corps (IRGC) even deploying to fight alongside Russian forces.[89]

History's warning against complacency

Given all these factors, the US military's advantages in a protracted war – whether in terms of its adaptability, logistical advantages or geographical positioning – might seem self-evident. That said, both history and the pace and scale of China's current reforms should warn against complacency. Indeed, the very fact that the PRC is engaged in such a vigorous bout of self-criticism provides a clear indication of its willingness and determination to adapt and reform. As Rome's remarkable exercise in maritime transformation over the course of the First Punic War demonstrates, determined adversaries, when operating under the innervating pressures of a major war, can sometimes overcome their initial lack of expertise to attain competitive levels of proficiency. And while, in a limited war, an early defeat might prove critical, within the context of a more protracted confrontation, such a humiliation may simply serve as the required stimulus for creative reform, much as when Gonzalo Fernández de Córdoba was motivated to radically overhaul Spanish force structure in the wake of his losses at Seminara. As RAND's Timothy Heath rightly observes when commenting on China's lack of combat experience:

> As wars drag on and both sides accumulate experience, factors such as training, leadership, access to resources, civil–military relations, and the institutional ability to draw and implement lessons learned are likely to prove more decisive. Combat experience thus matters for China at the operational and strategic levels, but its significance can be overstated. At the operational level, other factors such as leadership, training, preparation,

and motivation are more responsible for determining military effectiveness on the battlefield. Weaknesses in these areas are more likely to impair the PLA's performance than inexperience. Inexperience matters mainly in that it obscures the extent of the PLA's deficiencies, impairing an accurate assessment of all the factors that contribute to combat readiness.[90]

After all, the American doughboys of the First World War were initially deeply inexperienced in comparison with their weary but far more seasoned allied counterparts.[91] Only 3,885 of the United States' 5,791 officers serving in 1917 had spent more than a year in the army, and General John Pershing was the only senior officer with experience in commanding a force larger than a brigade.[92] Their GI successors were almost equally green when they entered the Second World War, despite the Herculean efforts by figures such as General George C. Marshall and Lieutenant General Lesley McNair to inculcate much greater realism in their training.[93] And yet in both cases, American forces learned from their first harrowing trials by fire and relatively rapidly improved their general combat proficiency, both on land and at sea.[94]

China's civil–military relations and somewhat unconventional command structure might exert a more damaging effect on its prospects of victory than its initial lack of experience. That said, politicised or highly ideological armies are not uniformly ineffective, and 'political intervention is not an unalloyed evil'.[95] On certain rare occasions, politicisation can indeed strong-arm otherwise sclerotic military bureaucracies into adopting more effective war practices or inculcating greater discipline into their ranks – the performance of the People's Army of Vietnam (PAVN) during the Vietnam War is one such example.[96] Moreover, China's leadership seems to have some awareness, however limited, of the risks tied to the PLA's duopolistic command structure, and to have initiated efforts to make combat officers and commissars more interchangeable, or at least better acquainted with each other's specific area of competency.[97] If, however, Xi Jinping's concerns over regime stability become more chronic, leading to sweeping corruption purges and constant changes in military leadership, this is likely to lead to suboptimal military performance, and work to the United States' advantage.[98]

Finally, although the PRC suffers from a clear vulnerability with regard to shielding its distant SLOCs from adversarial predation, the sheer scale of its current shipbuilding effort – in addition to its colossal investment in global maritime infrastructure – raises questions as to whether this state of affairs will endure. As the following section will illustrate, there comes a time when quantity has a quality of its own. Moreover, the PRC might not need to steam vulnerable surface action groups (SAGs) into the Indian Ocean in order to punch a hole in a US-led blockade – indeed, it could adopt a more limited form of counter-blockading action by dispatching small 'wolf packs' of submarines or by employing long-range precision strikes to 'conduct far-seas sabotage-raid warfare on exterior lines'.[99] The epicentres of the most conceivable Sino-US conflict scenarios – from a war in defence of Taiwan to a clash over the Senkaku/Diaoyu islands – are all well within the PRC's increasingly formidable inner maritime defence perimeter. If Chinese planners begin to feel confident that, in the wake of their initial 'joint firepower strikes' campaign, they can deny US sustainment and reinforcement from flowing into the prime area of operations – that is, effectively lock follow-on forces out of the first island chain – they may come to see their relative inability to wage a multi-theatre war as a secondary, or even tertiary, strategic concern. Beijing's continued – and flawed – perception that a war with the US would remain compressed in time and space would probably only reinforce this more sanguine attitude toward extra-regional power projection.

In sum, while the US military appears, at present, to be better positioned to prevail in a protracted war, a certain degree of historically informed caution is warranted. Indeed, an extended Sino-US confrontation would, first and foremost, be a war of moral and economic attrition, one in which each nation's degree of socio-economic resiliency would play a preponderant role.

Socio-economic power and resiliency

Which country appears best positioned to meet the industrial requirements and weather the socio-economic effects of a protracted war? In order to engage in a tentative comparative analysis of the United States' and China's socio-economic resiliency within such a context, it is helpful to disaggregate the lines of inquiry into two broad categories: the structural elements and long-term trends likely to exert a decisive impact on each competitor's broader societal resiliency; and the factors that would more specifically affect Washington's and Beijing's capacity for military mobilisation, sustainment and recuperation.

Structural factors, long-term trends and national resilience

In addition to its privileged geographic position, the US would be able to draw on several pre-existing socio-economic advantages in the event of a protracted war with China. The US is a vast, fertile land, which enjoys one of the highest food self-sufficiency rates in the world, producing, for example, roughly 1.4 times more grain than it consumes. In the event of a major disruption of international markets and food supply lines, the American population would thus be able to rely largely on domestic production to satisfy its nutritional needs.[100] While certain food products might be less available or more expensive, Americans would not suffer from the chronic deprivation and widespread malnutrition that have afflicted millions of hapless civilians during previous protracted wars. Indeed, as one historian has noted, during the Second World War more individuals perished of starvation, malnutrition and associated diseases than from military combat.[101] The war in Ukraine has served as a brutal reminder of the importance of food security – a grim and enduring aspect of attritional warfare since antiquity.[102] From Sparta's efforts, during the Peloponnesian War, to cut off Athens from its overseas grain supplies to the current famine in the war-torn Ethiopian region of Tigray, strategies of starvation – or what Roman military jargon termed 'kicking an enemy in the belly' – have often featured at the heart of drawn-out conflicts.[103]

Meanwhile, China's food dependence has only grown with its consumption habits.[104] The mass consumption of meat has led to an explosion in the cultivation of livestock, which has in turn increased China's demand for imported grain. Not insignificantly, much of this grain is currently imported from the US.[105] China's steadily shrinking proportion of arable land and its heavily polluted groundwater have exacerbated its reliance on foreign grain.[106] According to the Chinese government in 2018, almost 26% of surface water in Chinese river basins was unfit for human consumption.[107] There are indications that the CCP leadership is increasingly concerned about the issue of food security, as a series of high-profile campaigns have been launched to reduce food waste, and to protect the nation's dwindling patches of nutrient-rich black soil by providing subsidies to farmers in exchange for eschewing the heavy use of fertilisers.[108] Memories of past famines – from the so-called Incredible Famine of the late 1800s to the terrible years of the Great Leap Forward (1958–62), when an estimated 30 million people died of starvation – are seared into the Chinese collective consciousness, adding extra urgency to the CCP's food-supply-related anxieties.[109]

Since 2019, the US has also attained nominal 'energy independence', that is, it produces more energy than it uses, and exports more oil and petroleum products than it imports. This remarkable milestone – a result of both advances in domestic fracking technology and far greater levels of energy efficiency – came after an 'uninterrupted petroleum deficit for at least seven straight decades, from 1949 through 2019'.[110] This offers Washington a powerful advantage. Meanwhile, China is the world's largest importer of oil, relying on imports for more than 70% of its needs. It is also the world's largest importer of natural gas.[111]

In addition to its food and energy independence, the US enjoys a decisive demographic advantage over its great-power rival. China's population is rapidly ageing. Within about 25 years, more than one-third of its people will be retirees, with one Chinese government study estimating that elderly care may devour up to 25% of the country's total GDP within this time, potentially leading to a decline in general living standards, while siphoning away resources from military modernisation.[112] The country's fertility rate stands at 1.18 and it is unlikely that Beijing's recent efforts to arrest the rapid decline in birth rates – most notably by allowing all married couples to have three children from 2021 – will prove successful in forestalling a looming demographic crisis.[113] Indeed, ageing societies have been shown to be less dynamic and innovative, while concerns have been aired within China itself over the potential military implications of its long-standing one-child policy. Indeed, 70% of the PLA is composed of only children. While some Chinese commentary has criticised the generation of 'little emperors' for being overly pampered, one could also query how thousands of families losing their only child in a protracted war would affect the nation's morale and resiliency.[114] Nicholas Eberstadt and Ashton Verdery, two of America's most perceptive experts on Chinese demography, have pointed to another, less recognised side effect of China's precipitous demographic decline – its devastating effect on China's traditional family-structured social networks, and thus on the Chinese civic compact writ large.[115]

The US, on the other hand, has long boasted one of the healthiest demographic profiles among all the industrialised countries.[116] In 2020, there were some early signs that this may be changing, with that year's census showing a marked decline in fertility, in addition to the precipitous drop in immigration to half of what it was five years earlier.[117] This may have been a simple epiphenomenon of the COVID-19 pandemic and of Trump-era immigration restrictions, however, as the resident population has now begun to crawl back up, registering a 0.4% increase in 2022.[118] Nevertheless, even if the downward trajectory of 2020 reasserted itself and then persisted over the long term, the US would still maintain a strong demographic position for at least another generation.[119]

A somewhat more speculative question is that regarding each population's respective capacity for extreme hardship and mass casualties. This is not easily measurable and is therefore somewhat beyond the ambit of this book, barring a few quick reflections. Firstly, as is often pointed out, America's civilian populace has not experienced high-intensity conventional warfare on its soil since the Civil War. Unlike within populations in Europe and Asia, there are no generational transmissions or shared familial memories of widespread domestic destruction, territorial occupation, mass starvation or economic upheaval. As Andrew Krepinevich remarks in his own reflections on the future potential for a protracted great-power war:

The Chinese have an expression for it: 'eating bitterness'. How much bitterness would the American people be willing to swallow? What factors might exert an important influence on this aspect of the competition? … Americans would be asked to sacrifice on a level they had never before experienced. There are, however, different kinds of sacrifice. Which would be easiest to extract over an extended period? Material deprivation, such as rationing? Financial constraints, such as higher taxes and war bond drives? 'Taxing' manpower, such as a return to the draft and enduring high casualty rates? Limiting access to information and free speech, such as by restricting aspects of social media and coverage of military operations by the press? Obviously, a mix of these sacrifices might be required. And the kinds of sacrifices U.S. allies would be willing and able to bear should inform the kinds of costs the American people would be asked to shoulder.[120]

Recent developments in American politics and society might incline one toward pessimism over the republic's societal unity and resiliency in the event of a conflict. After all, one could glumly point to the United States' currently unprecedented levels of political polarisation, or to the irrational and panicked behaviour of ordinary citizens during even relatively minor crises such as the May 2021 cyber attack that briefly interrupted the flow of fuel along Colonial Pipeline (an 8,850-kilometre pipeline that transports approximately 45% of the fuel consumed along the eastern coast of the US).[121] Meanwhile, the initial mismanagement and politicisation of the COVID-19 pandemic resulted in the US suffering one of the highest mortality rates per capita in the industrialised world.[122] The pandemic also exposed troubling vulnerabilities in US supply-chain security – particularly with regard to certain key pharmaceutical products such as antibiotics and hydrocortisone, a large proportion of which are manufactured in China.[123] In recent years, various bills have therefore been introduced to lessen the country's perceived dependence on Chinese imports for medical supplies, which some legislators fear could provide the PRC with a powerful source of leverage in the event of a protracted conflict.[124]

At the same time, however, in the speed and efficacy of its vaccine roll-out, the US also displayed some of its most formidable qualities: its unparalleled technological and scientific prowess, and its occasional ability to engage, through the invocation of the Truman-era Defense Production Act, in industrial production on a massive scale.[125] (Whether the US could display a similarly spectacular level of efficiency in rapidly ramping up military platforms and munitions production will be addressed in the following section.)

While the American people may be domestically polarised, they also have a long-standing tendency to rally round the flag in times of perceived peril.[126] Asia policy is one of the few legislative areas where there is meaningful bipartisan action, with concern over the deteriorating security environment in the Indo-Pacific still serving something of a unifying function. Recent polling by the Pew Research Center indicates that there is now a broad societal consensus on the threat posed by a rising and more assertive China.[127]

Meanwhile, only a diminishing portion of Chinese citizens were alive during the dark years of the Japanese invasion or the civil wars. Within a few years, the average urban Chinese citizen may not have a greater cultural familiarity with the experience of war-related hardship than the average American. Moreover, due to the opacity of the Chinese regime, there are few means of measuring (whether via publicly conducted polls or other tools) the true degree of civic unity and solidarity animating Chinese society. There are certain tentative indications, however, that Chinese society may in many ways be far more atomised and fractured than US society, largely due to the crisis in social trust inherent to so many authoritarian regimes. Over recent years, many commentators and sociologists have drawn attention to China's so-called 'bystander problem', whereby passers-by walk by fellow citizens in states of physical distress – and sometimes in clear mortal peril – and refuse to provide them with any assistance. As some Chinese commentators have volunteered, this mysteriously ingrained tendency to steer clear of others' misfortunes and not volunteer assistance appears to be the result of a complex combination of factors, and of the generalised sense of societal anomie that is often the hallmark of life under rigidly authoritarian rule.[128]

While these discussions may seem somewhat anecdotal, they do appear to point to some broader underlying truths and suggest that, contrary to what one may believe, Chinese society would not necessarily be more unified and resilient in the event of a conflict, especially if it were subjected to a lengthy blockade that accentuated social stresses and competition. The recent rash of popular protests in China following years of draconian 'zero-COVID' policies served as a vivid reminder of the deeper tensions and frustrations that may seethe under a seemingly placid surface.[129] The demonstrations may have been short-lived, but in the space of a few days they compelled a frazzled Chinese government to engage in a complete policy U-turn, precipitately jettisoning its zero-COVID approach in favour of a near-total relaxation of quarantine and travel restrictions. Such a dizzying about-turn, when combined with its continued refusal to accept more effective Western-made mRNA vaccines for reasons of nationalist pride, furnishes valuable insights into the various pathologies of ossified dictatorships, along with their tendency to adopt self-defeating courses of action.[130]

Capacity for military sustainability, regeneration and mobilisation

The United States' geographical, demographic, technological and economic fundamentals appear remarkably robust in the context of a protracted competition. When it comes to evaluating both nations' current capacities to sustain and regenerate military strength over the course of a protracted war, however, China appears to hold the upper hand.

Since the end of the Cold War, the US industrial base has severely atrophied, as has its merchant fleet.[131] The country's capacity to rapidly replenish munitions stocks in the event of a protracted conflict is in serious doubt, and a combination of cyber and supply-chain vulnerabilities – in critical materials such as rare earths, for example – have rendered US procurement far more exposed to external disruption.[132] Meanwhile, ongoing military operations in Ukraine have reminded American policymakers of the importance of mass, magazine depth and large-scale production in high-intensity, 'industrial' warfare.[133] These defence-industrial-base-related concerns are hardly confined to Washington. Whether in Paris, London or Tokyo, allied security managers are all increasingly concerned over the parlous state of their logistical slack capacity, their dwindling munitions reserves and the steady decline in their domestic manufacturing capacity.[134] As one report recently observed, at the height of the fighting in the Battle for the Donbas during late spring and early summer 2022, Russia was expending more ordnance in two days than the entire British armed forces currently have in stock.[135]

Image 6: **Ukrainian soldiers along the front line near the town of Zolote-4, January 2022**

(Wolfgang Schwan/Anadolu Agency via Getty Images)

Defence planners in the US, which, at the time of writing, has supplied Ukraine with – among other items – approximately one million 155 mm artillery shells and thousands of *Javelin* anti-tank missiles and *Stinger* man-portable air-defence systems (MANPADS), now fret that it may take several years to replenish their depleted reserves, even when operating at heightened 'surge' rates of production.[136]

As one excellent report on the United States' reduced industrial-mobilisation capacity has rightly cautioned:

> When strategists and planners think of industrial mobilization, they think of World War II and all that came with it: conversion of civilian industry to military use, mass production, a long buildup of forces, and, finally, well-equipped, massive armies that overwhelm opponents. However, future wars

are unlikely to have the long strategic warning that the United States had before World War II. Existing industrial mobilization capabilities are all that will likely be available.[137]

Unlike today, during the Second World War, the US, as the world's leading producer of manufactured goods and steel, could rely on the colossal latent capacity of its industrial sector. As President Franklin D. Roosevelt proudly stated in one of his most famous 'fireside chats', 'manufacturers of watches, of farm implements, of linotypes and lawn mowers and locomotives' were mobilised to produce 'fuses and bomb packing crates and telescope mounts and shells and pistols and tanks'. This nationwide conversion of civilian industrial plants to weaponry manufacturers was, in reality, far from straightforward. Indeed, as Richard Overy notes in his magisterial recent history of the Second World War, some military aircraft relied on more than 100,000 separate parts, which meant that 'volume production represented an extraordinary challenge simply in terms of organizing the flows from hundreds of subcontractors to ensure that final assembly could proceed relatively smoothly'.[138] Whether in Germany, the United Kingdom or the US,

> the establishment of long production runs, and the corresponding economies of scale, were regularly frustrated by unpredictable shifts in strategy, or the need to match or exceed enemy technical accomplishments, or to interrupt production runs because of military insistence on short-term tactical modifications to an established weapon.[139]

Nevertheless, the US soon outpaced its competitors. By 1943, its output was greater than that of all its adversaries combined.

A key determinant of its triumph was the superiority of American production culture, which prized efficiency in rapid mass production, over that of Nazi Germany's, which was both more decentralised and inflexibly attached to the most exacting standards of craftsmanship and engineering. The net result was that even though the American *Sherman* was, without a doubt, an inferior tank to the German *Panther* or *Tiger*, it was churned out at such speed and scale that qualitative differences no longer mattered. 'American ground combat', remarks Overy, 'succeeded chiefly because there was simply so much equipment to compensate for any deficiencies in the quality of the product'.[140]

In the event of another protracted great-power war, Washington could no longer draw on such a sprawling industrial base. Indeed, even though the US manufacturing sector has been experiencing something of a revival in recent years, it remains a far cry from what it was in the 1950s and 1960s, when almost one in three Americans toiled on an assembly line.[141] (Now that figure is closer to one in ten.)[142] Furthermore, given the growing sophistication of modern weapons systems, converting civilian industries into arms manufacturers – under the aegis, say, of a twenty-first-century version of the War Production Board – is likely to prove far more demanding. Perhaps most importantly, the size of the US defence-industrial base has significantly diminished, following several decades of corporate mergers and downsizing. Over the past decade, it is estimated that the number of small enterprises conducting business with the US DOD has declined by over 40%.[143] As production lines have continued to contract and consolidate, they present greater risks of succumbing to single points of failure, while major arms providers, operating under perverse industrial incentives, have felt less pressure to focus on competitive pricing

Image 7: **Production line of B-24E *Liberator* bombers at Ford's huge Willow Run plant, Michigan, during the Second World War**

(PhotoQuest/Getty Images)

and speed of delivery.[144] Troublingly, in one recent study produced by the US National Defense Industrial Association (NDIA), 42% of NDIA member companies reported being the sole eligible producer of a defence product.[145]

At the same time, defence companies have had to grapple with a chronic shortage of skilled labour, from shipyard welders to software engineers, and concerns have grown over the vulnerability of supply chains for critical sub-components such as semiconductors.[146] An emphasis on low-volume production efficiency and just-in-time delivery, when combined with residual concerns over the somewhat erratic nature of US defence funding in recent decades, have also naturally rendered it more challenging to persuade companies to invest in the workers and infrastructure required for ramping up mass armaments production at scale.

The US Navy, which would play a lead role in any US–China contingency, is already overstretched, overworked and hobbled by an ever-growing backlog of maintenance delays.[147] In the event of a protracted, high-intensity war, it would struggle, given the United States' current shipyard limitations, to replace its losses in a timely manner.[148] Intensifying production rates for some of the most critical US Navy assets in a Sino-US conflict – such as nuclear-powered attack submarines (SSNs) – could prove particularly arduous, due to their added complexity and the chronic dearth of qualified workers.[149] Meanwhile, China now boasts the largest navy in the world, with 'an overall battle force of approximately 340 ships and submarines, including approximately 125 major surface combatants', and is the top ship-producing nation in the world by tonnage, manufacturing more than half the world's commercial ships and 96% of the world's dry shipping containers.[150] In the event of conflict, China could call on this massive excess industrial capacity to ramp up naval production, with its largest shipyards already surpassing in their capacity all of America's shipyards combined. Some estimates indicate that the PLAN may swell to 440 ships by 2030, with up to five aircraft-carrier groups and more than 60 cruisers and destroyers.[151] In comparison, the US Navy, as of August 2023, has approximately 297 battle-force ships, and is unlikely – given current production, maintenance and decommissioning rates – to greatly exceed, or even reach, 300 crewed battle-force ships by 2030.[152] As the former commandant of the US Marine Corps candidly remarked in 2020:

> Replacing ships lost in combat will be problematic, inasmuch as our industrial base has shrunk, while peer adversaries have expanded their shipbuilding capacity. In an extended conflict, the United States will be on the losing end of a production race

> – reversing the advantage we had in World War II
> when we last fought a peer competitor.[153]

Uncrewed systems, it has been suggested, could serve something of a compensatory function, adding mass and operational flexibility to an increasingly anaemic and overextended fleet, all while helping to fill 'gaps brought on from world conflicts, or industrial base challenges at a more affordable cost'.[154] There is no doubt that uncrewed systems will come to play an increasingly critical role across the US joint force structure, including within the US Navy. Families of unmanned surface vessels (USVs) and unmanned underwater vehicles (UUVs), working in concert with crewed ships under the aegis of a 'hybrid' fleet, can, and will, greatly expand the US Navy's magazine depth, reach and persistence, in addition to offering the option, in some instances, of taking on greater degrees of operational risk with less potential for heavy casualties.[155] The clear war-fighting benefits of the use of uncrewed systems, however, will not be reserved for the US. Moreover, the notion that the solution to a widening quantitative naval gap with China lies in a more hybridised US fleet structure appears somewhat unrealistic, given the PLAN's own enormous investments in robotics, autonomy and AI.[156] In all likelihood, both naval competitors will rely on ever larger numbers of uncrewed vessels in the decades to come, and China may well come to outpace the US in the mass production of USVs and UUVs. Indeed, while experts believe that Washington still has a narrow lead over Beijing in the field of AI, China largely dominates the commercial drone market, and is the world's largest exporter of weaponised uncrewed systems.[157]

That said, some of the most positive ramifications of the US Navy's induction of uncrewed vessels at scale may relate to cross-regional force adjudication. Indeed, dispatching flotillas of USVs to lesser-priority theatres for presence or constabulary missions may enable the US Navy to more easily deploy or forward-station high-end, multi-mission crewed platforms to the Indo-Pacific. To provide one telling example, Washington currently aims to have a fleet of well over 100 US and allied USVs patrolling the waters of the Gulf in the near future.[158] The duplication of similar such initiatives across a wide array of maritime regions where the threats primarily consist of activities such as illegal fishing, trafficking or piracy could do much to alleviate the Navy's global forward-presence burden, thereby improving crewed vessels' readiness and availability for redeployment to the Indo-Pacific theatre.

Meanwhile, even as the People's Liberation Army Air Force (PLAAF) and PLAN Aviation continue to modernise – with fourth- and fifth-generation platforms now comprising an ever-growing proportion of their combined inventory of 2,300 combat aircraft – the US Air Force (USAF) has sought to divest more planes than it has added.[159] Although the USAF remains the strongest air force in the world, its previously wide qualitative gap with the PLAAF is rapidly narrowing. Furthermore, its declining squadron levels mean that it is now increasingly spread thin between various high-tempo theatres, while its forward-deployed fighters in Asia are both vulnerable to Chinese missile barrages and heavily outnumbered by Beijing's localised concentration of aerospace power.[160] In recent years, USAF weapons-systems sustainment costs have increased approximately 40% above inflation, and, as of May 2022, the average American fighter aircraft in service was 29 years old, with many continuing to fly well beyond their projected lifespan.[161] Repeatedly falling short of its professed acquisition target of 72 new fighters a year, the USAF now has, according to its own definitions, around half of the fighters and one-third of the bombers it possessed at the end of the

Cold War.[162] Meanwhile, the US Navy has been grappling with a chronic strike-fighter shortfall, an issue that has provoked much frustration in Congress and which, due to a combination of factors ranging from service-life modernisation backlogs to delayed or reduced aircraft reductions, is unlikely to be remedied any time soon.[163]

With the great bulk of the US joint force still based in the continental US (CONUS), the issue of contested logistics would loom large in any protracted, large-scale war with China. Decades of underinvestment in logistics – from forward-positioned stocks to air and maritime connectors – have resulted, one recent report rightly notes, in a 'logistical system that is stretched thin supporting peacetime operations, and wholly unsuited to the demands of warfare with China or Russia'.[164] The 44 roll-on/roll-off ships US Transportation Command (TRANSCOM) currently relies upon to surge forces from CONUS to overseas theatres are more than 40 years old on average.[165] Finding newly qualified engineers for some of these vintage steam-powered vessels is challenging: many of those currently servicing Military Sealift Command's ships are in their sixties, or even seventies.[166] In the event of a conflict with China, US follow-on forces would have to 'fight to get into the fight', and logistical assets – from tanker aircraft to military cargo vessels – would constitute prime targets of opportunity for the PLA. With the United States' finite number of combat assets already spread thin, they would be hard-pressed to provide continuous aerial escort or convoy duty to more vulnerable, less stealthy logistical connectors.[167] Attrition levels could be severe, and the US might initially struggle to replace personnel such as mariners with critical skills.

In short, when it comes to guaranteeing its capacity for industrial resiliency, mobilisation, military production, sustainment and regeneration, all factors that would prove increasingly critical in the event of a protracted conflict with China, the US is facing a severe uphill battle. Increasingly aware of the urgency and daunting nature of the challenge, the US executive and legislative branches have acted with heightened resolve and dispatch, working to rectify some of these stark imbalances under the aegis of a revitalised industrial policy.[168] In recent years, the US has made considerable efforts to reshore or 'friendshore' supply chains for critical goods and technologies, ranging from rare earths to information and communication technologies (ICT) to semiconductors.[169] Most notably, in January 2023, Amsterdam, Tokyo and Washington signed a trilateral pact restricting the export of advanced chip-making machinery to China.[170]

Meanwhile, the Biden administration has launched, through the passage of landmark legislation such as the Infrastructure Investment and Jobs Act, the CHIPS and Science Act and the Inflation Reduction Act, a once-in-a-generation endeavour to reinvest in domestic infrastructure and manufacturing. Somewhat revealingly, these domestic reforms have been repeatedly and publicly framed as positioning the US to prevail in an increasingly existential long-term competition with China – partly, no doubt, as a means of securing solid bipartisan approval.[171] These reforms should, indeed, be interpreted as forming part of a much broader competitive strategy, as they aim not only to strengthen the defence-industrial base of the US, but also to drain talent and manufacturing away from that of its principal rival. Under the so-called 'Clawback Requirement' of the CHIPS and Science Act, for instance, any entity that benefits from the freshly instituted US Department of Commerce's financial-assistance programme for semiconductor-facility development in the US must also commit to not manufacturing in China 'or any other foreign country of concern' for at least a decade, or they must forfeit the award.[172] And in October 2022, shortly after the Department of Commerce announced a new package of stringent restrictions on the sale of advanced computing chips and chip-making machinery to China, a spokesman for the Chinese Embassy in Washington publicly complained that the US was 'trying to use its technological prowess as an advantage' to hobble China's progress.[173]

In this he was not wrong, as export controls over sensitive military technologies have increasingly overshadowed already fraught Sino-US trade relations. In July 2023, Beijing implemented its own set of export restrictions on gallium and germanium (and their related chemical compounds), two rare metals critical to US military supply chains.[174] Little more than a month later, the Biden administration unveiled a new executive order (EO 14105) prohibiting certain categories of US outbound investments to China on 'technologies critical to the next generation of military innovation' in three key sectors: semiconductors and microelectronics, quantum information technologies, and AI.[175] The White House has framed EO 14105 as forming part of what it has dubbed a 'small yard, high fence' approach to addressing the national-security threat posed by 'countries of concern' (i.e., China) suddenly leapfrogging their way to military dominance.[176] And despite its seemingly groundbreaking nature, historians of the early twenty-first century will no doubt view it as merely an opening salvo in an ever more zero-sum struggle to deny the PRC any form of game-changing technological supremacy.

Efforts have also been undertaken to re-energise the defence-industrial base, with numerous observers noting that if US production lines are already struggling to keep pace with the exigencies of arming Ukraine, with consumption rates far outstripping slack capacity, they would be completely overwhelmed in the event of an actual protracted, peer-to-peer conflict with an adversary such as China. Concerns have grown in some quarters not only over the condition of the Pentagon's own weapon stocks, but also over its ability to provide other key partners, such as Taiwan, with the military aid they urgently need in a timely fashion.[177] Meanwhile, the US Federal Trade Commission has begun to display a growing willingness to stymie or unwind further large-scale mergers within the defence industry.[178]

In addition to pouring funds into supply-chain investments and workforce training and retention programmes, the US is seeking ways to reform its cumbersome and outdated acquisition process, most notably by giving military services the authority to award multi-year contracts, typically reserved for large-scale naval or aircraft programmes, for the purchase of munitions and launcher lines.[179] Creating a strong, consistent demand signal through such multi-year contracts and block purchases will prove essential in convincing arms manufacturers of the value of making such costly – and risk-laden – capital investments in plant modernisation and expansion. Looking beyond the immediate, practical utility of acquisitions reform, this will inevitably require a continued and steady increase in the overall defence budget – one that continuously exceeds inflation – along with a broader willingness of US taxpayers to approve the purchase of munitions and platforms in greater excess volume, both as a form of security down payment, and as a means of keeping vital production lines up and running.

Strengthening US shipbuilding capacity will necessitate, as one report avers, a willingness to 'break with maritime strategies that assume commercial and national security contributions of the maritime industry are largely distinct', along with the recognition that the US Merchant Marine, as in the Second World War, would play a vital long-term sustainment and sealift role in the event of a US–China war.[180] Under the Maritime Security Program (MSP), established in 1996, and the Voluntary Intermodal Sealift Agreement (VISA), first authorised under the Defense Production Act of 1950, the US Department of Transportation's Maritime Administration (MARAD) administers two commercial sealift programmes intended to guarantee that Merchant Marine vessels, crews, port infrastructure and logistics-management services will be available in times of conflict or national emergencies.[181] For the time being, only 60 militarily useful commercial ships are maintained under the MSP. To add insult to injury, a 'turbo' wartime sealift stress test conducted in September 2019 revealed that only 33 of the 61 activated vessels were able to demonstrate immediate availability for inter-theatre force deployment.[182] In order to immediately increase the number of MSP-affiliated vessels, the US government should consider raising the annual stipends it pays ships that sail under the US flag – a decision that can often prove somewhat onerous for mariners in comparison to opting for other, more heavily subsidised and less tightly regulated foreign-flagged fleets. In addition to passing supportive legislation such as the recently introduced bipartisan Shipyard Act, which sought to make larger amounts of funding available for the improvement and development of both public and private shipyards, various programmes such as MARAD's Small Shipyard Grant Program, or the Federal Ship Financing Program ('Title XI') – which offers a full faith and credit loan guarantee by the federal government for private-sector debt accrued in the construction and/or reconstruction of ships and shipyards – could be revamped and sizeably expanded in the next few years.[183]

When it comes to the issue of contested logistics, there is a growing recognition of the need to minimise forward-based forces' dangerous dependence on continuous resupply from the CONUS. By deepening, hardening and dispersing forward-positioned munitions stocks and fuel-storage tanks, and working to improve in-theatre capabilities such as under-way replenishment and at-sea reloading, US military planners aim to both increase their forward, persistent combat power and enhance their general resiliency to disruption.[184] In the future, this resiliency could be bolstered by improvements in digital engineering and additive manufacturing, with 3D printers capable of rapidly producing spare parts aboard ships or on base, thus pushing part of the maintenance and repair cycle to the forward edge of battle.[185] Developments in renewable-energy technology could eventually reduce US forces' voracious appetite for fuel shipments, while advances in AI could help generate a more agile and effective inventory-maintenance and management system. Finally, the development of cheaper, more expendable uncrewed connectors and delivery systems would render the US logistical web far less brittle and vulnerable to disruption – provided, of course, these systems can be produced at sufficient speed and scale.[186]

Another important consideration is that of mass human mobilisation. Under the leadership of Xi Jinping, Chinese authorities have been placing a revived emphasis on this issue, which falls under the general rubric of 'civil–military integration', by strengthening the reserve element of the PLA as well as local militias such as the People's Armed Forces Committees and People's Air Defence System. As one close observer of Chinese military developments has noted, 'there are now reserve units at airports, ship repair yards and important factories, all designed for forms of military logistics support or to supplement the active PLA'.[187] All these initiatives would appear to indicate that the CCP has, slowly but surely, been resurrecting the kind of 'architecture for whole-of-nation mobilisation' that it so heavily relied upon in earlier periods of its history.[188]

In the US, fevered debates over the civic and military virtues of the draft, or some other variant of compulsory service, have swirled since the nation's founding. However, since the announcement by the Selective Service System on 27 January 1973 that there would be no further draft calls and that the US would move toward an all-volunteer force, there has been little appetite for its reintroduction. A reintroduction of the draft a full half-century after its disappearance hardly seems politically feasible – even in light of growing threat perceptions – or judicious, considering the enormous burden, both financial and logistical, that such a drastic step would place on the volunteer force. That said, US military planners will eventually need to think more strategically about the question of mass manpower mobilisation, whether in terms of expanding the size and capabilities of its military reserve forces, better integrating those same, fully mobilised reserves into emergent operational constructs, or in terms of reforming the current Selective Service machinery, which has remained in place, largely unchanged, for several decades. Under US law, virtually all male citizens and male aliens aged 18–25 residing in the US are required to register with the Selective Service. In the future, the US may need to consider extending this registration in duration (up to age 35, or even 40, for instance) and in scope (by requiring females to register as well). Indeed, while as of 1 January 2016, all gender-based military restrictions on military service were officially removed, allowing women to serve in combat roles, the Selective Service still, somewhat anachronistically, only applies to men. If, however, the US was ultimately compelled, under dire circumstances, to reintroduce conscription, it might struggle to find enough young men and women fit for immediate deployment. Indeed, a recent study showed that, with more than two-thirds of American adults classified as either overweight or obese, along with other reasons for disqualification such as drug and alcohol abuse, only 23% of 17–24-year-olds are currently considered eligible to serve – an alarming state of affairs that has rendered military recruitment increasingly challenging.[189]

Last but not least, Washington will need to focus on intensifying its efforts to prevail in the global competition for talent. In the decades since its rise to superpowerdom, the US has reaped enormous technological, economic and national-security advantages from immigration. From the refugee scientists who spearheaded the Manhattan Project to the extraordinary proportion (more than 45%) of Fortune 500 companies founded either by immigrants or their children, the lasting dividends drawn from these influxes of foreign talent appear self-evident.[190] No other industrialised country can boast such a distinguished roster of foreign-born, naturalised citizens having played such a central role in the formulation of its national-security policy – from the German-born Henry Kissinger, to the Polish-born Zbigniew Brzezinski, to the late, Czech-born, Madeleine Albright. Meanwhile, through the remarkable contributions of key figures such as the Bulgarian-born aeronautical-engineering genius Assen 'Jerry' Jordanoff, or Hyman G. Rickover, the Polish-American 'father of the nuclear navy', the American military-innovation enterprise has equally benefited from the drive, ingenuity and patriotism of naturalised immigrants.

While immigration issues can be highly contentious in the US, there may be some room in the years ahead for bipartisan compromise and legislative action on the narrower issue of skills-based immigration reform, particularly if the broader defence-policy community works to raise awareness of its criticality to US interests and security. Unlike China or Russia, the US – with its high white-collar wages, deep and liquid capital markets, world-class universities and reliable legal system – holds enormous appeal for foreign scientists, engineers, academics and entrepreneurs. America has traditionally captured 40–50% of the global inflow of college-educated migrants to OECD nations, followed by the UK, Canada and Australia, and more than half of all Nobel Prize winners moved to the US for professional reasons.[191] As of 2022, some 42% of all PhD students in STEM subjects (science, technology, engineering and maths) disciplines in US universities were foreign-born, as was approximately 69% of the Silicon Valley tech workforce, with the largest shares coming from India (25%) and China (14%).[192]

Even as the US continues to exert a strong gravitational pull on foreign talent, its domestic pool of skilled or highly specialised workers has become too shallow to properly compete with its most formidable rival, China. In international assessments, America's K–12 education system (so named because it stretches from kindergarten to 12th grade, or the end of secondary school) continues to lag behind those of most other industrialised nations, especially in STEM subjects.[193] Meanwhile, in addition to recently outpacing the US in several key scientific metrics and in its contribution to global R&D funding, Beijing is now projected to produce nearly twice as many STEM PhD graduates as the US by 2025.[194] As the US National Security Commission on Artificial Intelligence observed in its 2021 report, Washington is confronted with a daunting workforce deficit, and 'AI and digital talent is simply too scarce in the United States'.[195] In 2020, 'there were more than 430,000 open computer science jobs in the United States, while only 71,000 new computer scientists graduate from American universities each year'. These qualified-workforce deficiencies extend well beyond the field of computer science and AI, to affect the entirety of the US defence-industrial base. A sense of genuine alarm has begun to permeate the national-security establishment, with the 2021 Industrial Capabilities Report of the US DOD describing the current STEM shortage in the defence-industrial base as 'another Sputnik moment we can't afford to ignore'.[196]

In short, the US needs large numbers of highly skilled immigrants – and preferably large numbers of naturalised highly skilled immigrants, who can take the oath of allegiance and serve the US government – to compete and prevail in the twenty-first century. Efforts should certainly be made to improve the quality of the K–12 education system, and to upscale the skills of its native-born workforce, but such reforms will inevitably take years, if not decades, to fully bear fruit, and will therefore provide no short- to medium-term solution to the United States' widening talent gap with China. Streamlining immigration and naturalisation processes for foreign citizens with coveted competencies should therefore be a bipartisan national-security priority, and disentangled from other, more domestically contentious immigration-based issues.[197]

Grand strategy and diplomatic dexterity

This is an area where the US continues to hold a key advantage by virtue of its extensive alliance portfolio, both in Asia and in Europe. Although these alliances come with their own sets of security commitments and burden-sharing issues, they also provide the US with extensive global reach through a dense web of basing arrangements, and with considerable additive military, diplomatic and intelligence capabilities. Six treaty allies (Canada, France, Germany, Italy, Japan and the UK) feature among the top ten largest economies by nominal GDP.[198] Two of these allies permanently sit on the United Nations Security Council, and possess their own robust strategic deterrents, which has the added benefit of complicating adversaries' nuclear planning. Many, to include Japan and Germany, are now finally beginning to sizeably reinvest in their militaries after decades of relative risk aversion and underinvestment. This new and more proactive approach to defence has been partially motivated by recent events, with fears in both European and Asian capitals that Russia's brutal invasion of Ukraine might form a dangerous precedent, and, ultimately, a system-shattering event.[199] And indeed, the United States' democratic allies have displayed a remarkable, and some might say unexpected, level of shared resolve since the beginning of the war, both in their willingness to supply Kyiv with weaponry and financial assistance, and in their determination to sap Russia's economic strength though the application of unprecedently severe economic sanctions.[200]

The strong levels of support offered by Asian democracies such as Australia, Japan and South Korea to US-led efforts in Ukraine have served as a valuable reminder that, when push comes to shove, fellow liberal democracies remain America's strongest and most reliable allies. Similarly, the willingness of many of the most repressive and revisionist authoritarian regimes – from North Korea to Iran and Syria – to side militarily with Moscow appears to validate, to a certain degree, the notion that the collective geopolitical landscape continues to be traversed, and to a certain degree defined, by major ideational fault lines, even though it would be simplistic to reduce world affairs to a cosmic clash between democracy and authoritarianism. Meanwhile, Beijing's regional assertiveness and bombastic 'wolf warrior' diplomacy, combined with its recent actions in Hong Kong and lack of transparency regarding the origins of COVID-19, have only succeeded in denting its soft power, with public perceptions of China precipitously, and perhaps irredeemably, cratering across both Asia and Europe.[201]

Unlike the US, China has no formal allies. There are no immediate signs that it intends to reverse its long-standing policy of 'independence and self-reliance', preferring, in lieu of rigid alliances, to tout the more flexible and ambiguous concept of a 'new type of security partnership'.[202] Perspectives in Beijing, however, could suddenly change, particularly if concerns grow over Japanese rearmament, or over Washington's invigorated efforts to thicken its network of alliances in Asia beyond the traditional hub and spokes model – whether via 'minilateral' initiatives such as the Quad (Australia, India, Japan, US), AUKUS (Australia, UK, US) and the US–Japan–South Korea Trilateral, or through its remarkable recent string of successes in negotiating new basing arrangements in places ranging from Palau to the Philippines.[203]

If Beijing does shed its traditional mistrust of alliances, with the current China–Russia *entente* morphing into a proper, formalised mutual security arrangement, this could pose a significant and lasting challenge to US military dominance and allied strategy in the region.[204] Moscow might, for example, opt to provide Beijing with several of the apex military technologies it so desperately needs to overcome some of its few remaining sectoral weaknesses, either in ASW and nuclear-submarine design, or in high-performance aircraft engines.[205] The prospect of Chinese military assets freely ranging from Russian submarine and air bases would severely complicate US and allied operational planning. If Beijing were to gain permanent access to Russian Pacific Fleet facilities, notes one excellent recent study, this would 'facilitate a sustained PLAN presence in the sea of Japan', thus allowing Beijing to both break out of the United States' defensive perimeter and potentially outflank it.[206] Finally, in the event of a Sino-US war, Russia, with its bountiful reserves of energy and grain, could emerge as China's great continental resource reservoir, providing it with the energy and foodstuffs it would require to mitigate the most damaging effects of a US-led maritime blockade.[207] This would engender a veritable 'Eurasian nightmare' for American strategic planners,

Image 8: **Russian President Vladimir Putin greets Chinese PLA soldiers at the 2018 *Vostok* exercises, Tsugol range, Russia, 13 September 2018**

(Photo by Russian Presidential Press and Information Office/Handout/Anadolu Agency/Getty Images)

who would need to contend with a newly formed authoritarian 'fortress economy' squatting over much of the world's continental landmass, which the early twentieth-century British geographer Halford Mackinder memorably termed the great 'world island' or 'pivot area'.[208]

Even in the absence of a formally coordinated Sino-Russian campaign, one cannot discard the possibility of an opportunistic Russian, Iranian or North Korean act of aggression during a Sino-US protracted war. Indeed, under the opportunistic and congenitally hostile leadership of a Vladimir Putin or Kim Jong-un, it seems highly unlikely that Moscow, Tehran or Pyongyang would simply stand still and not try to draw advantage from Washington's distraction. Once again, there is nothing especially novel about this daunting dilemma. Even when locked in what initially appeared to be strictly dyadic struggles, great powers have frequently had to grapple with the reality or prospect of third-party intervention and scavenging, opportunistic 'war joiners', and have thus been compelled to update their war plans and posture their forces accordingly. During the Hundred Years War with France, English monarchs fretted constantly over the possibility of opportunistic Scottish assaults along their kingdom's northern border. Similarly, during the darkest days of the Second Punic War, Roman senators lived in fear of Philip V of Macedon's phalanxes taking advantage of Rome's state of weakness, suddenly disembarking on Italian soil to reinforce the reviled Carthaginian invaders.[209] Meanwhile, contemporary defence planners in Delhi sombrely talk of their need to plan for a two-front war, arguing that if large-scale hostilities were to break out along the Sino-Indian border, Islamabad would most likely opt to engage in an opportunistic act of aggression along the viciously disputed Line of Control (LoC), thus tying down large numbers of Indian troops along India's western front.[210]

If, however, Washington wishes to fully leverage the formidable potential of its alliance system, it will need to pursue three interrelated lines of effort.

Firstly, it must engage in deft alliance management, shoring up intra-alliance ties and ensuring that lingering historical sources of discord among allies such as South Korea and Japan, or Greece and Turkiye, do not dilute or even undermine the effectiveness of its overarching grand strategy. Understanding the complex domestic politics of friendly societies, or the variegated political constraints that shape the decision-making of allied leaders – for example, when it comes to advancing security cooperation or negotiating new basing arrangements – will prove crucial to shaping the military balance in America's favour. Efforts to reinforce relations with one key partner should not be seen as acting to the detriment of another. The way the AUKUS deal was unveiled, for example, was an example of ineffectual alliance management: while the trilateral security pact undoubtedly served both US interests and regional security, dissembling and hiding its development from

Paris needlessly antagonised one of the United States' most important allies.[211] On the other hand, Washington's discreet chaperoning of Japan–South Korea relations, with the major US allies holding their first bilateral summit in 12 years in March 2023, is a perfect example of quietly effective statesmanship.

Secondly, Washington should continue to enhance military cooperation with its major allies, and work to better integrate them into its operational constructs and war planning. At the same time, given the countries' sizeable differences in resources, investments and capabilities, it will need to ensure that technological gaps do not widen, preventing US and allied platforms from being truly inter-operable. As several leading US defence analysts have urged, this may require the negotiation of ambitious new intelligence- and information-sharing agreements to ensure that key allies are not shut out of the United States' emergent, and increasingly sophisticated, battle-network architectures.[212] In addition to revising and extending the rules governing foreign military sales and International Traffic in Arms Regulations (ITAR) exemptions, the US should also more actively pursue or build on joint weapons and munitions production programmes with countries ranging from Taiwan to Australia, Japan and Norway.[213] The recent agreement signed between Canberra and Washington to engage in the joint manufacture of guided weapons, ranging from Guided Multiple Launch Rocket Systems (GMLRS) to M795 155 mm artillery shells, surface-to-air missiles and heavyweight torpedoes, has the potential to be transformational in this regard, and is clearly a step in the right direction.[214]

Within Asia itself, intensified cooperation will be particularly important not only with regard to negotiating new basing arrangements, but also when it comes to more tightly enmeshing the United States' Indo-Pacific logistics system with those of its local allies and partners, thus allowing forward-stationed US forces to 'live off the land' and depend far less on external provisions.[215] As the US Army Pacific commander General Charles Flynn recently noted, heightened rotational US force deployments throughout the first island chain can serve as a useful diplomatic tool as well as having a deterrent function: not only do they 'thicken US interior lines' by improving US and allied training and readiness across a vast region, they can also help advance non-allied regional relationships, which, in times of major crisis, might prove absolutely critical.[216] Emphasis was laid, in Chapter Two, on the key additive role allies have historically played during protracted conflicts – whether in terms of lending vital economic or military capabilities, or niche specialisations. Within the context of contemporary Sino-US competition, one of the most vital potential allied contributions could be their industrial capacity – and more specifically shipyard capacity. Indeed, while the steady atrophy of the United States' shipbuilding industry is certainly cause for grave concern, Washington is also fortunate in that South Korea and Japan, two of its closest allies in Asia, are also, respectively, the second- and third-largest shipbuilders in the world.[217] The US should seek to better leverage its Indo-Pacific partners' industrial prowess, for example by using private Japanese and South Korean shipyards to maintain and repair US warships in theatre, rather than repatriating them thousands of miles across the Pacific for costly refits at US facilities.[218] This would have the added benefit of easing maintenance backlogs at chronically overwhelmed American shipyards, thus contributing to both US fleet readiness and forward presence in Asia. Finally, given the genuinely alarming state of the Military Sealift Command (MSC), TRANSCOM should seek to recapitalise its inventory as fast as possible, and without limitation on number, even if this requires prioritising the long-term lease of large numbers of foreign (preferably South Korean, Japanese or European) cargo vessels over the purchase of US-built ships.[219]

Finally, the US will need to advance a more affirmative free-trade agenda and work to convince its European and Asian allies that its revitalised industrial policy is not wholly protectionist in nature.[220] There is a danger that the United States' ambitious – and strategically judicious – efforts to strengthen its own economic competitivity and resiliency might jeopardise relations with some of its closest allies and trading partners, through 'indiscriminately discriminatory' trade policies that siphon investment and production away from their shores.[221] The US will therefore need to make efforts to better harmonise trade and economic approaches, secure ally-specific exemptions within certain key industrial sectors, and more generally reassure partners in Berlin, Paris and Seoul that its domestic rejuvenation will not be at their economic expense.

Conclusion

On the evening of 22 March 2023, Xi Jinping suddenly paused at the door of the Kremlin. Leaning toward his Russian host to bid him farewell, he stood for a moment in the chill night air, patiently waiting for his interpreter to translate his parting message to Vladimir Putin: 'Right now there are changes – the likes of which we haven't seen for 100 years – and we are the ones driving these changes together.'[1] Caught on camera, and coming at the end of a lavish three-day state visit during which both autocrats repeatedly highlighted the growing strength of the Sino-Russian *entente*, Xi's portentous ruminations only seemed to further underscore the tectonic nature of contemporary geopolitical shifts. Meanwhile, as both despots engaged in their demonstrative displays of bonhomie, Japanese Prime Minister Kishida Fumio made a surprise visit to Ukraine, pledging millions of dollars of additional aid, and touring the devastated town of Bucha. The contrast was striking, and for some historically minded observers, the early 2020s might now bring to mind other seemingly crepuscular moments in global affairs – from the dim twilight of the Edwardian era to the troubled interwar period, or the fraught early years of the Cold War.

In 1947, then US secretary of state Dean Acheson, pointing with alarm to the increasingly venomous state of US–Soviet relations, with the powers 'divided by an unbridgeable ideological chasm', also found himself turning to history, making the dramatic observation that 'not since Rome and Carthage' had 'there been such a polarization of power on this earth'.[2] It might seem somewhat premature or excessive to state that China and the US are now caught in the throes of a similarly bipolar and existential struggle, and yet there is little doubt that the evolving Sino-US rivalry has already begun to shape the contours of the twenty-first century. As relations between China and the United States have continued along their seemingly inexorable downward trajectory, concerns have grown in Washington over the state of the military balance, and over America's ability, after years of military downsizing, industrial consolidation and costly counter-insurgency campaigns, to prevail in a large-scale conflict against a peer competitor as redoubtable as China.

Since the end of the Cold War, America's military planning has placed a strong emphasis on winning short, sharp wars, and on using its technological prowess to rapidly seize the initiative in an era marked by the ubiquity of exquisite sensor and precision-strike networks. But military planners are now increasingly recognising the need to think beyond the first salvo, and that an armed conflict with an adversary as large, wealthy and powerful as the People's Republic of China would most likely evolve into a protracted war of attrition – one that would span several interlocking theatres, directly threaten the American homeland and civilian populace, and draw on all dimensions of national power.

In such a grim eventuality, how might the US and China both fare? This is no easy question, but it is one that this *Adelphi* book has attempted to answer at least partially, by engaging in an exercise of applied history and examining various aspects of protracted conflict across space and time. Protracted great-power wars are immensely destructive, whole-of-society affairs, the effects of which typically extend well beyond their point of origin, spilling across multiple regions and siphoning huge amounts of personnel, materiel and resources. When thinking about how to prevail in such draining marathons, neat quantifiable metrics such as ships, munitions stockpiles and logistical inventories certainly matter – but so do less easily measurable factors such as a state's capacity for scientific innovation, its societal resilience and the quality and robustness of its alliances. Ultimately, protracted great-power wars usually only end when an adversary faces total annihilation, or collapses under the weight of its own exhaustion. Final victory, this book has argued, therefore rests on a combination of three core factors: a state's military effectiveness and adaptability, its socio-economic power and resiliency, and the soundness of its alliance management and grand strategy.

A detailed comparative analysis of Beijing and Washington based on these three factors has shown that Washington seems quite well positioned to ultimately prevail, contrary to what some vocal declinists may believe. The world's oldest democracy remains its largest and most innovative economy.[3] Indeed, despite the meteoric ascent of China and other Asian juggernauts such as India, the United States' share of global GDP, somewhat remarkably, remains the same as it was in the early 1990s, at the height of the so-called unipolar era. The geopolitical fundamentals of its continued primacy remain strong: its favoured geographical position, its abundant natural resources and relatively healthy demographic profile, and its unparalleled network of allies and partners across the globe. To this one can add its new-found status as a net energy exporter, and the continued dominance of the dollar as the global reserve currency. Its formidable armed forces remain, by far, the world's most experienced, and appear – by virtue of their training, command structure and doctrinal philosophy – to be in a much better position to engage in rapid intra-war adaptation than their People's Liberation Army counterparts. Yet there is no room for hubris on this front: history has shown time and time again how determined adversaries can occasionally overcome an initial lack of expertise to attain competitive levels of combat proficiency.

China, meanwhile, suffers from several severe and growing challenges, including resources, demography and maintaining the sustained levels of economic growth essential to its regime's perceived legitimacy. Unlike the Soviet Union in its heyday, Beijing's ideational appeal remains limited, and it can draw on no formalised alliance structures or large-scale overseas basing networks that would enable it to truly magnify its military reach overseas.

Two aspects of the Sino-US competition, however, should foster grave and immediate concern in Washington, as well as in allied capitals.

The first is China's raw industrial might, and the sheer scale and scope of its military build-up, which, in many ways, is historically unprecedented. If the US wishes to maintain a viable conventional deterrent in Asia, it will need to launch a once-in-a-generation construction and procurement effort, all while encouraging its even more industrially atrophied allies in Europe and Asia to do the same. In addition to reinvesting massively in its defence-industrial base, merchant marine and logistical enablers, Washington will need to focus on enlarging and upskilling its labour force, both through accelerated domestic education and training programmes, and via a revamped, bipartisan immigration policy. Given the level of investments required to even approach the intensity of China's frantic shipbuilding efforts, the US may need to raise defence spending to well above its current levels. In the absence of a return to continuous Cold War levels of expenditure of 5–10% of GDP, it may prove necessary to engage in the ever-delicate bureaucratic exercise of re-evaluating the current intra-service budget share, with the aim of directing more funding to the services that would play the lead role in any China-related conflict scenario (i.e., the navy and air force).

Secondly, the evolving Sino-Russian *entente* offers another cause for anxiety, or at least a combination of guarded wariness and careful contingency planning. There appears to be little that the US or its allies can do to generate fissures within this rapidly solidifying authoritarian axis. Indeed, both parties appear firmly united in their detestation of the West, believing that they have far more to gain than to lose from tightening their security cooperation. Whether this perception will prove accurate, especially in the case of the weaker partner, Russia, remains to be seen. For now, however, Washington can do little other than closely monitor the relationship's development while attempting to consider the military ramifications of its potential maturation into a fully fledged alliance.

Finally, it goes without saying that none of these observations will obtain should the US succumb to powerful internal trends towards illiberalism, fall victim to extreme polarisation or slip into an extended period of domestic dysfunction. In any protracted war with an authoritarian challenger, some of the United States' most formidable competitive advantages would be its civic resilience; its values of openness, tolerance and innovation; its network of democratic allies; and its capacity to engage in unified, long-term planning. An America unmoored from its foundational values, estranged from its most capable long-standing allies, unable to pass a budget in time, and more generally riven by internal divisions would have little chance of prevailing over its most formidable peer competitor.

Chapter One

1   For a stimulating discussion of the 2018 NDS and its revived focus on great-power competition, see 'Policy Roundtable: A Close Look at the 2018 National Defense Strategy', *Texas National Security Review*, 26 January 2018, https://tnsr.org/roundtable/policy-roundtable-close-look-2018-national-defense-strategy.

2   Most notably, the 2022 NSS baldly states that the US has now 'broken down the dividing line between foreign policy and domestic policy. We understand that if the United States is to succeed abroad, we must invest in our innovation and industrial strength, and build our resilience, at home.' See The White House, 'National Security Strategy', October 2022, p. 8, https://www.whitehouse.gov/wp-content/uploads/2022/10/Biden-Harris-Administrations-National-Security-Strategy-10.2022.pdf.

3   For a small sampling of these growing concerns, see Conrad Crane, 'Too Fragile to Fight: Could the US Military Withstand a War of Attrition?', War on the Rocks, 9 May 2022, https://warontherocks.com/2022/05/too-fragile-to-fight-could-the-u-s-military-withstand-a-war-of-attrition; Anna Jean Wirth et al., 'Keeping the Defense Industrial Base Afloat During COVID-19: A Review of the Department of Defense and Federal Government Policies and Investments in the Defense Industrial Base', RAND Corporation, 2021, https://www.rand.org/pubs/research_reports/RRA1392-1.html; and Hal Brands, 'Ukraine War Shows the US Military Isn't Ready for War with China', Bloomberg, 18 September 2022, https://www.bloomberg.com/opinion/articles/2022-09-18/ukraine-war-shows-the-us-military-isn-t-ready-for-war-with-china#xj4y7vzkg.

4   For a good overview of China's growing tendency to resort to economic coercion, see Evan Feigenbaum, 'Is Coercion the New Normal in China's Economic Statecraft?', MacroPolo, 25 July 2017,

https://macropolo.org/coercion-new-normal-chinas-economic-statecraft. For an excellent examination of China's coercive diplomatic behaviour writ large, see Fergus Hanson, Emilia Currey and Tracy Beattie, 'The Chinese Communist Party's Coercive Diplomacy', Australian Strategic Policy Institute, 2020, https://www.aspi.org.au/report/chinese-communist-partys-coercive-diplomacy.

5   On the drivers and implications of this renewed 'overconcentration of power', see Susan L. Shirk, 'China in Xi's "New Era": The Return to Personalistic Rule', *Journal of Democracy*, vol. 29, no. 2, 2018, pp. 22–36, https://www.journalofdemocracy.org/articles/china-in-xis-new-era-the-return-to-personalistic-rule/; and Bjorn Alexander Duben, 'Xi Jinping and the End of Chinese Exceptionalism', *Problems of Post-Communism*, vol. 67, no. 2, 2020, pp. 111–28.

6   On China's growing jingoism and increasingly confrontational public diplomacy, see, for example, Jessica Chen Weiss, *Powerful Patriots: Nationalist Protest in China's Foreign Relations* (New York: Oxford University Press, 2014); Jude D. Blanchette, *China's New Red Guards: The Return of Radicalism and the Rebirth of Mao Zedong* (New York: Oxford University Press, 2019); and Peter Martin, *China's Civilian Army: The Making of Wolf Warrior Diplomacy* (New York: Oxford University Press, 2021). As Susan Shirk notes in her excellent recent analysis of Chinese foreign policy, clear signs of China's growing truculence, or hubris, could already be detected in the 2000s, particularly in the wake of the 2008 financial crisis. See Susan Shirk, *Overreach: How China Derailed Its Peaceful Rise* (New York: Oxford University Press, 2023).

7   See Ben Blanchard and Yew Lun Tian, 'Polishing the Gun: China, US Tensions Raise Taiwan Conflict Fears', Reuters, 26 August 2020, https://www.reuters.com/article/us-taiwan-china-security-analysis/polishing-the-gun-china-u-s-tensions-raise-taiwan-conflict-fears-idUSKBN25M0VE; 'Philippines Flags Incursion by Nearly 300 Chinese Militia Boats', Reuters, 12 May 2021, https://www.reuters.com/world/asia-pacific/philippines-flags-incursions-by-nearly-300-chinese-militia-boats-2021-05-12; and 'China Faces Fateful Choices, Especially Involving Taiwan', *The Economist*, 20 February 2021, https://www.economist.com/china/2021/02/20/china-faces-fateful-choices-especially-involving-taiwan.

8   Oriana Skylar Mastro, 'The Taiwan Temptation: Why Beijing May Resort to Force', *Foreign Affairs*, July/August 2021, https://www.foreignaffairs.com/articles/china/2021-06-03/china-taiwan-war-temptation.

9   For a discussion of the notion of 'windows of opportunity', see Richard Ned Lebow, 'Windows of Opportunity: Do States Jump Through Them?', *International Security*, vol. 9, no. 1, Summer 1984, pp. 147–86.

10 See, for example, the compelling arguments laid out by Michael Beckley and Hal Brands in *Danger Zone: The Coming Conflict with China* (New York: W. W. Norton, 2022).

11 There is an extensive literature on preventive war. See, for example, Jack S. Levy, 'Preventive War: Concept and Propositions', *International Interactions*, vol. 37, no. 1, 2011, pp. 87–96. On the drivers undergirding the fateful decision to launch a preventive war, see, for example, Dale Copeland, 'A Tragic Choice: Japanese Preventive Motivations and the Origins of the Pacific War', *International Interactions*, vol. 37, no. 1, 2011, pp. 116–26; James D. Fearon, 'Rationalist Explanations for

War', *International Organization*, vol. 49, no. 3, 1995, pp. 379–414; Marc Trachtenberg, 'Preventive War and U.S. Foreign Policy', *Security Studies*, vol. 15, no. 1, 2007, pp. 1–31; and J. Kugler and A.F.K. Organski, *The War Ledger* (Chicago, IL: University of Chicago Press, 1980).

12 See Kirstin Huang, 'US Marines Chief Calls China the Pacing Threat for the Next Decade', *South China Morning Post*, 4 March 2021, https://www.scmp.com/news/china/diplomacy/article/3123944/us-marines-chief-calls-china-pacing-threat-next-decade; and Jim Garamone, 'Official Talks DOD Policy Role in Chinese Pacing Threat, Integrated Deterrence', DOD News, 2 June 2021, https://www.defense.gov/Explore/News/Article/Article/2641068/official-talks-dod-policy-role-in-chinese-pacing-threat-integrated-deterrence.

13 The White House, 'National Security Strategy', October 2022.

14 On how ongoing shifts in the balance of power call for a revised military approach, see Christopher M. Dougherty, 'Why America Needs a New Way of War', Center for a New American Security, 2019, https://www.cnas.org/publications/reports/anawow; and Thomas G. Mahnken, Grace Kim and Adam Lemon, 'Piercing the Fog of Peace: Developing Innovative Operational Concepts for a New Era', Center for Strategic and Budgetary Assessments, 2019, https://csbaonline.org/research/publications/piercing-the-fog-of-peace-developing-innovative-operational-concepts-for-a-/publication/1.

15 See, for example, David C. Gompert, Astrid Stuth Cevallos and Cristina L. Garafola, 'War with China: Thinking Through the Unthinkable', RAND Corporation, 2016, pp. 71–3, https://www.rand.org/pubs/research_reports/RR1140.html.

16 Jim Mitre, 'A Eulogy for the Two-war Construct', *Washington Quarterly*, vol. 41, no. 4, 2018, pp. 7–30.

17 See David Vergun, 'DOD Focuses on Aspirational Challenges in Future Warfighting', DOD News, 26 July 2021, https://www.defense.gov/News/News-Stories/Article/Article/2707633/dod-focuses-on-aspirational-challenges-in-future-warfighting; and Frank Wolfe, 'Joint Warfighting Concept Assumes "Contested Logistics"', Defense Daily, 6 October 2020, https://www.defensedaily.com/joint-war fighting-concept-assumes-contested-logistics/pentagon/.

18 The commonly employed acronym C4ISR stands for command, control, communications and computers (C4) intelligence, surveillance and reconnaissance (ISR).

19 Joshua Rovner, 'A Long War in the East: Doctrine, Diplomacy, and the Prospects for a Protracted Sino-American Conflict', *Diplomacy and Statecraft*, vol. 29, no. 1, 2018, pp. 129–42.

20 These include Mao Zedong's own writings on protracted and guerrilla warfare, derived from the Chinese Communist Party's combat experience during the Chinese civil war and the Sino-Japanese War. For a useful compilation and discussion of these seminal texts, see Arthur Waldron (ed.), *Mao on Warfare: On Guerilla Warfare, On Protracted War, and Other Martial Writings* (New York: CN Times Books, 2013).

21 One influential and much-cited DOD-commissioned document from the late 1990s provided a particularly memorable definition of network-centric warfare (NCW) as it was perceived at the time: 'We define NCW as an information superiority-enabled concept of operations that generates increased combat power by networking sensors, decision-makers, and shooters to

achieve shared awareness, increased speed of command, higher tempo of operations, greater lethality, increased survivability, and a degree of self-synchronization. In essence, NCW translates information superiority into combat power by effectively limiting knowledgeable entities in the battlespace.' See David S. Alberts et al., *Network Centric Warfare: Developing and Leveraging Information Superiority*, 2nd ed. (Washington DC: DOD C4ISR Cooperative Research Program, 1999). There is a vast literature on the centrality of technology to the American way of war. For a balanced and nuanced perspective, see Thomas G. Mahnken, *Technology and the American Way of War Since 1945* (New York: Columbia University Press, 2008).

22 See US Department of Defense, 'Summary of the Joint All-domain Command and Control (JADC2) Strategy', March 2022, https://media.defense.gov/2022/Mar/17/2002958406/-1/-1/1/SUMMARY-OF-THE-JOINT-ALL-DOMAIN-COMMAND-AND-CONTROL-STRATEGY.PDF.

23 Nina A. Kollars, 'War at Information Speed', in Stenn Rynning, Oliver Schmitt and Amelie Theussen (eds), *War Time: Temporality and the Decline of Western Military Power* (Washington DC: Brookings Institution Press, 2021), pp. 230–52.

24 For a stimulating take on timing in combat operations and John Boyd's famed focus on the observe–orient–decide–act (OODA) loop, or iterative feedback loop, see Alastair Luft, 'The OODA Loop and the Half-beat', The Strategy Bridge, 17 March 2020, https://thestrategybridge.org/the-bridge/2020/3/17/the-ooda-loop-and-the-half-beat.

25 China Aerospace Studies Institute, 'In Their Own Words: Science of

Military Strategy', p. 238, https://www.airuniversity.af.edu/CASI/Display/Article/2485204/plas-science-of-military-strategy-2013/.

26 See Alison A. Kaufman and Daniel M. Hartnett, 'Managing Conflict: Examining Recent PLA Writings on Escalation Control', CNA China Studies, February 2016, https://www.cna.org/cna_files/pdf/DRM-2015-U-009963-Final3.pdf; and Forrest E. Morgan et al., 'Dangerous Thresholds: Managing Escalation in the 21st Century', RAND Corporation, 2008, p. 54.

27 See Jeffrey Engstrom, 'Systems Confrontation and System Destruction Warfare: How the Chinese People's Liberation Army Seeks to Wage Modern Warfare', RAND Corporation, 2018, https://www.rand.org/pubs/research_reports/RR1708.html; and David C. Gompert and Martin Libicki, 'Cyber Warfare and Sino-American Crisis Instability', *Survival: Global Politics and Strategy*, vol. 56, no. 4, 2014, pp. 7–22. On the tendency in Chinese writings to simply skirt the issue of protraction in order to focus more on short-lived conflict scenarios, see also Timothy R. Heath, Kristen Gunness and Tristan Finazzo, 'The Return of Great Power War: Scenarios of Systemic Conflict Between the United States and China', RAND Corporation, 2022, https://www.rand.org/pubs/research_reports/RRA830-1.html.

28 Mao Zedong, *On Protracted Warfare*, cited in John Costello and Peter Mattis, 'Electronic Warfare and the Renaissance of Chinese Information', in Joe McReynolds (ed.), *China's Evolving Military Strategy* (Washington DC: Jamestown Foundation, 2016), p. 75. Mattis and Costello both note that pre-emption and system-of-system paralysis form the two structural pillars of Chinese information-warfare operational strategy.

29 For more background on Chinese
'blinding' concepts, see Zi Yang,
'Blinding the Enemy: How the PRC
Prepares for Radar Countermeasures',
China Brief, vol. 18, no. 6, April 2018,
https://jamestown.org/program/
blinding-the-enemy-how-the-prc-
prepares-for-radar-countermeasures;
Elsa B. Kania and John Costello,
'Seizing the Commanding Heights:
The PLA Strategic Support Force in
Chinese Military Power', *Journal of
Strategic Studies*, vol. 44, no. 2, 2021, pp.
218–64; and Edmund J. Burke et al.,
'People's Liberation Army Operational
Concepts', RAND Corporation, 2020,
https://www.rand.org/pubs/research_
reports/RRA394-1.html.

30 Basil Liddell Hart, *Strategy: The Indirect
Approach* (New York: Praeger, 1954),
ch. 15. For Fuller's description of
how armoured thrusts could unleash
a 'barrage of demoralisation' and
trigger 'strategic paralysis', see J.F.C.
Fuller, *The Reformation of War* (London:
Hutchinson and Company, 1923), p.
89. On how the British school's focus
on the psychological impact endures
in some of the ideas underpinning
so-called 'effects-based operations' in
American strategic thought, see Brian
Holden Reid, *Studies in British Military
Thought: Debates with Fuller and Liddell
Hart* (Lincoln, NE: University of
Nebraska Press, 1998).

31 As Aaron L. Friedberg has noted, the
possibility of a tense confrontation
between opponents 'armed with
highly capable, but potentially
fragile, conventional precision-
strike complexes could replicate the
"two scorpions in a bottle" problem
that so troubled nuclear strategists
during the Cold War'. See Aaron L.
Friedberg, *Beyond Air–Sea Battle: The
Debate over US Military Strategy in
Asia* (London: IISS, 2014), p. 90.

32 On the escalatory pressures inherent
in both states' concepts of operation,
see Craig Neuman, 'The Cult of

Accelerated War: How US and
Chinese Warfighting Doctrines
Increase the Risk of Escalation',
Center for Strategic and International
Studies, 2020, https://www.jstor.org/
stable/resrep24234.9.

33 Justin Kelly and Michael Brennan,
'Alien: How Operational Art
Devoured Strategy', US Army
War College Press, 2009, p. 58,
https://press.armywarcollege.edu/
monographs/620.

34 Gordon W. Prange with Donald M.
Goldstein and Katherine V. Dillon,
*At Dawn We Slept: The Untold Story
of Pearl Harbor* (New York: McGraw-
Hill, 1981), p. 21.

35 Klaus Knorr, 'Strategic Surprise: The
Incentive Structure', in Klaus Knorr
and Patrick Morgan, *Strategic Military
Surprise: Incentives and Opportunities*
(London: Transaction Books, 1983),
pp. 173–95.

36 See Patrick Morgan, 'The
Opportunity for Strategic Surprise',
in Knorr and Morgan, *Strategic
Military Surprise: Incentives and
Opportunities*, pp. 195–247.

37 On the PLA's historic fondness for
strategic surprise, see Mark A. Ryan
et al. (eds), *Chinese Warfighting: The
PLA Experience Since 1949* (New York:
Routledge, 2003); and Mark Burles and
Abram N. Shulsky, 'Patterns in China's
Use of Force: Evidence from History
and Doctrinal Writings', RAND
Corporation, 2000, https://www.
rand.org/pubs/monograph_reports/
MR1160.html. On how this intellectual
predilection is still manifest in Chinese
military writings, see Toshi Yoshihara,
'Chinese Views of Future Warfare in
the Indo-Pacific: First Strike and US
Forward Bases in Japan', in John H.
Maurer and Erik Goldstein (eds), *The
Road to Pearl Harbor: Great Power War
in Asia and the Pacific* (Annapolis, MD:
Naval Institute Press, 2022), pp. 162–82.

38 For a good overview of Chinese
operational concepts regarding

Taiwan, see Lonnie Henley, 'PLA Operational Concepts and Centers of Gravity in a Taiwan Conflict: Testimony Before the U.S.–China Economic and Security Review Commission Hearing on Cross-strait Deterrence', 18 February 2021, https://www.uscc.gov/sites/default/files/2021-02/Lonnie_Henley_Testimony.pdf.

39 See, for example, Bonny Lin and John Culver, 'China's Taiwan Invasion Plans May Get Faster and Deadlier', *Foreign Policy*, 19 April 2022, https://foreignpolicy.com/2022/04/19/china-invasion-ukraine-taiwan.

40 See Antulio J. Echevarria II, 'Toward an American Way of War', US Army War College, 2004, p. 10, https://www.files.ethz.ch/isn/14216/Toward%20and%20American%20Way%20of%20War.pdf; Phillip S. Meilinger, 'Time in War', *Joint Force Quarterly*, vol. 87, no. 4, 2017, pp. 93–100, https://ndupress.ndu.edu/Media/News/News-Article-View/Article/1326002/time-in-war; and Thomas Hughes, 'The Cult of the Quick', *Aerospace Power Journal*, vol. 15, no. 4, 2001, pp. 57–68, https://go.gale.com/ps/i.do?p=AONE&u=googlescholar&id=GALE|A82777339&v=2.1&it=r&sid=AONE&asid=895d2708.

41 For two useful examinations of various scenarios that could lead to Sino-US conflict, see Gompert et al., 'War with China: Thinking Through the Unthinkable'; and Todd South, 'What War with China Could Look Like', *Military Times*, 1 September 2020, https://www.militarytimes.com/news/your-army/2020/09/01/what-war-with-china-could-look-like. It is important to note that this study does not argue that the victim of the first salvo would necessarily be severely crippled, or that each protagonist is equally vulnerable to a pre-emptive strike – indeed, as we shall see, the PLA may well possess a 'localised

hardening advantage' vis-à-vis the US military's more dispersed and less well-defended basing structure. That said, there is no question that the combat environment would be radically transformed and universally more degraded in the wake of the first multi-domain battle network exchanges, regardless of who the pre-emptor was.

42 On the importance of deterring a Chinese or Russian fait accompli, see Elbridge Colby, 'How to Win America's Next War', *Foreign Policy*, 5 May 2019, https://foreignpolicy.com/2019/05/05/how-to-win-americas-next-war-china-russia-military-infrastructure. For an excellent examination of the concept of fait accompli, see Daniel W. Altman, 'By Fait Accompli, Not Coercion: How States Wrest Territory from Their Adversaries', *International Studies Quarterly*, vol. 61, no. 4, 2017, pp. 881–91, https://academic.oup.com/isq/article/61/4/881/4781720.

43 See, for example, Lawrence Freedman's analysis of the literature on the future of warfare in the nineteenth and early twentieth centuries. Lawrence Freedman, *The Future of War: A History* (New York: Hachette Books, 2017).

44 There is a vast literature on war termination as well as on the rhetoric and psychology of sunk costs in foreign policy. For a brief sampling of some of the more relevant material, see B.M. Staw, 'Knee-deep in the Big Muddy: A Study of Escalating Commitment to a Chosen Course of Action', *Organizational Behavior and Human Performance*, vol. 16, no. 1, June 1976, pp. 27–44, https://www.sciencedirect.com/science/article/abs/pii/0030507376900052; William A. Boettcher III and Michael D. Cobb, '"Don't Let Them Die in Vain": Casualty Frames and Public Tolerance for Escalating Commitment

in Iraq', *Journal of Conflict Resolution*, vol. 53, no. 5, 2009, pp. 677–97; and H.R. Arkes and Catherine Blumer, 'The Psychology of Sunk Cost', *Organizational Behavior and Human Decision Processes*, vol. 35, 1985, pp. 124–40, https://www.researchgate. net/publication/4812596_The_ psychology_of_sunk_cost.

45 Fred Charles Iklé, *Every War Must End* (New York: Columbia University Press, 1991), p. 42.

46 For 'calculated act of terror', see Joseph Strayer, *The Albigensian Crusades* (Ann Arbor, MI: University of Michigan Press, 1992), p. ix. See also Elaine Graham-Leigh, 'Justifying Deaths: The Chronicler Pierre des Vaux-De-Cernay and the Massacre of Béziers', Mediaeval Studies, vol. 63, 2001, pp. 283–303. On the controversy surrounding Henry V's slaughter of the French prisoners at Agincourt, see Andy King, '"Then a Great Misfortune Befell Them": The Laws of War on Surrender and the Killing of Prisoners on the Battlefield in the Hundred Years War', *Journal of Medieval History*, vol. 43, no. 1, 2017, pp. 106–17. On brutalisation in protracted medieval warfare more broadly, see Sean McGlynn, *By Sword and Fire: Cruelty and Atrocity in Medieval Warfare* (London: Weidenfeld and Nicolson, 2014).

47 See Marion Girard, *A Strange and Formidable Weapon: British Responses to World War I Poison Gas* (Lincoln, NE: University of Nebraska Press, 2008); and L.F. Farber, *The Poisonous Cloud: Chemical Warfare in the First World War* (New York: Oxford University Press, 1986).

48 Interestingly, during the Second World War, mutual restraint regarding the use of chemical weapons on the battlefield was observed by Germany and the Allies (although not by Germany's Italian ally in Ethiopia, or by the Japanese in China). Jeffrey Legro has argued that the Wehrmacht's restraint, rather unsurprisingly, was primarily for practical and bureaucratic, rather than ethical, reasons. See Jeffrey W. Legro, 'Military Culture and Inadvertent Escalation in World War II', *International Security*, vol. 18, no. 4, 1994, pp. 108–42.

49 See Williamson Murray and Kevin M. Woods, *The Iran–Iraq War: A Military and Strategic History* (Cambridge: Cambridge University Press, 2014); Efraim Karsh, *The Iran–Iraq War: 1980–1988* (Oxford: Osprey Publishing, 2002); and Pierre Razoux, *The Iran–Iraq War* (Cambridge, MA: Harvard University Press, 2015).

50 Detailed historical examples of such instances – when defeat in protracted war was either precipitated or was the result of internal political upheaval – will be provided later in this study. For some academic examinations of how shifts in governing coalitions or political leadership can accompany war termination, see Elizabeth A. Stanley, *Paths to Peace: Domestic Coalition Shifts, War Termination and the Korean War* (Stanford, CA: Stanford University Press, 2009); Harold Calahan, *What Makes a War End?* (New York: Vanguard Press, 1944); and Bruce Bueno de Mesquita and David Lalman, *War and Reason: Domestic and International Imperatives* (New Haven, CT: Yale University Press, 1992).

51 Cathal J. Nolan, *The Allure of Battle* (New York: Oxford University Press, 2017), p. 7.

52 Philippe Contamine, *La Guerre de Cent Ans* (Paris: Presses Universitaires de France, 1968), pp. 118–99. Author's translation from the French.

53 On this categorisation issue, see Jack S. Levy, *War in the Modern Great Power System: 1495–1975* (Lexington, KY: University Press of Kentucky, 1983), pp. 50–76.

54 For two excellent biographies of Bismarck, see A.J.P. Taylor, *Bismarck: The Man and the Statesman* (New York: Vintage, 2011); and Jonathan Steinberg, *Bismarck: A Life* (New York: Oxford University Press, 2011). For a good overview of the literature on early German nationalism and its anti-French emotional stimulants, see Mark Hewitson, 'Belligerence, Patriotism and Nationalism in the German Public Sphere, 1792–1815', *English Historical Review*, vol. 128, no. 533, 2013, pp. 839–76.

55 The term 'Hundred Years War' was first employed by the French historian Chrysanthe-Ovide des Michels in his *Tableau Chronologique de L'histoire du Moyen Âge*. It was then imported into English historiography by the English historian Edward Freeman. For a good retracing of the genealogy of this descriptor, see George Minois, *La Guerre de Cent Ans: Naissance de Deux Nations* (Paris: Éditions Perrin, 2008), pp. 10–11.

56 See Andrew Roth, 'Putin's Security Men: The Elite Group Who Fuel His Anxieties', *Guardian*, 4 February 2022, https://www.theguardian.com/world/2022/feb/04/putin-security-elite-siloviki-russia. For an excellent recent discussion of memory politics in today's Russia and the role certain key chapters in Soviet history play therein, see Jade McGlynn, *Memory Makers: The Politics of the Past in Putin's Russia* (London: Bloomsbury, 2023).

57 Polybius, *The Histories*, Book III.4, Loeb Classical Library edition, 1922, https://penelope.uchicago.edu/Thayer/E/Roman/Texts/Polybius/3*.html.

58 See Andrew Sweet, *The Strength of the City: Morale in Thucydides' Histories*, PhD dissertation, Cornell University, 2011, https://ecommons.cornell.edu/handle/1813/29224.

59 See, for example, Rachel M. Stein, *Vengeful Citizens, Violent States: A Theory of War and Revenge* (New York: Cambridge University Press, 2019); Peter Liberman, 'An Eye for an Eye: Public Support for War Against Evildoers', *International Organization*, vol. 60, no. 3, 2006, pp. 687–722; Peter Liberman and Linda J. Skitka, 'Revenge in US Public Support for War Against Iraq', *Public Opinion Quarterly*, vol. 81, no. 3, 2017, pp. 636–60; and Peter Liberman, 'War and Torture as "Just Deserts"', *Public Opinion Quarterly*, vol. 78, no. 1, 2014, pp. 47–70.

60 For an excellent examination of national sentiment (and revanchism) during this fraught period in French history, see Karine Varley, *Under the Shadow of Defeat: The War of 1870–71 in French Memory* (London: Palgrave Macmillan, 2008).

61 See Daniel Markey, 'Prestige and the Origins of War: Returning to Realism's Roots', *Security Studies*, vol. 8, no. 4, 1999, pp. 126–72; Richard Ned Lebow, *A Cultural Theory of International Relations* (Cambridge: Cambridge University Press, 2008); Mark L. Haas, *The Ideological Origins of Great Power Politics 1789 1989* (Ithaca, NY: Cornell University Press, 2007); and Stacie E. Goddard, 'Uncommon Ground: Indivisible Territory and the Politics of Legitimacy', *International Organization*, vol. 60, no. 1, 2006, pp. 35–68.

62 And, more specifically, the desire to regain the lost continental holdings of the former Angevin Empire. See Malcolm Vale, *The Angevin Legacy and the Hundred Years War, 1250–1340* (London: Blackwell, 1990). On the development of French royal exceptionalism in the centuries leading up to the Hundred Years War, see Robert Fawtier, *The Capetian Kings of France: Monarchy and Nation, 987–1328* (London: Palgrave Macmillan, 1960); John W. Baldwin, *The Government of Philip Augustus: Foundations of French Royal Power in the Middle Ages* (Berkeley,

CA: University of California Press, 1986); and James Naus, *Constructing Kingship: The Capetian Monarchs of France and the Early Crusades* (Manchester: Manchester University Press, 2016).

63 See Marjorie Reeves, *The Prophetic Sense of History in Medieval and Renaissance Europe* (New York: Routledge, 1999); and Alexandre Y. Haran, *Le Lys et le Globe: Messianisme Dynastique et Rêve Impérial en France aux XVIᵉ et XVIIᵉ Siècles* (Paris: Éditions Champ Vallon, 2016).

64 Michael Howard, 'The Forgotten Dimensions of Strategy', *Foreign Affairs*, vol. 57, no. 5, 1979, pp. 975–86, https://www.foreignaffairs.com/articles/1979-06-01/forgotten-dimensions-strategy.

65 Two exceptions, which both provide compelling and useful intellectual points of departure, are Andrew F. Krepinevich Jr, 'Protracted Great-power War: A Preliminary Assessment', Center for a New American Security, 5 February 2020, https://www.cnas.org/publications/reports/protracted-great-power-war; and Hal Brands, 'Getting Ready for a Long War with China: Dynamics of Protracted Conflict in the Western Pacific', American Enterprise Institute, 25 July 2022, https://www.aei.org/research-products/report/getting-ready-for-a-long-war-with-china-dynamics-of-protracted-conflict-in-the-western-pacific.

66 For three examples of Cold War-era thinking on the issue of conflict protraction, see Robert Strausz-Hupe et al., *Protracted Conflict* (New York: Harper and Brothers, 1959); John K. Setear, 'Protracted Conflict in Central Europe: A Conceptual Analysis', RAND Corporation, 1989; and Joseph W. Russel, 'Concepts for Protracted War: A Report Prepared for the Director of the Defense Nuclear Agency', Boeing Aerospace Company, 1 December 1980, https://apps.dtic.mil/dtic/tr/fulltext/u2/a956120.pdf.

67 For an excellent overview of US grand strategy during the Cold War and how it can inform present-day thinking on great-power competition, see Hal Brands, *The Twilight Struggle: What the Cold War Teaches Us About Great-power Rivalry Today* (New Haven, CT: Yale University Press, 2022).

68 See, for example, Ali Wyne, 'America's Blind Ambition Could Make It a Victim of Global Competition', *National Interest*, 11 February 2019, https://nationalinterest.org/feature/americas-blind-ambition-could-make-it-victim-global-competition-44227; and Katie Bo Williams, 'What's Great Power Competition? No One Really Knows', Defense One, 13 May 2019, https://www.defenseone.com/news/2019/05/whats-great-power-competition-no-one-really-knows/156969. On the debate over whether China and the US are currently caught in the throes of a new cold war, see Iskander Rehman et al., 'Policy Roundtable: Are the United States and China in a New Cold War?', *Texas National Security Review*, 15 May 2018, https://tnsr.org/roundtable/policy-roundtable-are-the-united-states-and-china-in-a-new-cold-war.

69 See, for example, Peter Trubowitz, Emily O. Goldman and Edward Rhodes (eds), *The Politics of Strategic Adjustment: Ideas, Institutions, and Interests* (New York: Columbia University Press, 1999); and Emily O. Goldman, *Power in Uncertain Times: Strategy in the Fog of Peace* (Stanford, CA: Stanford University Press, 2010).

70 On the importance and utility of applied history, see Iskander Rehman, 'Why Applied History Matters', Engelsberg Ideas, 20 November 2021, https://engelsbergideas.com/essays/why-applied-history-matters/;

Hal Brands and William Inboden, 'Wisdom Without Tears: Statecraft and the Uses of History', *Journal of Strategic Studies*, vol. 41, no. 7, 2018, pp. 916–46; and Robert Crowcroft (ed.), *Applied History and Contemporary Policymaking: School of Statecraft* (London: Bloomsbury, 2022).

71 On the Clausewitzian *coup d'oeil*, 'an intellect that, even in the darkest hour, retains some glimmerings of the inner light which leads to truth', see Carl von Clausewitz, *On War*, Book I. On Patton's passion for history, see J. Furman Daniel III, *Patton: Battling with History* (Columbia, MO: University of Missouri Press, 2020). For an excellent examination of the power the myth of Alexander exerted over Roman elites, and most famously Julius Caesar, see Diana Spencer, 'Roman Alexanders: Epistemology and Identity', in Waldemar Heckel and Lawrence A. Tritle (eds), *Alexander the Great: A New History* (Chichester: Blackwell, 2009), pp. 251–75.

72 Polybius, *The Histories*, Book I.36, Loeb Classical Library edition, 1922, https:// penelope.uchicago.edu/Thayer/E/ Roman/Texts/Polybius/1*.html.

73 Jim Mattis and Bing West, *Call Sign Chaos: Learning to Lead* (New York: Random House, 2019), p. 12.

74 Quoted in Jay Luvaas, 'Military History and Officer Education: Some Personal Reflections', The Army Historian, no. 6, Winter 1985, pp. 9–11, https://www.jstor.org/ stable/26303404?seq=1.

75 See, for example, Toshi Yoshihara, 'Chinese Lessons from the Pacific War: Implications for PLA Warfighting', Center for Strategic and Budgetary Assessments, 5 January 2023, https://csbaonline. org/research/publications/chinese-lessons-from-the-pacific-war-implications-for-pla-warfighting;

Lyle Goldstein, 'China's Falklands Lessons', *Survival: Global Politics and Strategy*, vol. 50, no. 3, 2008, pp. 65–82; Lyle Goldstein, 'Why China's View of the Battle of Guadalcanal Matters', *National Interest*, 21 October 2021, https:// nationalinterest.org/blog/ reboot/why-chinas-view-battle-guadalcanal-matters-194825; and Fumio Ota, 'Sun Tzu in Contemporary Chinese Strategy', Joint Force Quarterly, no. 73, April 2014, pp. 76–80, https:// ndupress.ndu.edu/JFQ/Joint-Force-Quarterly-73/Article/577507/sun-tzu-in-contemporary-chinese-strategy.

76 On the importance of leveraging asymmetries and identifying enduring sources of advantage as part of a strategy of long-term cost imposition – including by exacerbating an adversary's select tendencies toward self-damaging patterns of behaviour – see Stephen Peter Rosen, 'Competitive Strategies: Theoretical Foundations, Limits, and Extensions', in Thomas G. Mahnken (ed.), *Competitive Strategies for the 21st Century: Theory, History, and Practice* (Stanford, CA: Stanford University Press, 2012), pp. 12–28.

77 See James G. Roche and Thomas G. Mahnken, 'What Is Net Assessment?', in Thomas G. Mahnken (ed.), *Net Assessment and Military Strategy: Retrospective and Prospective Essays* (New York: Cambria Press, 2020), pp. 11–27; Andrew W. Marshall, 'The Nature and Scope of Net Assessments', National Security Council Memorandum, 16 August 1972, p. 1; and Stephen Peter Rosen, 'Net Assessment as an Analytical Concept', in Andrew W. Marshall et al. (eds), *On Not Confusing Ourselves: Essays on National Strategy in Honor of Albert and Roberta Wohlstetter* (Boulder, CO: Westview Press, 1991), pp. 283–301.

Chapter Two

1 As Frank Hoffman observes in an
excellent recent study, 'war is an
arbiter of how military institutions
and states perceive the future of
conflict, how they prepare for war,
and how well their intelligence and
force-generation processes succeed
in capturing emerging technologies
and foreign military innovations.
But the ultimate test of military
preparation and effectiveness does
not end once a war begins. On the
contrary, history strongly reflects
the enduring phenomena of learning
and implementing change during
war as well. You may go to war with
the army you have, but you do not
necessarily win with the same army. It
has to adapt itself.' Frank G. Hoffman,
*Mars Adapting: Military Change During
War* (Annapolis, MD: Naval Institute
Press, 2021), pp. 5–6. For another
interesting recent examination of the
phenomenon of wartime adaptation,
see David Barno and Nora Bensahel,
*Adaptation Under Fire: How Militaries
Change in Wartime* (New York: Oxford
University Press, 2020).

2 Hoffman, *Mars Adapting: Military
Change During War*, pp. 8–9.

3 See John Lazenby, *The First Punic
War* (New York: Routledge, 2006), ch.
5; and J.H. Thiel, *A History of Roman
Sea-power Before the Second Punic
War* (Amsterdam: North Holland
Publishing Co., 1954).

4 Most notably, according to Livy, the
Roman Senate voted to create two
coastal-defence squadrons of ten
ships each. See Livy, *The History of
Rome*, Book IX, 30.3, https://www.
perseus.tufts.edu/hopper/text?doc
=Perseus%3Atext%3A1999.02.0155

%3Abook%3D9%3Achapter%3D30.
A good discussion of Rome's early
naval efforts can be found in Bernard
Combet Farnoux, *Les Guerres Puniques*
[The Punic Wars] (Paris: Presses
Universitaires de France, 1967), ch. 2.

5 See Raffaele d'Amato, *Republican
Roman Warships 509–27 BC* (Oxford:
Osprey Publishing, 2015), pp. 9–19;
and John Morrison, *Greek and Roman
Oared Warships 399–30 BC* (Oxford:
Oxbow, 2016), ch. 2.

6 See Cassius Dio, *An Epitome of the Lost
Books 1–21 as Found in the Chronicon of
Ionnes Zoanaras*, XI, 8.9, Loeb Classical
Library edition, 1914, https://
penelope.uchicago.edu/Thayer/E/
Roman/Texts/Cassius_Dio/11*.html.

7 Didorus Siculus, *The Library of
History*, Fragments of Book XXIII.2.
Loeb Classical Library edition, 1957,
https://penelope.uchicago.edu/
Thayer/E/Roman/Texts/Diodorus_
Siculus/23*.html.

8 Imperial Rome's later willingness to
experiment and selectively adopt the
foreign military equipment and tactics
from lesser military competitors
validates the arguments of Timothy
Hoyt, who has argued that the
diffusion and emulation process can
occur from the periphery to the centre
– rather than simply 'downward'
from the hegemon toward lesser-
ranking military powers. See Timothy
Hoyt, 'Revolution and Counter-
revolution: The Role of the Periphery
in Technological and Conceptual
Innovation', in Emily Goldman and
Leslie Eliason (eds), *The Diffusion of
Military Technology and Ideas* (Stanford,
CA: Stanford University Press, 2003),
pp. 179–201.

9   See Polybius, *The Histories,* Book I. Loeb Classical Library edition, 1922, https://penelope.uchicago.edu/Thayer/E/Roman/Texts/Polybius/1*.html. One could argue that Rome profoundly reshaped the pre-existing security equation, which had been characterised by a land–sea equilibrium that fostered stalemate, with neither power able to neutralise its opponent's key source of comparative advantage. On how this state of affairs – involving sea powers ranged against land powers, with each unable to strike at their foe's centre of gravity – can lead to protraction, see Colin S. Gray, 'Sea Power: The Great Enabler', *Naval War College Review,* vol. 47, no. 1, 1994, pp. 18–27; and Joshua Rovner, 'Sea Power Versus Land Power: Cross-domain Deterrence in the Peloponnesian War', in Erick Gartzke and Jon R. Lindsay (eds), *Cross-domain Deterrence: Strategy in an Era of Complexity* (New York: Oxford University Press, 2019). Rovner argues that Athens and Sparta's respective advantages (at sea for Athens and on land for Sparta) prolonged their contest, as both nations struggled to implement decisive campaigns within their opponent's favoured domain of operations.

10 The classicist Dexter Hoyos posits that Polybius's account, however sensationalist it may seem, is wholly plausible. Indeed, the remains of a smaller Carthaginian vessel that sank over the course of the First Punic War indicated that it was built with the aid of special marked timbers, in other words, notes Hoyos, 'following the ancient equivalent of a blueprint – and the same could have been done by (Roman) craftsmen after taking apart the captured quinquereme'. Dexter Hoyos, *Mastering the West: Rome and Carthage at War* (New York: Oxford University Press, 2015), p. 41.

11 As Emily O. Goldman observes, 'the competitive logic governing the international system creates a powerful incentive for actors to adopt the military practices of the most successful states in the system. ... but while states have a powerful incentive to adopt innovative military methods, full emulation may not be the most efficient way to provide security given their geography, particular factor endowments, demographic pressures and strategic circumstances'. Emily O. Goldman, 'Introduction: Military Diffusion and Transformation', in Emily O. Goldman and Thomas G. Mahnken (eds), *The Information Revolution in Military Affairs in Asia* (New York: Palgrave Macmillan, 2004), p. 14. In this case, Rome was clearly engaging in a combination of emulation and innovation: emulating Carthaginian shipbuilding practices, while engaging in its own innovation effort, one better tailored to its preference for the heavy infantry melees characteristic of land warfare. In short, Rome was forcing Carthage's navy to play by its continental rules. On military emulation more broadly, see Colin Elman, *The Logic of Emulation: The Diffusion of Military Practices in the International System,* PhD dissertation, Columbia University, 1999.

12 As Paul Erdkamp notes, 'it is not that Carthage did not want to support Hannibal's army (by sea) – there was simply no way to do so in a

meaningful way'. Paul Erdkamp, 'Manpower and Food Supply in the First and Second Punic Wars', in Dexter Hoyos (ed.), *A Companion to the Punic Wars* (Hoboken, NJ: Wiley-Blackwell, 2011), p. 75.

13 The first full-scale invasion of Africa, led by Marcus Atilius Regulus in 256 BCE, however, was a costly failure, resulting in the defeat of the Roman invasion force and Regulus's capture. On the importance of Regulus as both a cautionary tale and a symbol of heroic virtue in Roman historiography, see G.K. Tipps, 'The Defeat of Regulus', *The Classical World*, vol. 96, no. 4, Summer 2003, pp. 375–85.

14 For a superb examination of the logistical challenges confronted by Hannibal, see John F. Shean, 'Hannibal's Mules: The Logistical Limitations of Hannibal's Army and the Battle of Cannae, 216 B.C.', *Historia: Zeitschrift für Alte Geschichte*, vol. 45, no. 2, 1996, pp. 159–87.

15 One of the most balanced analyses of Rome's maritime threat perceptions leading up the First Punic War, and of the subsequent historiographical interpretations and debates surrounding Rome's remarkable naval build-up, can be found in Matthew Leigh, 'Early Roman Epic and the Maritime Moment', *Classical Philology*, vol. 105, no. 3, July 2010, pp. 265–80.

16 As Williamson Murray notes, 'in peacetime, time poses few significant challenges to the innovator; he may lack significant resources, but he has time to form, test and evaluate his ideas and perceptions. The opposite is true in war. There, those involved in combat usually possess a plethora of resources, but time is not one of them; those pursuing serious changes in doctrine, technology, or tactics in the midst of a conflict have only a brief opportunity to adapt. Adding to their difficulties is the fact that as their organization adapts, so, too will the enemy.' See Williamson Murray, *Military Adaptation in War: With Fear of Change* (New York: Cambridge University Press, 2011), p. 1.

17 See Demosthenes, *First Philippic*, The Bibliotheke, https://cmuntz.hosted.uark.edu/texts/demosthenes/4-first-philippic.html.

18 Carl von Clausewitz, *On War*, Book I, 'On the Nature of War' (Princeton, NJ: Princeton University Press, 1976).

19 Meir Finkel, *On Flexibility: Recovery from Technological and Doctrinal Surprise on the Battlefield* (Stanford, CA: Stanford Security Studies, 2011). In the field of psychology, a helpful distinction has been made between 'proactive adaptation' and 'reactive adaptation'. Rome's maritime transformation during the First Punic War could be described as a case of proactive adaptation, whereas Spain's decision to profoundly reorganise its infantry in the wake of Seminara can be presented as an example of reactive adaptation. On proactive versus reactive adaptation, see Christian D. Schunn and Lynne M. Reder, 'Individual Differences in Strategy Adaptivity', *Psychology of Learning and Motivation*, vol. 38, no. 1, 1998, pp. 115–54.

20 Michael Howard, 'Military Science in an Age of Peace', *RUSI Journal*, vol. 119, no. 1, 1974, p. 7.

21 For an excellent overview of the Italian Wars, see Christine Shaw and Michael Mallett, *The Italian Wars 1494–1559: War, State and Society in Early Modern Europe*, 2nd edition (London: Routledge, 2019).

22 On the conquest of Granada and how its campaigns contributed to state formation and centralisation in early modern Spain, see Joseph F. O'Callaghan, *The Last Crusade in the West: Castile and the Conquest of Granada* (Philadelphia, PA: University of Pennsylvania Press, 2014); and Weston F. Cook Jr, 'The Cannon Conquest of Nasrid Spain and the End of the Reconquista', *Journal of Military History*, vol. 57, no. 1, 1993, pp. 43–70. On how Córdoba and his soldiers were initially 'better equipped and trained to fight in the sierras of Granada and against the lightly equipped Muslim forces than to effectively face the heavily armed and fierce infantry and cavalry forces of the French', see Idan Sherer, *Warriors for a Living: The Experience of the Spanish Infantry in the Italian Wars, 1494–1559* (Leiden: Brill, 2017), p. 194.

23 See Gabriele Esposito, *Renaissance Armies in Italy 1450–1550* (Oxford: Osprey Publishing, 2020), p. 60.

24 'Gonzalo Fernandez de Cordoba to the Catholic Monarchs', Reggio, 2 July 1495, Biblioteca Nacional de España, MS/20211/1.

25 See Paul Stewart, 'The Santa Hermandad and the First Italian Campaign of Gonzalo de Cordoba, 1495–1498', *Renaissance Quarterly*, vol. 28, no. 1, 1975, pp. 29–37; and Rene Quatrefages, *La revolución militar moderna: el crisol español* [The modern military revolution: the Spanish crucible] (Madrid: Spanish Ministry of Defense, 1996).

26 For a classic, if perhaps somewhat outdated, analysis of the Battle of Cerignola, see Charles Oman, *A History of the Art of War in the Sixteenth Century* (New York: Dutton and Co., 1937), pp. 52–4.

27 On the importance of arquebusiers in early Spanish force structure, see Fernando Gonzalo de Leon, 'Spanish Military Power and the Military Revolution', in Geoff Mortimer (ed.), *Early Modern Military History, 1450–1815* (London: Palgrave Macmillan, 2004), pp. 25–42.

28 To give another contemporary example, the German *Leopard* 2 tank's diesel-powered engine is far easier for Ukrainian troops to maintain and refuel than the complex jet-fuel-powered turbine engine of the American M1A2 *Abrams*. The *Leopard* 2 is therefore far better suited to the Ukrainian war effort than the (arguably) better but more maintenance-heavy *Abrams*. On the logistical virtues of the *Leopard* 2, see Adam Taylor, William Neff and Daniel Wolfe, 'For Ukraine, What's So Special About Germany's Leopard Tanks?', *Washington Post*, 25 January 2023, https://www.washingtonpost.com/world/2023/01/24/leopard-2-ukraine-germany-m1-abrams/; and 'What Makes Germany's Leopard 2 Tank the Best Fit for Ukraine?', *The Economist*, 25 January 2023, https://www.economist.com/the-economist-explains/2023/01/25/what-makes-germanys-leopard-2-tank-the-best-fit-for-ukraine.

29 The *rodeleros* were eventually phased out in favour of larger numbers of arquebusiers.

30 See Ignacio and Iván Notario López, *The Spanish Tercios: 1536–1704* (Oxford: Osprey Publishing, 2012); Esposito, *Renaissance Armies in Italy 1450–1550*; Rene Quatrefages, 'The Military System of the Spanish Habsburgs', in Rafael Banon Martinez and Thomas M. Barker (eds), *Armed Forces and Society in Spain: Past and Present* (New York: Columbia University Press, 1988);

Luna Nájera, 'The Deployment of the Classics in Early Modern Spanish Military Manuals', *Sixteenth Century Journal*, vol. 46, no. 3, 2015, pp. 607–27; and Mark R. Geldof, 'The Pike and the Printing Press: Military Handbooks and the Gentrification of the Early Modern Military Revolution', in Matthew McLean and Sara K. Barker (eds), *International Exchange in the Early Modern Book World* (Leiden: Brill, 2016).

31   For a more in-depth analysis of the military reasons behind France's defeat in the Italian Wars, see Michael Mallett, 'The Transformation of War, 1494–1530', in Christine Shaw (ed.), *Italy and the European Powers: The Impact of War, 1500–1530* (Leiden: Brill, 2006), pp. 3–21.

32   For a good overview of French military strategy and force structure during this period, see David Potter, *Renaissance France at War: Armies, Culture and Society, c.1480–1560* (Woodbridge: Boydell Press, 2008).

33   For more literature on this period, see David Parrott, *The Business of War: Military Enterprise and Military Revolution in Early Modern Europe* (Cambridge: Cambridge University Press, 2012); and Thomas F. Arnold, *The Renaissance at War* (London: Cassell, 2006).

34   For the contrast in attitudes between the French and Castilian higher nobilities on fighting alongside the lower social orders, see Sherer, *Warriors for a Living: The Experience of the Spanish Infantry in the Italian Wars, 1494–1559*, p. 246; and Treva J. Tucker, 'Eminence over Efficacy: Social Status and Cavalry Service in Sixteenth-century France', *Sixteenth Century Journal*, vol. 32, no. 4, 2001, pp. 1057–95.

35   See Idan Sherer, '"When War Comes They Want to Flee": Motivation and Combat Effectiveness in the Spanish Infantry During the Italian Wars', *Sixteenth Century Journal*, vol. 48, no. 2, 2017, pp. 385–411.

36   On the importance of cultural factors in military adaptation and change, see Theo Farrell and Terry Terriff, 'The Sources of Military Change', in Theo Farrell and Terry Terriff (eds), *The Sources of Military Change: Culture, Politics, Technology* (London: Lynne Rienner, 2002), pp. 3–21.

37   See Robert T. Foley, 'A Case Study in Horizontal Military Innovation: The German Army, 1916–18', *Journal of Strategic Studies*, vol. 35, no. 6, 2012, pp. 799–827.

38   See Paddy Griffith, *Battle Tactics of the Western Front: The British Army's Art of Attack 1916–18* (New Haven, CT: Yale University Press, 1994); Gary Sheffield, *Forgotten Victory: The First World War: Myths and Realities* (London: Headline, 2001); Michel Goya, *La Chair et l'Acier: L'Armee Française et l'Invention de la Guerre Moderne (1914–1918)* [Flesh and steel: the French army and the invention of modern warfare (1914–1918)] (Paris: Tallandier, 2004); and Mark Grotelueschen, *The AEF Way of War: The American Army and Combat in World War I* (Cambridge: Cambridge University Press, 2007).

39   On the lasting influence throughout the Middle Ages of the fourth-century Roman military theorist Publius Flavius Vegetius, with his emphasis on battle avoidance, exhaustion and logistical harassment, see Clifford J. Rogers, 'The Vegetian "Science of Warfare" in the Middle Ages', *Journal of Medieval Military History*, vol. 1, no. 1, 2002, pp. 1–20;

Christopher Allmand, *The* De Re Militari *of Vegetius: The Reception, Transmission and Legacy of a Roman Text in the Middle Ages* (Cambridge: Cambridge University Press, 2011); and Bernard Bachrach, 'The Practical Use of Vegetius' "De Re Militari" During the Early Middle Ages', *The Historian*, vol. 47, no. 2, February 1985, pp. 239–55.

40   These tactics had been honed to perfection by Edward III in the Scottish theatre during the early years of his reign. See Ranald Nicholson, *Edward III and the Scots: The Formative Years of a Military Career, 1327–1335* (Oxford: Oxford University Press, 1965); and Jonathan Sumption, *The Hundred Years War, Vol. 1: Trial by Battle* (Philadelphia, PA: University of Pennsylvania Press, 1990). In the earliest years of the Hundred Years War, Edward III's campaign efforts were largely inconclusive, with the English king struggling to finance his onerous system of alliances in the Low Countries, and unable to make any significant military gains in the face of Philip VI's Fabian strategy. As Anne Curry has observed, 'the English appeared to be losing the war in its first stages'. See Anne Curry, *The Hundred Years War: 1337–1453* (Oxford: Osprey Publishing, 2002), p. 25.

41   Moreover, once Philip's great rival Edward III took the fateful decision, in 1340, to formally and publicly lay claim to the French throne, the conflict between the two monarchs took on a far greater symbolic and political resonance, one that called for some form of clear denouement in the form of a decisive battle. See Craig Taylor, 'Edward III and the Plantagenet Claim to the French Throne', in James

Bothwell (ed.), *The Age of Edward III* (York: York Medieval Press, 2001), pp. 155–71. On the issue of chivalry and its relation to war fighting and national sentiment, see Craig Taylor, *Chivalry and the Ideals of Knighthood in France During the Hundred Years War* (Cambridge: Cambridge University Press, 2013).

42   On the importance of cultural interpretations of honour and how honour-related considerations can trigger escalation or shape a decision-maker's actions in war, see Allan Defor and Devin Caughey, 'Honor and War: Southern US Presidents and the Effects of Concern for Reputation', *World Politics*, vol. 68, no. 2, April 2016, pp. 341–81; and Barry O'Neill, *Honor, Symbols, and War* (Ann Arbor, MI: University of Michigan Press, 1999).

43   See A.K. McHardy, 'Some Reflections on Edward III's Use of Propaganda', in Bothwell (ed.), *The Age of Edward III*, pp. 171–92. On strategies of deliberate or tailored provocation during periods of tension or conflict, see Hyun-Binn Cho, *Tying the Adversary's Hands: Provocation, Crisis Escalation, and Inadvertent War*, PhD Dissertation, University of Pennsylvania, 2018, https://repository. upenn.edu/edissertations/3100/.

44   Charles V, one of the more intriguing and accomplished rulers of the late medieval era, remains a curiously underexamined figure in the English-language academic literature. For two excellent French examinations of his approach to statecraft and grand strategy, see Francoise Autrand, *Charles V: Le Sage* (Paris: Fayard, 1994) and Georges Bordonove, *Charles V: 1364–1380* (Paris: Pygmalion, 2012).

45   For a landmark examination of the wartime performance of modern

authoritarian regimes, see Caitlin Talmadge, *The Dictator's Army: Battlefield Effectiveness in Authoritarian Regimes* (Ithaca, NY: Cornell University Press, 2015). On autocratic audience costs, and the need for many authoritarian regimes to also cater to the demands and expectations of their domestic elites, see Jessica L. Weeks, 'Autocratic Audience Costs: Regime Type and Signaling Resolve', *International Organization*, vol. 62, no. 1, 2008, pp. 35–64.

46 See Efraim Karsh, *The Iran–Iraq War: 1980–1988* (Oxford: Osprey Publishing, 2002), p. 36. For a seminal history of the IRGC, see Afshon Ostovar, *Vanguard of the Imam: Religion, Politics, and Iran's Revolutionary Guards* (New York: Oxford University Press, 2016).

47 As Williamson Murray and Kevin M. Woods rightly point out, 'throughout the conflict, Khomeini and his hardline advisors believed their religious enthusiasm, engendered by their revolution, could replace military expertise, weapons systems, and technology. While this "way of war" may have affected a few tactical engagements, it was a recipe for disaster as a strategy.' Williamson Murray and Kevin M. Woods, *The Iran–Iraq War: A Military and Strategic History* (Cambridge: Cambridge University Press, 2014), p. 18.

48 See Veronika Melkozerova, 'Zelensky Slams Kremlin for Sacrificing Troops in the "Meat Waves" of Bakhmut', Politico, 20 December, 2022, https://www.politico.eu/article/volodymyr-zelenskyy-ukraine-war-bakhmut-russia-sacrificing-troops-meat-waves/; Katie Bo Lillis et al., 'Russian Mercenaries Jockey for Influence amid Military Struggles in Ukraine', CNN, 2 November 2022, https://www.cnn.com/2022/11/02/politics/yevgeny-prigozhin-ukraine-putin-kremlin-war-ukraine/index.html; and Paul Mozur, Adam Satariano and Aaron Krolik, 'An Alternate Reality: How Russia's State TV Spins the Ukraine War', *New York Times*, 15 December 2022, https://www.nytimes.com/2022/12/15/technology/russia-state-tv-ukraine-war.html.

49 As Theo Farrell observes, 'when at war, a military has strong incentives to stick with those ways of operating that have been tried and tested, and for which the organization has trained and equipped: the opportunity costs of introducing new ways of operating in the midst of war are high, especially if the new way does turn out to not be so effective'. See Theo Farrell, 'Introduction: Military Adaptation in War', in Theo Farrell et al. (eds), *Military Adaptation in Afghanistan* (Stanford, CA: Stanford University Press, 2013), p. 7.

50 Clausewitz, *On War*, ch. 14.

51 Some classicists deem this to have been one of the major causes behind Carthage's defeat during the Punic Wars, arguing that, with the notable exception of Hannibal and his father Hamilcar, Carthaginian generals and statesmen were unwilling or unable to take sufficient risks, or seize clear opportunities when they presented themselves. See, for example, Combet Farnoux, *Les Guerres Puniques*. Adrian Goldsworthy notes that this was in part due to differences in recruitment practices – as 'Carthage was never able to field troops in anything like the quantities of the Romans', the 'difficulty of replacing a tried and

tested army often encouraged a tentative approach to campaigning on the part of Punic generals, who, with a few notable exceptions, tended to be far less aggressive than their Roman counterparts'. See Adrian Goldsworthy, *The Fall of Carthage: The Punic Wars 265–146 BC* (London: Orion Books, 2000), p. 36. On how 'the lack of precedent makes wartime innovation risky, and with the risk comes a justified aversion', see Stephen Peter Rosen, *Winning the Next War: Innovation and the Modern Military* (Ithaca, NY: Cornell University Press, 1991), pp. 24–5.

52 Barno and Bensahel, *Adaptation Under Fire: How Militaries Change in Wartime*, p. 9.

53 For a seminal study of the evolution of infantry warfare during the Hundred Years War, see Kelly DeVries, *Infantry Warfare in the Early Fourteenth Century: Discipline, Tactics, and Technology* (Woodbridge: Boydell Press, 1996). On the notion of military revolutions during the Hundred Years War, see Clifford J. Rogers, 'The Military Revolutions of the Hundred Years War', *Journal of Military History*, vol. 57, no. 2, 1993, pp. 241–78; and Clifford J. Rogers, 'As If a New Sun Had Arisen: England's Fourteenth Century RMA', in MacGregor Knox and Williamson Murray (eds), *The Dynamics of Military Revolution, 1300–2050* (Cambridge: Cambridge University Press, 2001), pp. 15–34.

54 The collapse of England's position in France was not solely due to the power of French artillery. France's more evolved system of recruitment and logistics, along with a wave of defections among previously Lancastrian-aligned French nobles,

also played a key role. Nevertheless, it is hard to overemphasise the game-changing nature of France's royal siege trains toward the end of the Hundred Years War. See David Nicolle, *The Fall of English France: 1449–53* (Oxford: Osprey Publishing, 2012), pp. 11–12; R.D. Smith, 'Artillery and the Hundred Years War: Myth and Interpretation', in Anne Curry and Michael Hugues (eds), *Arms, Armies and Fortifications in the Hundred Years War* (Woodbridge: Boydell Press, 1994), pp. 151–60; and Anne Curry, 'Guns and Goddams: Was There a Military Revolution in Lancastrian Normandy 1415–1450?', *Journal of Medieval Military History*, vol. 8, 2010, pp. 171–88.

55 See the superb analysis of strategic decision-making in Wanli's court during the Imjin War in Kenneth M. Swope, 'As Close as Lips and Teeth: Debating the Ming Intervention in Korea', in Peter A. Lorge (ed.), *Debating War in Chinese History* (Leiden: Brill, 2013), pp. 163–90.

56 See Christopher Bell, 'Winston Churchill, Pacific Security, and the Limits of British Power, 1921–41', in John H. Maurer (ed.), *Churchill and the Strategic Dilemmas Before the World Wars: Essays in Honor of Michael I. Handel* (New York: Routledge, 2013), pp. 51–88; and John Pritchard, 'Winston Churchill, the Military, and Imperial Defence in East Asia', in Saki Dockrill (ed.), *From Pearl Harbor to Hiroshima: The Second World War in Asia and the Pacific, 1941–45* (London: Palgrave Macmillan, 1994), pp. 26–54.

57 As Bruce A. Elleman and S.C.M Paine wisely note, 'peripheral operations figure prominently in strategy because among the most important

decisions in wartime is the decision to open, not to open, to contest, or not to contest a new theater'. See Bruce A. Elleman and S.C.M Paine, 'Conclusions: Naval Expeditionary Warfare and the Future of Sea Power', in Bruce A. Elleman and S.C.M Paine (eds), *Naval Power and Expeditionary Warfare: Peripheral Campaigns and New Theaters of Naval Warfare* (New York: Routledge, 2011), p. 202.

58 For an excellent and nuanced examination of some of the vivid historiographical debates relating to the rationale behind Truman's fateful decision, see J. Samuel Walker, 'Historiographical Essay: Recent Literature on Truman's Atomic Bomb Decision: A Search for Middle Ground', *Diplomatic History*, vol. 29, no. 2, April 2005, pp. 311–34.

59 John David Lewis, *Nothing Less than Victory: Decisive Wars and the Lessons of History* (Princeton, NJ: Princeton University Press, 2010), ch. 3.

60 For some absorbing discussions of how Fabius's generalship and political leadership during Rome's darkest hour has traditionally been interpreted and perceived, see Sophia Xenophontos, 'Περὶ ἀγαθοῦ στρατηγοῦ: Plutarch's Fabius Maximus and the Ethics of Generalship', *Hermes*, vol. 140, no. 2, 2012, pp. 160–83; and Paul Erdkamp, 'Polybius, Livy and the Fabian Strategy', *Ancient Society*, vol. 23, 1992, pp. 127–47. For a good overview of Rome's strategy during this period, see Klaus Zimmerman, 'Roman Strategy and Aims in the Second Punic War', in Hoyos (ed.), *A Companion to the Punic Wars*, pp. 280–98.

61 Livy, *The History of Rome*, Book XXVIII, ch. 41. Loeb Classical Library

edition, https://www.loebclassics.com/view/LCL381/2021/volume.xml.

62 *Ibid*.

63 For a detailed analysis of Scipio's political and military decision-making during this period, see Arthur M. Eckstein, *Senate and General: Individual Decision-making and Roman Foreign Relations, 264–194 BC* (Berkeley, CA: University of California Press, 1987), ch. 8.

64 Lewis, *Nothing Less than Victory: Decisive Wars and the Lessons of History*, ch. 3.

65 Quoted in Carl Jacob Burckhardt, *Richelieu and His Age: Power Politics and the Cardinal's Death* (London: Allen & Unwin, 1971), p. 10.

66 On Richelieu's grand strategy, see Iskander Rehman, 'Raison d'Etat: Richelieu's Grand Strategy During the Thirty Years' War', *Texas National Security Review*, vol. 2, no. 3, June 2019, pp. 38–75, https://tnsr.org/2019/06/raison-detat-richelieus-grand-strategy-during-the-thirty-years-war/.

67 See Jean-Vincent Blanchard, *Eminence: Cardinal Richelieu and the Rise of France* (London: Bloomsbury, 2011), p. 163.

68 For a good discussion of the concept and measurement of national power, see Ashley J. Tellis et al., 'Measuring National Power in the Postindustrial Age: Analyst's Handbook', Rand Corporation, 1 January 2000, https://doi.org/10.7249/MR1110. On the importance of geography, and how it largely conditions the acquisition and exercise of national power, see D.G. Hansen, 'The Immutable Importance of Geography', *Parameters*, vol. 27, no. 1, Spring 1997, pp. 55–64; and Jakub J. Gyrgiel, *Great Powers and Geopolitical*

Change (Baltimore, MD: Johns Hopkins University Press, 2006).

69   See the introductory chapter to Geoffrey Sloan, *Geopolitics, Geography and Strategic History* (New York: Routledge, 2017).

70   'The shape of the North American continent prevents Mexico from adding significantly to its size by southern expansion, and topography, and climate will make it forever impossible to build on its area a powerful economy. Canada, although larger in area than the United States, is by location and climate permitted to develop only a very small part of her territory as a base for economic and political life. The result is that the United States has been able to conduct its foreign policy for the last seventy-five years without giving any consideration to the problem of territorial security, and that its people are unable to understand the preoccupation of Europeans with security and power politics.' Nicholas J. Spykman, 'Geography and Foreign Policy, II', *The American Political Science Review*, vol. 32, no. 2, April 1938, p. 226.

71   He reportedly also told the Japanese premier, 'if I am told to fight regardless of consequence, I shall run wild for the first six months or a year, but I have utterly no confidence for the second and third years'. See Samuel Eliot Morison, *The Rising Sun in the Pacific, 1931–April 1943: History of United States Naval Operations in World War II, Vol. 3* (Annapolis, MD: Naval Institute Press, 2010), p. 126; and Ian W. Toll, *Pacific Crucible: War at Sea in the Pacific 1941–1942* (New York: W. W. Norton & Company, 2011), p. 46.

72   See Michael G. Carew, *Becoming the Arsenal: The American Industrial Mobilization for World War II, 1938–1942* (Lanham, MD: University Press of America, 2010); and Alan L. Gropman, *Mobilizing U.S. Industry in World War II: Myth and Reality* (Washington DC: Institute for National Strategic Studies, National Defense University, 1996).

73   As one study notes, 'over the course of the war, 733 merchant ships of over 1,000 tons were lost. It was not until 1943 that US cargo ship production finally outpaced losses. … In July 1942, it took 105 days to construct a Liberty ship. By 1943, it took just over 50 days. By the end of the war, it only took 40 days from laying the keel to delivery.' See Mark F. Cancian et al., 'Industrial Mobilization: Assessing Surge Capabilities, Wartime Risk, and System Brittleness', Center for Strategic and International Studies, 8 January 2021, https://www.csis.org/analysis/ industrial-mobilization-assessing- surge-capabilities-wartime-risk-and- system-brittleness. On the United States' broader maritime logistics network during the Second World War, see Worrall Reed Carter, *Beans, Bullets, and Black Oil: The Story of Fleet Logistics Afloat in the Pacific During World War II* (Washington DC: US Government Printing Office, 1953); and Thomas Wildenberg, *Gray Steel and Black Oil: Fast Tankers and Replenishment at Sea in the U.S. Navy, 1912–1992* (Annapolis, MD: Naval Institute Press, 1996).

74   Jeffrey Record, *Ends, Means, Ideology and Pride: Why the Axis Lost and What We Can Learn from Its Defeat* (Carlisle, PA: US Army War College, 2017), p. 24.

75   Adam Tooze, *The Wages of Destruction: The Making and Breaking of the Nazi Economy* (New York: Penguin Books, 2006), p. 17.

76 Quoted by Barry J. Dysart, 'Materialschlacht: The Materiel Battle in the European Theater', in Alan Gropman (ed.), *The Big L: American Logistics in World War II* (Washington DC: National Defense University Press, 1997), p. 339.

77 Quote from Plutarch, *The Parallel Lives*, ch. 21, 'The Life of Pyrrhus'. Loeb Classical Library edition, 1920, https://penelope.uchicago.edu/Thayer/E/Roman/Texts/Plutarch/Lives/Pyrrhus*.html. On Rome's talent for mass mobilisation largely through its unique system of military alliances and highly organised administrative and census system, see Luuk de Ligt, *Peasants, Citizens and Soldiers: Studies in the Demographic History of Roman Italy 225 BC–AD 100* (Cambridge: Cambridge University Press, 2012); and Michael J. Taylor, *Soldiers and Silver: Mobilizing Resources in the Age of Roman Conquest* (Austin, TX: University of Texas Press, 2020). For a sophisticated treatment of the Roman Republic's superior efficiency in extracting revenues and manpower during the First Punic War in particular, see Bret C. Deveraux, *The Material and Social Costs of Roman Warfare in the Third and Second Centuries B.C.E.*, PhD Dissertation, University of North Carolina, 2018, https://cdr.lib.unc.edu/concern/dissertations/3r074v31f.

78 The scale of the slaughter over the course of one single major engagement, some have claimed, was unrivalled until the great offensives of the First World War. For a detailed examination of one of history's most pored-over battles, see Gregory Daly, *Cannae: The Experience of Battle in the Second Punic War* (London: Routledge, 2002). For an excellent examination of Rome's attitude and adaptation to defeat, see Jessica H. Clark, *Triumph in Defeat: Military Loss and the Roman Republic* (Oxford: Oxford University Press, 2014). See also Erdkamp, 'Manpower and Food Supply in the First and Second Punic Wars', pp. 66–7.

79 Livy, in his *History of Rome*, describes how Fabius allegedly recruited 8,000 soldiers from the slave population of the city. On Rome's desperate recruitment efforts after Cannae, see John F. Lazenby, *Hannibal's War: A Military History of the Second Punic War* (Norman, OK: University of Oklahoma Press, 1997), p. 91.

80 Polybius, *The Histories*, Book VI, ch. 52. Loeb Classical Library edition, 1922, https://penelope.uchicago.edu/Thayer/E/Roman/Texts/Polybius/1*.html. This line of argument was famously reprised by Machiavelli in his arguments against mercenaries and in favour of a citizen army. See Mikael Hornqvist, 'Machiavelli's Military Project and the Art of War', in John M. Najemy (ed.), *The Cambridge Companion to Machiavelli* (Cambridge: Cambridge University Press, 2010), pp. 112–28; and Michael Mallett, 'The Theory and Practice of Warfare in Machiavelli's Republic', in Gisela Bock, Quentin Skinner and Maurizio Viroli (eds), *Machiavelli and Republicanism* (Cambridge: Cambridge University Press, 1990), pp. 173–80.

81 Especially in the cavalry, in which the ratio of Italian allied troops to Roman troops was sometimes to the order of 3:1. See Donald Walter Baronowski, 'Roman Military Forces in 225 BC (Polybius 2.23–24)', *Historia:*

Zeitschrift Fur Alte Geschichte, vol. 42, no. 2, 1993, pp. 181–202.

82 For an illuminating discussion of Hitler's strategic thinking leading up to and during *Operation Barbarossa*, see Stephen G. Fritz, *The First Soldier: Hitler as Military Leader* (New Haven, CT: Yale University Press, 2018), ch. 7.

83 Over 1,500 major industrial enterprises were relocated to remoter regions within the Soviet interior by rail, necessitating the requisition of over 1.5 million train wagons. The largest industrial evacuation point was the Urals region, which produced the first T-34 tank on 8 December 1941. See Frank Ellis, *Barbarossa 1941: Reframing Hitler's Invasion of Stalin's Soviet Empire* (Lawrence, KS: University Press of Kansas, 2015), p. 82.

84 See Mark Harrison, 'Resource Mobilization for World War II: The USA, UK, USSR, and Germany, 1938–1945', *Economic History Review*, vol. 41, no. 2, May 1998, pp. 171–92.

85 See *The State Defense Committee Decrees, 1941–1945: Figures and Documents* (Moscow: Olma Press, 2002), pp. 115–17.

86 In the first 18 months of conflict, Axis forces destroyed over 297 Red Army divisions. The best extant study on the titanic scale of Soviet mobilisation practices from the summer of 1941 is Walter S. Dunn Jr, *Stalin's Key to Victory: The Rebirth of the Red Army in WWII* (Mechanicsburg, PA: Stackpole Books, 2007).

87 Clausewitz, *On War*, ch. 3.

88 Alexander Watson, *Enduring the Great War: Combat, Morale and Collapse in the German and British Armies, 1914–1918* (Cambridge: Cambridge University Press, 2008), pp. 17–20.

89 See Luke Mogelson, 'Trapped in the Trenches in Ukraine', *New Yorker*, 26 December 2022, https://www.newyorker.com/magazine/2023/01/02/trapped-in-the-trenches-in-ukraine; and Siobhán O'Grady and Anastacia Galouchka, 'Traumatic Stress, an Invisible Wound, Hobbles Ukrainian Soldiers', *Washington Post*, 10 March 2023, https://www.washingtonpost.com/world/2023/03/10/ukraine-war-post-traumatic-stress./

90 H. Hofmann, 'Die Deutsche Nervenkraft im Stellungskrieg' [The German nerve in trench warfare], in F. Seeßelberg (ed.), *Der Stellungskrieg 1914–18* [Trench warfare 1914–18] (Berlin: E.S. Mittler & Sohn, 1926), p. 445.

91 In the end, however, only 49 executions were carried out. See Leonard V. Smith, 'War and Politics: The French Army Mutinies of 1917', *War in History*, vol. 2, no. 2, 1995, pp. 180–201; and Guy Pendroncini, *Les Mutineries de 1917* (Paris: Presses Universitaires de France, 1967).

92 See Daniel Horn, *The German Naval Mutinies of World War I* (New Brunswick, NJ: Rutgers University Press, 1969); and Nicolas Wolz, *Und Wir Verrosten im Hafen: Deutschland, Großbritannien Und Der Krieg Zur See 1914–1918* [And we're rusting in the harbour: Germany, Britain and the war at sea 1914–1918] (Berlin: Deustcher Taschenbuch Verlag, 2013).

93 See Deian Hopkin, 'Domestic Censorship in the First World War', *Journal of Contemporary History*, vol. 5, no. 4, 1970, pp. 151–69; Eberhard Demm, *Censorship and Propaganda in World War 1: A Comprehensive History* (London: Bloomsbury Academic, 2019); and John Horne, 'Introduction:

Mobilizing for Total War 1914–1918',
in John Horne (ed.), *State, Society and
Mobilization in Europe During the First
World War* (Cambridge: Cambridge
University Press, 1997), pp. 7–8.

94 P.E. Vernon, 'Psychological Effects
of Air-raids', *Journal of Abnormal and
Social Psychology*, vol. 36, no. 4, 1941,
pp. 457–76.

95 Edgar Jones et al. 'Civilian Morale
During the Second World War:
Responses to Air Raids Re-examined',
Social History of Medicine, vol. 17, no. 3,
2004, pp. 463–79; R. Mackay, *Half the
Battle: Civilian Morale in Britain During
the Second World* War (Manchester:
Manchester University Press, 2002);
J.T. MacCurdy, *The Structure of Morale*
(Cambridge: Cambridge University
Press, 1943); and Ian McLaine,
*Ministry of Morale: Home Front Morale
and the Ministry of Information in World
War II* (London: Allen & Unwin, 1979).

96 Edgar Jones et al., 'Public Panic and
Morale: Second World War Civilian
Responses Re-examined in the
Light of the Current Anti-terrorist
Campaign', *Journal of Risk Research*,
vol. 9, no. 1, 2006, p. 65.

97 Terence H. O'Brien, *Civil Defence:
History of the Second World War*
(London: H.M. Stationery Office,
1955), p. 184.

98 For an interesting recent examination
of the concept of resiliency in
conflict and of some of these same
trade-offs, see Eyal Lewin, *National
Resilience During War: Refining the
Decision-making Model* (Lanham, MD:
Lexington Books, 2012).

99 Quoted in Christopher C. Harmon,
'"Are We Beasts?" Churchill and
the Moral Question of World War
II "Area Bombing"', US Naval War
College Newport Papers, 1991,
https://digital-commons.usnwc.edu/
usnwc-newport-papers/1/.

100 On these debates and the history of
area or strategic bombing, see Herman
Knell, *To Destroy a City: Strategic
Bombing and Its Human Consequences
in World War II* (Cambridge, MA:
Berghahn Books, 2003). See also Phillip
S. Melinger, 'Trenchard and Morale
Bombing: The Evolution of Royal Air
Force Doctrine Before World War II',
in Geoffrey Jensen, *Warfare in Europe
1919–1938* (New York: Routledge,
2008), ch. 8; and Mark Connelly, 'The
British Debate', in Igor Primoratz
(ed.), *Terror from the Sky: The Bombing
of German Cities in World War II* (New
York: Berghahn Books, 2010), ch. 8.

101 Robert A. Pape, *Bombing to Win: Air
Power and Coercion in War* (Ithaca,
NY: Cornell University Press, 2014),
p. 36. For another good examination
of strategic bombing, see Gian P.
Gentile, *How Effective Is Strategic
Bombing? Lessons Learned from World
War II to Kosovo* (New York: New
York University Press, 2001).

102 As H.J. Hewitt notes, 'the enemy was to
be weakened by the destruction of his
resources. Devastation was a negative,
economic means for the attainment of
the ultimate, political end.' H.J. Hewitt,
*The Organization of War Under Edward
III* (Manchester: Manchester University
Press, 1966), p. 117.

103 Jonathan Sumption notes that 'the
Anglo-Gascons had destroyed about
500 villages lying in a band about 200
miles long by forty miles wide across
Southern France. They had ruined at
least a dozen walled towns and the
trading and residential quarters of
three major cities. The damage to the
economy of the southwest was very
serious. The English were well aware

that wars were fought with money
and they understood perfectly the
economic consequences of what they
were doing.' Jonathan Sumption,
*Trial by Fire: The Hundred Years War,
Vol. 2* (Philadelphia, PA: University of
Pennsylvania Press), p. 185.

104 Clifford J. Rogers, 'By Fire and
Sword: Bellum Hostile and Civilians
in the Hundred Years War', in Mark
Grimsley and Clifford J. Rogers (eds),
Civilians in the Path of War (Lincoln,
NE: University of Nebraska Press,
2002), pp. 33–78.

105 See, for example, the correspondence
of the Treasurer of England, the
Bishop of Winchester, with one of the
English nobles who accompanied the
Black Prince on his 1355 *chevauchée*,
in Edward Maunde Thompson
(ed.), *Robertus de Avesbury De Gestis
Mirabilus Regis Edwardi Tertii* [Robert
of Avesbury on the great acts of King
Edward III] (Cambridge: Cambridge
University Press, 2012), pp. 440–2.

106 See David Nicolle, *French Armies
of the Hundred Years Wars* (Oxford:
Osprey Publishing, 2000), pp. 34–5;
Boris Bove, *Le Temps de la Guerre de
Cent Ans 1328–1453* [The time of
the Hundred Years War 1328–1453]
(Paris: Editions Belin, 2014), pp.
163–4; and Nicholas Wright, *Knights
and Peasants: The Hundred Years War in
the French Countryside* (Rochester, NY:
Boydell, 1998), pp. 96–117.

107 On how protraction often leads to
civilian victimisation out of a desire
for war termination, see Alexander B.
Downes, 'Desperate Times, Desperate
Measures: The Causes of Civilian
Victimization in War', *International
Security*, vol. 30, no. 4, Spring
2006, pp. 152–95. On the difficulty
of measuring the effectiveness of

counter-civilian targeting for coercive
purposes in inter-state war, see
Michael Horowitz and Dan Reiter,
'When Does Aerial Bombing Work?
Quantitative Empirical Tests, 1917–
1999', *Journal of Conflict Resolution*,
vol. 45, no. 2, April 2001, pp. 147–73.

108 See R.J. Reinhart, 'Ukrainians Support
Fighting Until Victory', Gallup, 18
October 2022, https://news.gallup.
com/poll/403133/ukrainians-support-
fighting-until-victory.aspx.

109 The blockade also eroded popular
support for the war effort, as
the starving civilian population
increasingly saw resources they
desperately needed redirected toward
the front lines, to be devoured by
Germany's ravenous war machine.
As G.C. Peden notes, 'Germany was
vulnerable to blockade because of the
strain of war on her economy. Had
nitrogen been available for fertilizers
instead of for military transport,
the population could have been fed
satisfactorily, even though a quarter
of pre-war German food consumption
had been imported.' G.C. Peden,
*Arms, Economics and British Strategy:
From Dreadnoughts to Hydrogen Bombs*
(Cambridge: Cambridge University
Press, 2007), p. 84. On the effectiveness
of the blockade, especially in its final
years, in depriving the German armed
forces of much-needed raw materials,
see Eric W. Osborne, *Britain's Economic
Blockade of Germany 1914–1919* (London:
Frank Cass, 2004); and David Janicki,
'The British Blockade During World
War I: The Weapon of Deprivation',
Inquiries Journal, vol. 6, no. 6, 2014.

110 See Jonathan J. Price, *Thucydides and
Internal War* (Cambridge: Cambridge
University Press, 2001); and Michael
Palmer, 'Stasis in the War Narrative',

in Sara Forsdyke, Edith Foster and Ryan Balot (eds), *The Oxford Handbook of Thucydides* (New York: Oxford University Press, 2017), pp. 409–27.

111 On the development of English and French nationalism during the Hundred Years War, see David Green, *The Hundred Years War: A People's History* (New Haven, CT: Yale University Press, 2014), pp. 230–48; and Ardis Butterfield, *The Familiar Enemy: Chaucer, Language and Nation in the Hundred Years War* (Oxford: Oxford University Press, 2009).

112 On how the Wars of the Roses were in many ways a direct consequence of England's humiliating defeat during the Hundred Years War, see Christine Carpenter, *The Wars of the Roses: Politics and the Constitution in England 1437–1509* (Cambridge: Cambridge University Press, 1997); and D. McCulloch and E.D. Jones, 'Lancastrian Politics, the French War, and the Rise of the Popular Element', *Speculum*, vol. 58, no. 1, 1983, pp. 95–138.

113 On the mercenary uprisings of the Truceless War, which erupted almost immediately after the First Punic War and took Carthage four years to suppress, see Dexter Hoyos, *The Truceless War: Carthage's Fight for Survival, 241 to 237 BC* (Leiden: Brill, 2007).

114 See the introductory chapter in Wolfgang Schivelbusch, *The Culture of Defeat: On National Trauma, Mourning, and Recovery* (London: Picador Books, 2013).

115 See, for example, Gary W. Gallagher and Alan T. Nolan (eds), *The Myth of the Lost Cause and Civil War History* (Bloomington, IN: Indiana University Press, 2000); and Allan Mitchell, 'The Xenophobic Style:

French Counterespionage and the Emergence of the Dreyfus Affair', *Journal of Modern History*, vol. 52, no. 3, September 1980, pp. 414–25.

116 See Seva Gunitsky, *Aftershocks: Great Powers and Domestic Reforms in the Twentieth Century* (Princeton, NJ: Princeton University Press, 2017), p. ix. Gunitsky charts how, over the course of the twentieth century, abrupt shifts in the distribution of relative power among leading powers in the international system frequently produced ideological shockwaves that shaped the spread and retreat of competing ideologies of democracy, communism or fascism.

117 For more details on these proxy conflicts, see L.J. Andrew Villalon, 'Spanish Involvement in the Hundred Years War and the Battle of Nájera', in L.J. Andrew Villalon and Donald J. Kagay (eds), *The Hundred Years War: A Wider Focus* (Leiden: Brill, 2005), pp. 3–74.

118 For an interesting recent examination of how state actors seek to externalise their defence by shifting the costs and burdens of war to surrogates, whether in the form of proxies, mercenaries or even unmanned systems, see Andreas Krieg and Jean-Marc Rickli, *Surrogate Warfare: The Transformation of War in the Twenty-first Century* (Washington DC: Georgetown University Press, 2019).

119 For an excellent collection of essays on how the French and Indian War was viewed by its varied participants, see Warren R. Hofstra (ed.), *Cultures in Conflict: The Seven Years' War in North America* (Lanham, MD: Rowman and Littlefield, 2007).

120 For an excellent examination of the Seven Years War and its effects on

North America, and one that places a refreshing emphasis on the role, strategies and agency of the native peoples, see Fred Anderson, *Crucible of War: The Seven Years' War and the Fate of Empire in British North America, 1754–1766* (New York: Vintage, 2007). See also William R. Nester, *The First Global War 1756–1775: Britain, France and the Fate of North America* (Westport, CT: Greenwood Publishing, 2000).

121 See Paul Kelton, 'The British and Indian War: Cherokee Power and the Fate of Empire in North America', *The William and Mary Quarterly*, vol. 69, no. 4, 2012, pp. 763–92. See also Matthew C. Ward, *Breaking the Backcountry: The Seven Years' War in Virginia and Pennsylvania, 1754–1765* (Pittsburgh, PA: University of Pittsburgh Press, 2003).

122 On the pivotal role of the Cherokees, see also David H. Corkran, *The Cherokee Frontier: Conflict and Survival, 1740–1762* (Norman, OK: University of Oklahoma Press, 1962); and Gregory Evans Dowd, 'Insidious Friends: Gift Giving and the Cherokee–British Alliance in the Seven Years' War', in Andrew R.L. Cayton and Fredrika J. Teute (eds), *Contact Points: American Frontiers from the Mohawk Valley to the Mississippi, 1750–1830* (Chapel Hill, NC: University of North Carolina Press, 1998), pp. 114–50.

123 For a seminal recent examination of the concept of lawfare, see Orde F. Kittrie, *Lawfare: Law as a Weapon of War* (Oxford: Oxford University Press, 2015). On contemporary China's practice of lawfare as one of the 'Three Warfares' (the other two forms being public-opinion

warfare and psychological warfare) at the basis of Chinese military influence operations, see Dean Cheng, 'Winning Without Fighting: Chinese Legal Warfare', The Heritage Foundation, 21 May 2012, https://www.heritage.org/asia/report/winning-without-fighting-chinese-legal-warfare; and Jill Goldenziel, 'Law as a Battlefield: The US, China and Global Escalation of Lawfare', *Cornell Law Review*, vol. 106, no. 5, September 2021, https://www.cornelllawreview.org/2021/09/23/law-as-a-battlefield-the-u-s-china-and-the-global-escalation-of-lawfare/.

124 For 'clogged up administrative processes and generally interfered with administrative activities', see Green, *The Hundred Years War: A People's History*, p. 53. For more context on the legalistic dimension to Franco-English competition in the decades leading up to the Hundred Years War, see G.P. Cuttino, 'Historical Revision: The Causes of the Hundred Years War', *Speculum*, vol. 31, no. 3, July 1956, pp. 463–77.

125 For a superb history of the role of mercantilism and coercive trade policy in a great-power rivalry, see John V.C. Nye, *War, Wine, and Taxes: The Political Economy of Anglo-French Trade, 1689–1900* (Princeton, NJ: Princeton University Press, 2018).

126 See E.B. Fryde, 'Edward III's Wool Monopoly of 1337: A Fourteenth Century Royal Trading Venture', *History*, vol. 37, no. 129, 1952, pp. 8–24; and Henry Stephen Lucas, *The Low Countries and the Hundred Years War: 1326–1347* (Ann Arbor, MI: University of Michigan Press, 1929), pp. 198–9.

127 For two stimulating historical examinations of state-directed

industrial espionage, see Gregory Afinogenov, *Spies and Scholars: Chinese Secrets and Imperial Russia's Quest for World Power* (Cambridge, MA: Harvard University Press, 2020) and J.R. Harris, *Industrial Espionage and Technology Transfer: Britain and France in the Eighteenth Century* (London: Ashgate Publishing, 1998).

[128] On the Megarian decree, whereby Athens imposed tight economic sanctions on Megara in retaliation for its support of Corinth, a Spartan ally, see P.A. Brunt, 'The Megarian Decree', *The American Journal of Philology*, vol. 72, no. 3, 1951, pp. 269–82; and Ronald P. Legon, 'The Megarian Decree and the Balance of Greek Naval Power', *Classical Philology*, vol. 68, no. 3, 1973, pp. 161–71. Thucydides claims that the Megarians' complaints to the Spartans regarding their unfair treatment played a lead role in the breakdown of Athens–Sparta relations in the period leading up to the Peloponnesian Wars, relating how 'there were many who came forward and made their several accusations; among them the Megarians, in a long list of grievances, called special attention to the fact of their exclusion from the ports of the Athenian Empire and the market of Athens'. See Thucydides, *The History of the Peloponnesian War*, Book I, ch. 67, paragraph 4, translated by Richard Crawley. Project Gutenberg, https://www.gutenberg.org/files/7142/7142-h/7142-h.htm. On Bismarck's weaponisation of tariffs and regulations, see Roland Vaubel, 'Comment: The Strategy of Raising Rivals' Costs by Federal Regulation Under Bismarck', in Peter Bernholz and Roland Vaubel (eds), *Political Competition and Economic Regulation* (New York: Routledge, 2007), pp. 194–9; and Otto Pflanze, *Bismarck and the Development of Germany, Vol. 2: The Period of Consolidation, 1871–1880* (Princeton, NJ: Princeton University Press, 1990 edition), ch. 16.

[129] See Adolf Burger, *The Devil's Workshop: A Memoir of the Nazi Counterfeiting Operation* (Barnsley: Frontline Books, 2009).

[130] On great-power competition as a two-level game, see Robert D. Putnam, 'Diplomacy and Domestic Politics: The Logic of Two-level Games', *International Organization*, vol. 42, no. 3, Summer 1988, pp. 427–60.

[131] See Geoffrey Parker, *The Grand Strategy of Philip II* (New Haven, CT: Yale University Press, 1998), pp. 345–6; Henry Kamen, *Philip of Spain* (New Haven, CT: Yale University Press, 1997), pp. 278–89; and N.M. Sutherland, 'The Foreign Policy of Philip II and the French Catholic League', *History*, vol. 51, no. 173, 1966, pp. 323–31.

[132] See Rehman, 'Raison d'Etat: Richelieu's Grand Strategy During the Thirty Years' War'; J.H. Elliott, *The Revolt of the Catalans: A Study in the Decline of Spain 1598–1640* (Cambridge: Cambridge University Press, 1984); and R.J. Knecht, *Richelieu* (New York: Routledge, 2014).

[133] Indeed, at one juncture, a combination of Castilian, Scottish and Italian allies comprised over 50% of the Armagnac army. See Philippe Contamine, *Guerre, État et Société à la Fin du Moyen Âge: Études sur les Armées des Rois de France, 1337–1494* [War, state and society in the Late Middle Ages: studies on the armies of the kings of France, 1337–1494] (Paris: Mouton & Co., 2004), ch. 4.

134 See G.J. Meyer, *The World Remade: America in World War I* (New York: Bantam Books, 2018); and Mitchell Yockelson, *Forty-seven Days: How Pershing's Warriors Came of Age to Defeat the German Army in World War I* (New York: Random House, 2016).

135 One interesting late Cold War study on a potential protracted and global war with the Soviet Union commented on the diversionary function of Sino-Soviet rivalry in the following terms: 'The Soviets already think enough of the threat to station about a quarter of the Soviet Army in the Far Eastern Theater of Military Operations. ... One must of course realize that the PRC might well wish to ensure that it did not become involved in a war between NATO and the Pact, but the potential for the PRC to act as a significant constraint on Soviet deployment of units in its interior to Europe means that the issue is one worthy of some consideration.' See John K. Setear, 'Protracted Conflict in Central Europe: A Conceptual Analysis', Report Prepared for the Office of Net Assessment, US Department of Defense, 1 November 1989, p. 20, https://apps.dtic.mil/sti/citations/ADA220000.

136 See Christine Isom-Verhaaren, *Allies with the Infidel: The Ottoman and French Alliance in the Sixteenth Century* (London: I.B. Tauris, 2011).

137 Philip de Commines, *The Memoirs of Philip de Commines, Lord of Argenton, Containing the Histories of Louis XI and Charles VIII, Kings of France, and of Charles the Bold, Duke of Burgundy, Vol. 1*(London: George Bell & Sons, 1883 edition), p. 381. First published in Paris, 1524.

138 *Ibid.*

139 On swing states, see Richard Fontaine and Daniel M. Kliman, 'International Order and Global Swing States', *Washington Quarterly*, vol. 36, no. 1, Winter 2013, pp. 93–109, https://www.csis.org/analysis/twq-international-order-and-global-swing-states-winter-2013.

140 See John Guy, *Henry VIII: The Quest for Fame* (London: Penguin Books, 2014), ch. 4; and Susan Doran, *England and Europe 1485–1603*, 2nd edition (New York: Routledge, 2013).

141 For a masterful account of the Jefferson administration's remarkably subtle diplomacy during this period, see James E. Lewis, 'A Tornado on the Horizon: The Jefferson Administration, the Retrocession Crisis, and the Louisiana Purchase', in Peter J. Kastor and Francois Weil (eds), *Empires of the Imagination: Transatlantic Histories of the Louisiana Purchase* (Charlottesville, VA: University of Virginia Press, 2009), pp. 117–40. See also Charles Cerami, *Jefferson's Great Gamble: The Remarkable Story of Jefferson, Napoleon and the Men Behind the Louisiana Purchase* (Naperville, IL: Sourcebooks, 2004).

142 On the function of buffer states in great-power rivalry and war, see John Chay and Thomas E. Ross (eds), *Buffer States in World Politics* (Boulder, CO: Westview Press, 1986); Marshall R. Singer, *Weak States in a World of Powers: The Dynamics of International Relationships* (New York: Free Press, 1972); and Michael G. Partem, 'The Buffer System in International Relations', *Journal of Conflict Resolution*, vol. 27, no. 1, March 1983, pp. 7–9.

143 Henry Foy, 'Vladislav Surkov: An Overdose of Freedom Is Fatal to a State', *Financial Times*, 18

June 2021, https://www.ft.com/
content/1324acbb-f475-47ab-a914-
4a96a9d14bac. Already in 2015,
Lawrence Freedman had correctly
diagnosed the Ukrainian conflict
as 'a war of exhaustion', in which
each side finds it 'preferable to live
with the conflict rather than make
irrevocable compromises'. See
Lawrence Freedman, 'Ukraine and
the Art of Exhaustion', *Survival:
Global Politics and Strategy*, vol. 57, no.
5, 2015, pp. 77–106.

144 See David Magie, *Roman Rule in
Asia Minor to the End of the Third
Century After Christ* (Princeton, NJ:
Princeton University Press, 1950);
Jason Schlude, *Rome, Parthia and the
Politics of Peace: The Origins of War in
the Ancient Middle East* (New York:
Routledge, 2020); and Rose Mary
Sheldon, *Rome's Wars in Parthia: Blood
and Sand* (Portland, OR: Valentine
Mitchell, 2010).

145 See Michael P. Fronda and Francois
Gauthier, 'Italy and Sicily in the
Second Punic War: Multipolarity,
Minor Powers, and Local Military
Entrepreneurialism', in Toni Ñaco Del
Hoyo and Fernando López Sánchez
(eds), *War, Warlords and Interstate
Relations in the Ancient Mediterranean*
(Leiden: Brill, 2017), pp. 308–25; and
Kathryn Lomas, 'Rome, Latins and
Italians in the Second Punic War', in
Hoyos (ed.), *A Companion to the Punic
Wars*, pp. 339–56.

146 Michael P. Fronda, *Between Rome
and Carthage: Southern Italy During
the Second Punic War* (Cambridge:
Cambridge University Press, 2010).

147 *Ibid.*, p. 51.

148 Hoyos, *Mastering the West: Rome and
Carthage at War*, p. 133.

Chapter Three

1 For an excellent examination of the
Sino-Soviet war, see Michael S. Gerson
(ed.), 'The Sino-Soviet Border Conflict:
Deterrence, Escalation, and the Threat
of Nuclear War in 1969', Center for
Naval Analyses, 2010, https://www.
cna.org/cna_files/pdf/d0022974.a2.pdf.

2 See, for example, John Mueller,
*Retreat from Doomsday: The
Obsolescence of Major War* (New York:
Basic Books, 1990).

3 Fiona S. Cunningham and M. Taylor
Fravel, 'Dangerous Confidence?
Chinese Views of Nuclear
Escalation', *International Security*,
vol. 44, no. 2, 2019, pp. 61–109,
https://direct.mit.edu/isec/article-
abstract/44/2/61/12244/Dangerous-
Confidence-Chinese-Views-on-Nucle
ar?redirectedFrom=fulltext.

4 *Ibid.* A 2008 RAND Corporation
study echoes these themes, stating
that 'Chinese military thinkers note
several changes in the global context
for armed conflict. … among nuclear-
armed states, unlimited warfare is
far too dangerous, and no major
power faces such a grave threat to its
existence that it would be willing to
escalate uncontrollably. A prominent
argument in Chinese writings about
war control is that conflict is far more
transparent in a globalized world,
and thus, it is subject to national and
international limits – some of which
constrain China and others that China
would seek to use to its advantage
during conflict. Chinese strategists
also argue that most nations possess
the material ability and political will

to control warfare; in other words, there is no ipso facto reason that warfare cannot be controlled.' See Forrest E. Morgan et al., 'China's Thinking on Escalation: Evidence from Chinese Military Writings', in Forrest E. Morgan et al., *Dangerous Thresholds: Managing Escalation in the 21st Century* (Santa Monica, CA: Rand Corporation, 2008), https://www.jstor.org/stable/10.7249/mg614af.10.

5 See Dean Cheng, 'How China's Thinking About the Next War', Breaking Defense, 19 May 2021, https://breakingdefense.com/2021/05/how-chinas-thinking-about-the-next-war.

6 See Yu Jin (ed.), *The Science of Second Artillery Operations* (Beijing: People's Liberation Army Press, 2004), pp. 294–6.

7 The commonly employed acronym C4ISR stands for command, control, communications and computers (C4) intelligence, surveillance and reconnaissance (ISR). See James M. Acton, 'Escalation Through Entanglement: How the Vulnerability of Command-and-control Systems Raises the Risks of an Inadvertent Nuclear War', *International Security*, vol. 43, no. 1, 2018, pp. 56–99, https://direct.mit.edu/isec/article/43/1/56/12199/Escalation-through-Entanglement-How-the.

8 Office of the Secretary of Defense, 'Annual Report to Congress: Military and Security Developments Involving the People's Republic of China 2019', p. 66, https://media.defense.gov/2019/May/02/2002127082/-1/-1/1/2019_CHINA_MILITARY_POWER_REPORT.pdf.

9 Caitlin Talmadge, 'Would China Go Nuclear? Assessing the Risk of Chinese Nuclear Escalation in a Conventional War with the United States', *International Security*, vol. 41, no. 4, Spring 2017, pp. 50–92.

10 These strategic debates are ably summarised in Aaron L. Friedberg, *Beyond Air–Sea Battle: The Debate over US Military Strategy in Asia* (London: IISS, 2014). For one of the best-known advocacies of the 'indirect approach', see T.X. Hammes, 'Offshore Control: A Proposed Strategy for an Unlikely Conflict', National Defense University, June 2012, https://ndupress.ndu.edu/Portals/68/Documents/stratforum/SF-278.pdf. For an argument in favour of carefully 'tailored conventional strike options', see Vincent A. Manzo, 'After the First Shots: Managing Escalation in Northeast Asia', *Joint Force Quarterly*, vol. 77, no. 2, 2015, pp. 91–100. For a noteworthy critique of overly relying on a strategy of horizonal escalation, see Elbridge Colby and David Ochmanek, 'How the United States Could Lose a Great-power War', *Foreign Policy*, 29 October 2019, https://foreignpolicy.com/2019/10/29/united-states-china-russia-great-power-war.

11 This point is ably made in Joshua Rovner, 'A Long War in the East: Doctrine, Diplomacy, and the Prospects for a Protracted Sino-American Conflict', *Diplomacy & Statecraft*, vol. 29, no. 1, 2018, pp. 129–42.

12 On how the continued evolution of the precision-strike regime has changed the character of warfare, see Barry D. Watts, 'The Evolution of Precision Strike', Center for Strategic and Budgetary Assessments, 2013, https://csbaonline.org/uploads/documents/Evolution-of-Precision-Strike-final-v15.pdf. On the concept of a 'maritime no-man's land', see Andrew Krepinevich, 'Maritime Competition in a Mature Precision-strike Regime', Center for Strategic and Budgetary Assessments, 2015, https://csbaonline.org/research/publications/maritime-competition-in-a-mature-precision-strike-regime.

13 Christian Brose, *The Kill Chain: Defending America in the Future of High-tech Warfare* (New York: Hachette Books, 2020).

14 On how this tenuous balance might stimulate competition in peripheral theatres via proxy, and what forms future Sino-US proxy wars might take, see Dominic Tierney, 'The Future of Sino-US Proxy War', *Texas National Security Review*, vol. 4, no. 2, Spring 2021, pp. 49–73, https://tnsr.org/2021/03/the-future-of-sino-u-s-proxy-war; and John Vrolyk, 'Insurgency, Not War, Is China's Most Likely Course of Action', War on the Rocks, 19 December 2019, https://warontherocks.com/2019/12/insurgency-not-war-is-chinas-most-likely-course-of-action.

15 See Mike Yeo, 'China's Missile and Space Tech Is Creating a Defensive Bubble Difficult to Penetrate', *Defense News*, 1 June 2020, https://www.defensenews.com/global/asia-pacific/2020/06/01/chinas-missile-and-space-tech-is-creating-a-defensive-bubble-difficult-to-penetrate.

16 John Speed Myers, 'Mainland Strikes and U.S. Military Strategy Towards China: Historical Cases, Interviews, and a Scenario-based Survey of American National Security Elites', RAND Corporation, 2019, pp. 146–7, https://www.rand.org/pubs/rgs_dissertations/RGSD430.html.

17 *Ibid.*

18 US Department of Defense, 'Air–Sea Battle: Service Collaboration to Address Anti-access and Area Denial Challenges', 2013, https://dod.defense.gov/Portals/1/Documents/pubs/ASB-ConceptImplementation-Summary-May-2013.pdf; US Joint Chiefs of Staff, 'Joint Concept for Entry Operations', 7 April 2014, https://www.jcs.mil/Portals/36/Documents/Doctrine/concepts/jceo.pdf%3fver%3d2017-12-28-162000-837; Michael E. Hutchens et al., 'Joint Concept for Access and Maneuver in the Global Commons: A New Joint Operational Concept', *Joint Force Quarterly*, vol. 84, 2017, pp.

134–9; Audrey Decker, 'Grady Eyes Third Iteration of JWC to Become Doctrine', *Inside Defense*, 3 November 2022, https://insidedefense.com/insider/grady-eyes-third-iteration-jwc-become-'doctrine'; US Department of the Navy, 'Commandant's Planning Guidance: 38th Commandant of the Marine Corps', 2020, https://www.hqmc.marines.mil/Portals/142/Docs/%20 38th%20Commandant%27s%20 Planning%20Guidance_2019.pdf?ver=2019-07-16-200152-700 and Barry Rosenberg, 'Distributed Maritime Operations: Dispersing the Fleet for Survivability and Lethality', Breaking Defense, 15 September 2021, https://breakingdefense.com/2021/09/distributed-maritime-operations-dispersing-the-fleet-for-survivability-and-lethality.

19 See US Department of Defense, 'Summary of the 2018 National Defense Strategy of the United States of America: Sharpening the American Military's Competitive Edge', 2018, p. 7, https://dod.defense.gov/Portals/1/Documents/pubs/2018-National-Defense-Strategy-Summary.pdf; and US Department of Defense, '2022 National Defense Strategy of the United States of America', 2022, p. 17, https://media.defense.gov/2022/Oct/27/2003103845/-1/-1/1/2022-NATIONAL-DEFENSE-STRATEGY-NPR-MDR.PDF.

20 David C. Logan, 'Are They Reading Schelling in Beijing? The Dimensions, Drivers, and Risks of Nuclear–Conventional Entanglement in China', *Journal of Strategic Studies*, November 2020, pp. 5–55.

21 *Ibid.*

22 US Department of Defense, 'Military and Security Developments Involving the People's Republic of China 2022: Annual Report to Congress', 2022, p. 160, https://media.defense.gov/2022/Nov/29/2003122279/-1/-1/1/2022-

MILITARY-AND-SECURITY-
DEVELOPMENTS-INVOLVING-
THE-PEOPLES-REPUBLIC-OF-
CHINA.PDF.

23 See Sky Lo, 'Could China's "Hot-
Swappable" Missile System Start an
Accidental Nuclear War?', *Bulletin
of the Atomic Scientists*, 8 April 2022,
https://thebulletin.org/2022/04/
could-chinas-hot-swappable-missile-
system-start-an-accidental-nuclear-
war/; and 'DF-26', CSIS Missile
Defense Project, 6 August 2021,
https://missilethreat.csis.org/missile/
dong-feng-26-df-26/.

24 See Fiona S. Cunningham, 'The
Unknowns About China's Nuclear
Modernization Program', *Arms
Control Today*, June 2023, https://
www.armscontrol.org/act/2023-06/
features/unknowns-about-chinas-
nuclear-modernization-program.

25 On the implications of such a shift
in warhead-handling infrastructure,
should it materialise, and on how
it could be indicative of a Chinese
move toward a launch-on-warning
posture or away from NFU, see
David C. Logan and Phillip C.
Saunders, 'Discerning the Drivers of
China's Nuclear Force Development:
Models, Indicators, and Data',
Institute for National Strategic
Studies, National Defense University
Press, July 2023, pp. 36–7, https://
ndupress.ndu.edu/Portals/68/
Documents/stratperspective/china/
chinaPerspectives-18.pdf?ver=vfq7ub
tJyhPAKNAaO21jkQ%3d%3d.

26 As Joshua Rovner notes, 'another
danger will arise even if Beijing and
Washington each prove reluctant
about going nuclear at the outset
of a crisis. It is one thing to possess
weapons of mass destruction but
another to use them, and past leaders
have blanched when faced with the
option. Yet they may have no interest
in backing down, even if they are
unwilling to go nuclear, and both
are likely to seek a quick decisive
victory using conventional forces.
The early days of such a campaign
may prove disappointing to Beijing
and Washington; the experience of
Great Power war rarely lives up to
pre-war expectations. In this way,
they may stumble into a prolonged
and mutually destructive struggle.
Thus, in the early days of the conflict,
the United States will face a grim
choice. If it tries to win quickly, it
might trigger nuclear war. If it tries
to reduce the risk of escalation, it
may end up in an exhausting war of
attrition.' Joshua Rovner, 'Two Kinds
of Catastrophe: Nuclear Escalation
and Protracted War in Asia', *Journal
of Strategic Studies*, vol. 40, no. 5, 2017,
pp. 696–730.

27 For a harsh critique of this approach,
see Raphael S. Cohen and Gian
Gentile, 'The U.S. Should Get Over its
Short War Obsession', *Foreign Policy*,
28 March 2023, https://foreignpolicy.
com/2023/03/28/us-russia-ukraine-
china-short-war-strategic-patience/.
At the time of writing, there is
evidence that the White House's
thinking regarding the targeting of
Crimea may be evolving. See Helene
Cooper, Eric Schmitt and Julian
E. Barnes, 'US Warms to Helping
Ukraine Target Crimea', *New York
Times*, 18 January 2023, https://www.
nytimes.com/2023/01/18/us/politics/
ukraine-crimea-military.html.

28 In his recent testimony before the
Senate Armed Services Committee,
Admiral Charles A. Richard, former
commander of US Strategic Command,
referred to China's expansion of its
nuclear arsenal as 'breathtaking' in
its scope, and fully 'inconsistent'
with its stated minimum deterrent
posture. See 'Statement of Charles A.
Richard, Commander United States
Strategic Command Before the Senate
Armed Services Committee', 8 March
2022, https://www.armed-services.

senate.gov/imo/media/doc/2022%20
USSTRATCOM%20Posture%20
Statement%20-%20SASC%20Hrg%20
FINAL.pdf.

29 US Department of Defense, '2022
Nuclear Posture Review', p. 4,
https://media.defense.gov/2022/
Oct/27/2003103845/-1/-1/1/2022-
NATIONAL-DEFENSE-STRATEGY-
NPR-MDR.PDF#page=33. Meanwhile,
the DOD's most recent annual report
to Congress on Chinese military
power predicts that, if current trend
lines continue, Beijing may boast a
'stockpile of about 1500 warheads by
its 2035 timeline'. See US Department
of Defense, 'Military and Security
Developments Involving the People's
Republic of China 2022: Annual
Report to Congress', 2022, p. 94.

30 Ibid.

31 See Chris Buckley, 'China Draws
Lessons from Russia's Losses in
Ukraine, and Its Gains', New York
Times, 1 April 2023, https://www.
nytimes.com/2023/04/01/world/asia/
china-russia-ukraine-war.html.

32 See, for example, the contrasting
arguments laid out in Elbridge
Colby, 'Against the Great Powers:
Reflections on Balancing Nuclear
and Conventional Power', Texas
National Security Review, vol. 2,
no. 1, pp. 143–50; Brandon M.
Patterson, 'The Navy Needs a
Low-yield Nuclear Weapon',
US Naval Institute, Proceedings,
vol. 148, no. 12, December 2022,
https://www.usni.org/magazines/
proceedings/2022/december/navy-
needs-low-yield-nuclear-weapon;
and Edward Geist, 'The U.S. Doesn't
Need More Nuclear Weapons to
Counter China's New Missile Silos',
Washington Post, 18 October 2021,
https://www.washingtonpost.com/
outlook/2021/10/18/china-silos-
missiles-nuclear/. On the cancellation
of the SLCM–N, see Valerie Insinna,
'Biden Administration Kills Trump-
era Nuclear Cruise Missile Program',
Breaking Defense, 28 March 2022,
https://breakingdefense.com/2022/03/
biden-administration-kills-trump-era-
nuclear-cruise-missile-program/.

33 This attitudinal shift is already
materialising in South Korea, in
large part due to swelling anxiety
over the nuclear threat from North
Korea. See Choe Sang-hun, 'In a
First, South Korea Declares Nuclear
Weapons a Policy Option', New York
Times, 12 January 2023, https://www.
nytimes.com/2023/01/12/world/asia/
south-korea-nuclear-weapons.html.
Meanwhile, in Japan, the former
prime minister Abe Shinzo, only a few
months before his assassination, called
for Tokyo to move away from its 'three
non-nuclear principles' (not producing,
possessing or hosting nuclear weapons
on its territory) and to consider hosting
US nuclear weapons. See Justin
McCurry, 'China Rattled by Calls for
Japan to Host US Nuclear Weapons',
Guardian, 1 March 2022, https://www.
theguardian.com/world/2022/mar/01/
china-rattled-by-calls-for-japan-to-host-
us-nuclear-weapons.

34 See The White House, 'Washington
Declaration', 26 April 2023, https://
www.whitehouse.gov/briefing-room/
statements-releases/2023/04/26/
washington-declaration-2/; Hyonhee
Shin and Josh Smith, 'US Nuclear
Missile Submarine Visits S.Korea as
Allies Talk War Planning', Reuters,
18 July 2023, https://www.reuters.
com/world/asia-pacific/us-skorean-
officials-huddle-new-nuclear-war-
planning-talks-2023-07-18/; and Ankit
Panda, 'The Washington Declaration
Is a Software Upgrade for the U.S.–
South Korea Alliance', Carnegie
Endowment for International
Peace, 1 May 2023, https://
carnegieendowment.org/2023/05/01/
washington-declaration-is-software-
upgrade-for-u.s.-south-korea-
alliance-pub-89648.

35 See Paula Hancocks et al., 'Exclusive: North Korea a "Clear and Present Danger", says South Korean Foreign Minister', CNN, 23 February 2023, https://www.cnn.com/2023/02/22/asia/south-korea-foreign-minister-interview-intl-hnk/index.html.

36 Evan Braden Montgomery and Toshi Yoshihara, 'The Real Challenge of China's Nuclear Modernization', *Washington Quarterly*, vol. 45, no. 4, 2022, pp. 45–60.

37 See Greg Austin, Kai Lin Tay and Munish Sharma, 'Great-power Offensive Cyber Campaigns: Experiments in Strategy', IISS, 2022, https://www.iiss.org/blogs/research-paper/2022/02/great-power-offensive-cyber-campaigns. The US Department of Defense's 2018 Cyber Strategy places a notable emphasis on 'defending forward' to 'disrupt or halt malicious cyber activity at its source', in addition to conducting cyberspace operations that enhance US military advantages. See US Department of Defense, 'Summary: Department of Defense Cyber Strategy 2018', 2018, p. 1, https://media.defense.gov/2018/Sep/18/2002041658/-1/-1/1/CYBER_STRATEGY_SUMMARY_FINAL.PDF.

38 For a good overview of this dogged state-sanctioned campaign of cyber espionage, see Nicole Perlroth, 'How China Transformed into a Prime Cyber Threat to the US', *New York Times*, 20 July 2021, https://www.nytimes.com/2021/07/19/technology/china-hacking-us.html.

39 See, for example, James M. Acton, 'Cyber Warfare & Inadvertent Escalation', *Daedalus*, vol. 149, no. 2, 2020, pp. 133–49. On the potential for opportunistic and covert third-party intervention in the cyber domain, see Andrew F. Krepinevich Jr, 'Protracted Great-power War: A Preliminary Assessment', Center for Strategic and Budgetary Assessments, 5 February 2020, https://www.cnas.org/publications/reports/protracted-great-power-war.

40 Stanford University's Jacquelyn Schneider rightly observes that 'measuring cyber capabilities is extremely difficult. Whereas in other domains capability is measured by orders of battle, performance in exercises, physical defense measures, or even the kinetic effects of different weapon systems – cyber capabilities are virtual, rarely static, difficult to predict their effect, and quite often classified.' Jacquelyn G. Schneider, 'US Military Strategy and Domestic Policy Coordination: Testimony Before the U.S.–China Economic and Security Review Commission: Hearing on China's Cyber Capabilities: Warfare, Espionage, and Implications for the United States', 17 February 2022, https://www.uscc.gov/sites/default/files/2022-02/Jacquelyn_Schneider_Testimony.pdf. While remaining mindful of these challenges, the IISS *Military Balance* is in the process of including cyber competencies in its assessment of national military capabilities.

41 These information-distribution challenges, notes Ben Buchanan, can exacerbate pre-existing security dilemmas, as no party can accurately gauge the full range of their opponent's capabilities. See Ben Buchanan, *The Cybersecurity Dilemma: Hacking, Trust, and Fear Among Nations* (New York: Oxford University Press, 2016), ch. 6.

42 See Steven M. Bellovin, Susan Landau and Herbert Lin, 'Limiting the Undesired Impact of Cyber Weapons: Technical Requirements and Policy Implications', in Herbert Lin and Amy Zegart (eds), *Bytes, Bombs and Spies: The Strategic Dimensions of Offensive Cyber Operations* (Washington DC: Brookings Institution Press, 2018), pp. 274–6.

43 President Xi has long warned that the 'control of core technology by

others is our [China's] biggest core danger', and that allowing foreign entities to gatekeep computer and cyber technology is akin to 'building a house on someone else's foundation'. See Rush Doshi et al., 'China as a "Cyber Great Power": Beijing's Two Voices in Telecommunications', Brookings Institution, April 2021, https://www.brookings.edu/research/china-as-a-cyber-great-power-beijings-two-voices-in-telecommunications/; and 'China's Cyber Capabilities: Warfare, Espionage, and Implications for the United States', in U.S.–China Economic and Security Review Commission, '2022 Report to Congress', 2022, ch. 3, Section 2, pp. 418–518, https://www.uscc.gov/sites/default/files/2022-11/2022_Annual_Report_to_Congress.pdf.

44 See Simone Dossi, 'On the Asymmetric Advantages of Cyberwarfare: Western Literature and the Chinese Journal *Guofang Keiji*', *Journal of Strategic Studies*, vol. 43, no. 2, 2020, pp. 281–308; and Dean Cheng, 'PLA Perspectives on Network Warfare', in '"Informationized Local Wars": Testimony Before the U.S.–China Economic and Security Review Commission, 17 February 2022, https://www.uscc.gov/sites/default/files/2022-02/Dean_Cheng_Testimony.pdf. Since the sweeping military reforms of late 2015, the newly formed Strategic Support Force is the PLA entity now responsible for 'fifth-generation information warfare' with a focus on cyber, electronic warfare, space and influence operations. For a good analysis of its evolving role, see John Chen, Joe McReynolds and Kieran Green, 'The PLA Strategic Support Force: A "Joint" Force for Information Operations', in Joel Wuthnow et al. (eds), *The PLA Beyond Borders: Chinese Military Operations in Regional*

and Global Context (Washington DC: National Defense University, 2021), pp. 151–79, https://ndupress.ndu.edu/Portals/68/Documents/Books/beyond-borders/990-059-NDU-PLA_Beyond_Borders_sp_jm14.pdf.

45 US Office of the Director of National Intelligence, 'Annual Threat Assessment of the U.S. Intelligence Community', February 2022, p. 8, https://www.dni.gov/files/ODNI/documents/assessments/ATA-2022-Unclassified-Report.pdf.

46 See Liu Zhen, 'US Military Urged to Act Faster on Interlinked Warfare System as China Catches Up', *South China Morning Post*, 9 January 2023, https://www.scmp.com/news/china/military/article/3206170/us-military-urged-act-faster-interlinked-warfare-system-china-catches.

47 A cyber attack which, for instance, either directly or indirectly affected healthcare facilities – a growing number of which have already experienced patient casualties due to ransomware attacks. See Maggie Miller, 'The Mounting Death Toll of Hospital Cyberattacks', Politico, 28 December 2022, https://www.politico.com/news/2022/12/28/cyberattacks-u-s-hospitals-00075638.

48 James Pearson and Jonathan Landay, 'Cyberattack on NATO Could Trigger Collective Defense Clause – Official', Reuters, 28 February 2022, https://www.reuters.com/world/europe/cyberattack-nato-could-trigger-collective-defence-clause-official-2022-02-28/.

49 For a classic examination of early modern privateering and its tight embeddedness within European grand strategy at the time, see Kenneth R. Andrews, *Elizabethan Privateering: English Privateering During the Spanish War, 1585–1603* (Cambridge: Cambridge University Press, 1964). On the role played by mercenaries in Angola's protracted civil wars, see W.

Martin James III, *A Political History of the Civil War in Angola, 1974–1990* (New York: Routledge, 2020); and Stephen Rookes, *CIA and British Mercenaries in Angola, 1975–76: From Operation IA/Feature to Massacre at Maquela* (Warwick: Helion and Company, 2021).

50 See Max Markusen, 'A Stealth Industry: The Quiet Expansion of Chinese Private Security Companies', Center for Strategic and International Studies, January 2022; and Paul Nantulya, 'Chinese Security Firms Spread Along the African Belt and Road', National Defense University Africa Center for Strategic Studies, 15 June 2021, https://africacenter. org/spotlight/chinese-security-firms-spread-african-belt-road/.

51 See Thomas Shugart, 'Mind the Gap: How China's Civilian Shipping Could Enable a Taiwan Invasion', War on the Rocks, 16 August 2021, https:// warontherocks.com/2021/08/mind-the-gap-how-chinas-civilian-shipping-could-enable-a-taiwan-invasion/.

52 See J. Michael Dahm, 'Chinese Ferry Tales: The PLA's Use of Civilian Shipping in Support of Over-the-shore Logistics', US Naval War College China Maritime Studies Institute, November 2021, https://digital-commons.usnwc.edu/cgi/viewcontent. cgi?article=1015&context=cmsi-maritime-reports; Kevin McCauley, 'Logistics Support for a Cross-strait Invasion: The View from Beijing', US Naval War College China Maritime Studies Institute, July 2022, https://digital-commons. usnwc.edu/cgi/viewcontent. cgi?article=1021&context=cmsi-maritime-reports; and H.I. Sutton and Sam LaGrone, 'Chinese Launch Assault Craft from Civilian Car Ferries in Mass Amphibious Invasion Drill, Satellite Photos Show', USNI News, 28 September 2022, https://news.usni. org/2022/09/28/chinese-launch-assault-craft-from-civilian-car-ferries-in-mass-amphibious-invasion-drill-satellite-photos-show.

53 See 'How Elon Musk's Satellites Have Saved Ukraine and Changed Warfare', *The Economist*, 5 January 2023.

54 See Michael Kahn, 'Ukraine's Tech Entrepreneurs Fight War on a Different Front', Reuters, 4 April 2023, https:// www.reuters.com/world/europe/ ukraines-tech-entrepreneurs-fight-war-different-front-2023-04-04/; and Shyam Sankar, 'Ukraine's Software Warrior Brigade', *Wall Street Journal*, 8 March 2023, https://www.wsj.com/ articles/ukraines-deadly-computer-science-brigade-russia-invasion-drone-engineer-software-wartime-weaponry-production-e0643979.

55 See Pierre Ayad and Pariesa Brody, 'Ukrainian Soldiers Are Turning Consumer Drones into Formidable Weapons of War', France 24, 8 August 2022, https://observers.france24. com/en/europe/20220808-ukraine-russia-modified-commercial-drones-battlefield-donations-weapons.

56 See Christopher Woody, 'Russian and Chinese Bombers Conducted Another Joint Patrol Between South Korea and Japan', Business Insider, 22 December 2020, https://www.businessinsider. com/russian-chinese-bombers-do-joint-patrol-between-south-korea-japan-2020-12; and Timothy Heath, 'Huge Military Drills Show Both the Limits, and the Durability, of China–Russia Ties', World Politics Review, 11 September 2018, https:// www.worldpoliticsreview.com/ articles/25845/huge-military-drills-show-both-the-limits-and-the-durability-of-china-russia-ties. For an interesting examination of how the PLA appears increasingly to emulate key aspects of Russian war-fighting doctrine and command philosophy, see Mandip Singh, 'How China Used Russian Models and Experiences to Modernize the PLA', Mercator Institute for China Studies, 23

September 2020, https://merics.org/sites/default/files/2020-09/Merics_ChinaMonitor_PLA-Russia_3.pdf.

57 See, for instance, Capts Walker Mills and Michael Rasmussen, 'Don't Reinvent the Wheel: Learning from Allies and Partners for EABO', *Marine Corps Gazette*, June 2021, pp. 106–9.

58 For example, the US Air Force's famed Red Flag exercises, which by 1987 had expanded to include 18 international participating countries and 15 foreign-observer countries. On how the most recent Red Flag exercises have focused specifically on a 'great-power air war' against China, see James Kitfield, 'Red Flag 2019: First Great Power Air War Test in Years', Breaking Defense, 6 March 2019, https://breakingdefense.com/2019/03/red-flag-2019-first-great-power-air-war-test-in-years/. On coalition training as a source of military effectiveness, see Nora Bensahel, 'International Alliances and Military Effectiveness: Fighting Alongside Allies and Partners', in Risa A. Brooks and Elizabeth A. Stanley (eds), *Creating Military Power: The Sources of Military Effectiveness* (Stanford, CA: Stanford University Press, 2007), ch. 8; and Olivier Schmitt, *Allies that Count: Junior Partners in Coalition Warfare* (Washington DC: Georgetown University Press, 2018).

59 See Dan Sabbagh, 'UK to Issue "Threat Alert" over China's Attempts to Recruit RAF Pilots', *Guardian*, 17 October 2022, https://www.theguardian.com/uk-news/2022/oct/18/uk-officials-threat-alert-china-attempts-to-recruit-raf-pilots; and Stefano D'Urso, 'Multiple Nations Investigating China's Efforts to Recruit Western Pilots', The Aviationist, 14 November 2022, https://theaviationist.com/2022/11/14/china-efforts-to-recruit-western-pilots/.

60 On Xi Jinping's reshaping of the PLA, see Chien-wen Kou, 'Xi Jinping in Command: Solving the Principal–Agent Problem in CCP–PLA Relations?', *China Quarterly*, vol. 232, 2017, pp. 866–85; 'China Issues Guideline on Ideological, Political Education of Military', Xinhua, 7 April 2021, http://www.xinhuanet.com/english/2021-04/07/c_139864797.htm; and Elsa Kania, 'In the "New Era", the PLA is Xi's Army', Center for Advanced China Research, 1 August 2019, https://www.ccpwatch.org/single-post/2019/08/01/In-the-New-Era-the-PLA-is-Xis-Army.

61 For more historical background, see Fyodor Tertitskiy, 'Evolutionary Patterns in the Institution of Political Officers in the North Korean Army: Coup-proofing Versus Military Effectiveness', *North Korean Review*, vol. 18, no. 1, Spring 2022, pp. 7–27; David Shambaugh, 'The Soldier and the State in China: The Political Work System in the People's Liberation Army', *China Quarterly*, vol. 127, September 1991, pp. 527–68; Dale R. Herspring and Roger N. McDermott, 'Chaplains, Political Officers, and the Russian Armed Forces', *Problems of Post-Communism*, vol. 57, no. 4, 2010, pp. 51–9; and Kenneth C. Cathey, 'Who Is the Commissar: Political Officers in the Chinese Communist Army', *Naval War College Review*, vol. 24, no. 9, 1971, pp. 55–72.

62 See Roger Reese, 'The Red Army and the Great Purges', in J. Arch Getty and Roberta T. Manning (eds), *Stalinist Terror: New Perspectives* (Cambridge: Cambridge University Press, 1993), pp. 198–214.

63 See James Mulvenon, 'Hotel Gutian: We Haven't Had That Spirit Here Since 1929', China Leadership Monitor, 19 March 2015.

64 For an invaluable recent report on this surprisingly understudied aspect of Chinese military command, see Jeff W. Beson and Zi Yang, 'Party on the Bridge: Political Commissars in the Chinese Navy', Center for

Strategic and International Studies, June 2020, https://csis-website-prod. s3.amazonaws.com/s3fs-public/ publication/200626_BensonYang_ PartyOnTheBridge_Web_v2.pdf. See also Amos Lee, 'China's Military Political Commissar System Under PLA Modernization/ Professionalization', *Fulbright Taiwan Online Journal*, 11 August 2020, https://journal.fulbright.org.tw/ chinas-military-political-commissar-system-under-pla-modernization-professionalization/.

65 As one granular recent analysis of these drastic changes astutely observes, 'aside from indicating a seeming lack of confidence in the PLA's reliability these changes will have a serious impact on how the PLA operates. If the PLA is serious about reinforcing and revitalizing the role of the party committee in the operational command process, then we must consider how its collective decision-making process is to be reconciled with the need for rapid decision-making in modern, informatized warfare.' Morgan Clemens and Benjamin Rosen, 'The Impact of Reform on the PLA's Political Work System', in Roy Kamphausen (ed.), *The People of the PLA 2.0* (Carlisle, PA: US Army War College, 2021), pp. 1–40.

66 The PLARF is a separate service with equivalent status to the army, navy and air force, overseeing a vast –and growing – inventory of both conventional and nuclear-armed land-based missiles. On the sudden and startling purge within the PLARF, see 'What to Make of a Surprise Shake-up in China's Nuclear Force', *The Economist*, 3 August 2022, https://www.economist.com/ china/2023/08/03/what-to-make-of-a-surprise-shake-up-in-chinas-nuclear-force; and Kathrin Hille, 'China Ousts Top Generals from Nuclear

Rocket Force', *Financial Times*, 31 July 2023, https://www.ft.com/ content/0375c760-7902-4a41-b8f4-1b41026a38fd.

67 See Minxin Pei, 'What the Ukraine War Should Teach China', Project Syndicate, 8 June 2022, https://www. project-syndicate.org/commentary/ ukraine-war-lessons-for-china-weaknesses-of-pla-and-russian-military-by-minxin-pei-2022-06; and Michael Schwirtz et al., 'Putin's War', *New York Times*, 18 December 2022, https://www.nytimes.com/ interactive/2022/12/16/world/europe/ russia-putin-war-failures-ukraine.html.

68 See, for example, Philip C. Saunders and Joel Wuthnow, 'Large and In Charge: Civil–Military Relations Under Xi Jinping', in Philip C. Saunders et al. (eds), *Chairman Xi Remakes the PLA: Assessing China's Military Reforms* (Washington DC: National Defense University Press, 2019), pp. 519–47, in which the authors note that 'CCP leaders have tried to compensate for the declining relevance of Marxist ideology by positioning the Party as the only vehicle for fulfilling nationalist goals such as building China into a powerful and respected state and resolving outstanding territorial disputes, including the status of Taiwan. However, this approach means that support for the Party based on nationalism is conditional on its performance in achieving nationalist goals. It is not hard to imagine deep resentment within the PLA toward leaders viewed as unduly soft toward China's perceived enemies and perhaps even talk about ineffectual Party leaders as national traitors.' On how the CCP's deliberate stoking of Chinese nationalism could end up being a double-edged sword, by 'boxing in' or even undermining China's leadership, see Li Yuan, 'Perils of Preaching Nationalism Play

Out on Social Media', *New York Times*, 4 August 2022, https://www.nytimes.com/2022/08/04/business/new-world-nancy-pelosi-taiwan-social-media.html; and 'Xi Jinping Has Nurtured an Ugly Form of Chinese Nationalism: It May Prove Hard to Control', *The Economist*, 13 July 2022.

69 Samuel P. Huntington, *The Soldier and the State: The Theory and Politics of Civil–Military Relations* (Cambridge, MA: Harvard University Press, 1957), p. 84.

70 Mission command, which finds its intellectual ancestry in nineteenth-century Prussian field-service regulations and doctrine, seeks – through the principles of subsidiarity and trust – to combine centralised intent with decentralised initiative and execution. The US military defines it more specifically in the following terms: 'Mission command is the conduct of military operations through decentralized execution based upon mission-type orders. Mission command exploits the human element, emphasizing trust, force of will, initiative, judgment, and creativity. Successful mission command demands that subordinate leaders at all echelons exercise disciplined initiative and act aggressively and independently to accomplish the mission. They focus their orders on the purpose of the operation rather than on the details of how to perform assigned tasks. Essential to mission command is the thorough understanding of the commander's intent at every level of command and a command climate of mutual trust and understanding.' See Deployable Training Division (DTD) of the Joint Staff J7, 'Mission Command: Second Edition', January 2020, https://www.jcs.mil/Portals/36/Documents/Doctrine/fp/missioncommand_fp_2nd_ed.pdf?ver=2020-01-13-083451-207.

71 David 'Cam' Smith, 'Mission Command in Multi-domain Operations', *OTH Journal*, 30 October 2017, https://othjournal.com/2017/10/30/mission-command-in-multi-domain-operations/. See also Heather Venable and Jared R. Donnelly, 'Scaling the Levels of War: The Strategic Major and the Future of Multi-domain Operations', War on the Rocks, 10 May 2019, https://warontherocks.com/2019/05/scaling-the-levels-of-war-the-strategic-major-and-the-future-of-multi-domain-operations/; and James K. Greer, 'Ulysses S. Grant, Command and Control, and the Multi-domain Battlespace of the Future', Modern War Institute at West Point, 11 November 2018, https://mwi.usma.edu/ulysses-s-grant-command-control-multi-domain-battlespace-future/.

72 Nathaniel Bowditch's *American Practical Navigator*, originally published in 1802. See Ken Moriyasu, 'Pentagon Turns to the Stars to Survive China's Electronic Warfare', Nikkei Asia, 14 April 2021, https://asia.nikkei.com/Politics/International-relations/Indo-Pacific/Pentagon-turns-to-the-stars-to-survive-China-s-electronic-warfare; and Geoff Brumfiel, 'US Navy Brings Back Navigation by the Stars for Officers', NPR, 22 February 2016, https://www.npr.org/2016/02/22/467210492/u-s-navy-brings-back-navigation-by-the-stars-for-officers.

73 See Ori Brafman and Rod A. Beckstrom, *The Starfish and the Spider: The Unstoppable Power of Leaderless Organizations* (New York: Penguin, 2006). The author first drew on this analogy when discussing, along with two former colleagues, possible reforms to Taiwanese military structure. See Jim Thomas, John Stillion and Iskander Rehman, 'Hard ROC 2.0: Taiwan and Deterrence Through Protraction', Center for Strategic and Budgetary Assessments, 2014, https://csbaonline.org/uploads/

documents/2014-10-01_CSBA-TaiwanReport-1.pdf.

74 Christopher Dougherty, 'More than Half the Battle: Information and Command in a New American Way of War', Center for a New American Security, 2021, https://s3.amazonaws.com/files.cnas.org/CNAS+Report-Command+and+Info-2021.pdf.

75 See Roderick Lee, 'Building the Next Generation of Chinese Military Leaders', *Journal of Indo-Pacific Affairs*, 31 August 2020, https://www.airuniversity.af.edu/JIPA/Display/Article/2331143/building-the-next-generation-of-chinese-military-leaders/.

76 See Kevin McCauley, 'The People's Liberation Army Attempts to Jump Start Training Reforms', *China Brief*, vol. 21, no. 3, 11 February 2021, https://jamestown.org/program/the-peoples-liberation-army-attempts-to-jump-start-training-reforms/.

77 *Ibid*. For example, by designing a new 'intelligent training support planning system platform' providing 'automated analysis of support requirements, automated planning of support tasks, and automated matching of resources to requirements to provide precision support'. See also Ryan Pickrell, 'China Says Its Fighter Pilots are Battling Artificial-intelligence Aircraft in Simulated Dogfights, and Humans Aren't the Only Ones Learning', Business Insider, 15 June 2021, https://www.businessinsider.com/china-pits-fighter-pilots-against-ai-aircraft-in-simulated-dogfights-2021-6; and Andrew Tate, 'Chinese Air Force Applying Artificial Intelligence to Air Combat Training', *Janes Defense Weekly*, 16 June 2021.

78 See Riccardo Cociani, 'PLA Improving Officers' Skills and Training to Conduct Joint Operations', *Janes Defense Weekly*, 27 January 2021; and Elsa B. Kania and Ian Burns McCaslin, 'Learning Warfare from the Laboratory: China's Progression in Wargaming and Opposing Force Training', Institute for the Study of War, September 2021.

79 Professors Andrew Erickson and Ian Burns McCaslin thus noted in 2019 that 'even with an increased focus on educating joint commanders and theater command staff, joint experience remains a widely acknowledged weakness of the PLA as a whole. Officers complain that the lack of joint command experience could reduce its joint commanders to mere "armchair strategists". The 2015 book *Theater Joint Operations Command* suggested that the PLA should engage more in exchanges and exercises with foreign militaries to compensate for this lack of experience. However, despite increasing PLA participation in international military exercises, only a few of these (a mere seven percent from 2003–2016) involve two or more PLA services.' Andrew Erickson and Ian Burns McCaslin, 'The Impacts of Xi-era Reforms on the Chinese Navy', in Saunders et al. (eds), *Chairman Xi Remakes the PLA: Assessing Chinese Military Reforms*, ch. 3, https://ndupress.ndu.edu/Portals/68/Documents/Books/Chairman-Xi/Chairman-Xi.pdf.

80 Minnie Chan, 'China's Army Infiltrated by "Peace Disease" After Years Without a War, Says Its Official Newspaper', *South China Morning Post*, 3 July 2018, https://www.scmp.com/news/china/diplomacy-defence/article/2153579/chinas-army-infiltrated-peace-disease-after-years.

81 See 'PLA Tweaks Rules to Get Top Recruits', *ANI*, 28 January 2020, https://www.business-standard.com/article/news-ani/pla-tweaks-rules-to-get-top-recruits-120012801156_1.html; and Steve Sacks, 'China's Military Has a Weakness', *Diplomat*, 20 April 2021, https://thediplomat.

com/2021/04/chinas-military-has-a-hidden-weakness/. On some of the challenges inherent to China's tardy embrace of joint operations, see Joel Wuthnow, 'A Brave New World for Chinese Joint Operations', *Journal of Strategic Studies*, vol. 40, no. 1, 2017, pp. 169–95.

82 On China's belief in the advent of a new revolution in military affairs structured around 'intelligent technologies', see Ben Noon and Chris Bassler, 'How Chinese Strategists Think AI Will Power a Military Leap Ahead', Defense One, 17 September 2021, https://www.defenseone.com/ideas/2021/09/how-chinese-strategists-think-ai-will-power-military-leap-ahead/185409/; Kevin McCauley, 'Cultivating Joint Talent: PLA Education and Training Reforms', Foreign Military Studies Office, February 2023, https://fmso.tradoc.army.mil/2023/2023-02-10-cultivating-joint-talent-pla-education-and-training-reforms-kevin-mccauley/; and Koichiro Takagi, 'New Tech, New Concepts: China's Plans for AI and Cognitive Warfare', War on the Rocks, 13 April 2022, https://warontherocks.com/2022/04/new-tech-new-concepts-chinas-plans-for-ai-and-cognitive-warfare/.

83 See Joel Wuthnow, Phillip C. Saunders and Ian Burns McCaslin, 'PLA Overseas Operations in 2035: Inching Toward a Global Combat Capability', National Defense University, May 2021, https://ndupress.ndu.edu/Portals/68/Documents/stratforum/SF-309.pdf; and Jean-Pierre Cabestan, 'China's Evolving Role as a UN Peacekeeper in Mali', United States Institute of Peace, September 2018, https://www.usip.org/sites/default/files/2018-09/sr432-chinas-evolving-role-as-a-un-peacekeeper-in-mali.pdf.

84 Indian troops stationed along the contested Sino-Indian border, or Line of Actual Control, for example. See Snehashish Roy, 'Army Looks to Recruit Those Proficient in Mandarin', *Hindustan Times*, 11 July 2022, https://www.hindustantimes.com/india-news/army-looks-to-recruit-those-proficient-in-mandarin-101657478071435.html.

85 As of 2019, China was dependent on foreign imports for 72% of its oil needs, and 41% of its gas needs. See International Energy Agency, 'Oil, Gas and Coal Import Dependency in China, 2007–2019', 18 December 2020, https://www.iea.org/data-and-statistics/charts/oil-gas-and-coal-import-dependency-in-china-2007-2019. See also Vanand Meliksetian, 'China's Energy Dependence to Grow Despite Major Oil Discoveries', OilPrice.Com, 25 December 2020, https://oilprice.com/Energy/Energy-General/Chinas-Energy-Dependence-To-Grow-Despite-Major-Oil-Discoveries.html; and Scott B. Macdonald, 'China, Food Security and Geopolitics', *Diplomat*, 30 September 2020, https://thediplomat.com/2020/09/china-food-security-and-geopolitics/.

86 Andrew Erickson, 'Power vs. Distance: China's Global Maritime Interests and Investments in the Far Seas', in Ashley J. Tellis, Alison Szalwinski and Michael Wills (eds), *Strategic Asia 2019: China's Expanding Strategic Ambitions* (Washington DC: National Bureau of Asian Research, 2019), p. 262.

87 For an excellent recent examination of how Chinese naval thinkers are grappling with the issue of SLOC protection, see Jeffrey Becker, 'Securing China's Lifelines Across the Indian Ocean', China Maritime Studies Institute, December 2020, https://digital-commons.usnwc.edu/cgi/viewcontent.cgi?article=1010&context=cmsi-maritime-reports. On the PLAN's

vigorous attempts to amend weaknesses in ASW and shipborne air defence, see Ronald O'Rourke, 'China Naval Modernization: Implications for US Navy Capabilities – Background and Issues for Congress', Congressional Research Service, 15 May 2023, https://sgp.fas.org/crs/row/RL33153.pdf.

88 Isaac B. Kardon, 'China's Global Maritime Access: Alternatives to Overseas Military Bases in the Twenty-first Century', *Security Studies*, vol. 31, no. 5, 2022, pp. 885–916.

89 See Alan Rappeport, 'North Korea Secretly Shipped Munitions to Russia Through the Middle East and North Africa, the US Says', *New York Times*, 2 November 2022, https://www.nytimes.com/2022/11/02/world/europe/russia-ukraine-north-korea-ammunition.html; Julian Borger, 'Iranian Advisors Killed Aiding Russians in Crimea, Says Kyiv', *Guardian*, 24 November 2022, https://www.theguardian.com/world/2022/nov/24/iranian-military-advisers-killed-aiding-moscow-in-crimea-kyiv; and Julian E. Barnes, 'Iran Sends Drone Trainers to Crimea to Aid Russian Military', *New York Times*, 18 October 2022, https://www.nytimes.com/2022/10/18/us/politics/iran-drones-russia-ukraine.html.

90 Timothy R. Heath, 'China's Military Has No Combat Experience: Does It Matter?', RAND Commentary, 27 November 2018, https://www.rand.org/blog/2018/11/chinas-military-has-no-combat-experience-does-it-matter.html.

91 For an excellent account of the American Expeditionary Forces' (AEF) performance during the First World War, see Edward M. Coffman, *The War to End All Wars: The American Military in World War I* (Lexington, KY: University Press of Kentucky, 1968).

92 Mark Ethan Grotelueschen, *The AEF Way of War: The American Army and Combat in World War I*

(Cambridge: Cambridge University Press, 2006), p. 12.

93 On some of these efforts, see Jennifer McArdle, 'Simulating War: Three Enduring Lessons from the Louisiana Maneuvers', War on the Rocks, 17 March 2021, https://warontherocks.com/2021/03/simulating-war-three-enduring-lessons-from-the-louisiana-maneuvers/. On McNair's pivotal role in developing a 'training-based army', capable of continuously learning from its ongoing campaigns, see Mark T. Calhoun, *General Lesley J. McNair: Unsung Architect of the US Army* (Lawrence, KS: University Press of Kansas, 2015).

94 See Trent Hone, *Learning War: The Evolution of Fighting Doctrine in the U.S. Navy, 1898–1945* (Annapolis, MD: US Naval Institute Press, 2018); and Patrick Rose, 'Allies at War: British and US Command Culture in the Italian Campaign, 1943–44', *Journal of Strategic Studies*, vol. 36, no. 1, 2013, pp. 42–75.

95 See Caitlin Talmadge, *The Dictator's Army: Battlefield Effectiveness in Authoritarian Regimes* (Ithaca, NY: Cornell University Press, 2015), p. 32.

96 Merle L. Pribbenow thus points to the central role played by North Vietnamese commissars in shoring up morale and enhancing military effectiveness during *Operation Rolling Thunder* and the air raids against Hanoi in particular, noting that 'to them [the North Vietnamese], it was because of the commissars, not in spite of them, that North Vietnam survived the three-year long American air offensive'. See Merle L. Pribbenow II, 'The -Ology War: Technology and Ideology in the Vietnamese Defense of Hanoi, 1967', *The Journal of Military History*, vol. 67, no. 1, 2003, pp. 175–200.

97 Mimi Lau, 'PLA Orders Combat Officers and Commissars to Trade Places to Boost Fighting

Capability', *South China Morning Post*, 11 January 2015, https://www.scmp.com/news/china/article/1678525/pla-orders-combat-officers-and-commissars-trade-places-boost-fighting. PLA-attached political cadres are now forced to periodically rotate into more conventional command roles, and to acquire core military competencies ranging from 'operating equipment, communicating via networks, instructing by means of technology platforms, organizing training in the field, and commanding in battle'. See Clemens and Rosen, 'The Impact of Reform on the PLA's Political Work System'.

98 On how 'coup-proofing' and a constant focus on internal threats negatively affect authoritarian regimes' military performance, see James T. Quinlivan, 'Coup-proofing: Its Practice and Consequences in the Middle East', *International Security*, vol. 24, no. 2, 1999, pp. 131–65.

99 PLA Navy commander Admiral Wu Shengli employed this term in a 2014 speech. Citation from Ryan D. Martinson, 'Counter-intervention in Chinese Naval Strategy', *Journal of Strategic Studies*, vol. 44, no. 2, 2021, pp. 265–87.

100 See Food and Agriculture Organization of the United Nations (FAO), 'The State of Agricultural Commodity Markets: Food Self-sufficiency and International Trade: A False Dichotomy?', 2016, http://www.fao.org/3/i5222e/i5222e.pdf; and Nicole Narea, 'The US Won't Run Out of Food During the Coronavirus Pandemic', Vox, 18 April 2020, https://www.vox.com/2020/4/18/21222028/america-food-meat-supply-chain-coronavirus.

101 Approximately 20m versus 19.5m. See Lizzie Collingham, *Taste of War: World War II and the Battle for Food* (New York: The Penguin Press, 2012), p. 2.

102 See Jake Epstein, 'Russian Troops Are Stealing Farm Equipment and Targeting Grain Warehouses to Cause a Famine, Ukraine Alleges', Business Insider, 2 May 2022, https://www.businessinsider.com/russian-forces-targeting-grain-storage-to-cause-famine-ukraine-alleges-2022-5; and 'The Looming Food Catastrophe: Why Food Insecurity Is a Global Threat', *The Economist*, 19 July 2022.

103 See John Nash, 'Sea Power in the Peloponnesian War', *Naval War College Review*, vol. 71, no. 1, 2018, pp. 119–39; Peter Garnsey, *Famine and Food Supply in the Graeco-Roman World: Responses to Risk and Crisis* (Cambridge: Cambridge University Press, 1988); and Rodney Muhumuza, 'In Tigray, Food Is Often a Weapon of War as Famine Looms', Associated Press, 11 June 2021, https://apnews.com/article/only-on-ap-united-nations-africa-business-897bed43c6743c4575298ba5cf7bdd1c. For 'kicking in the belly', see Plutarch's description of Lucullus's ruthless scorched-earth campaigns during the decade-long Third Mithridatic War (73–63 BCE), Plutarch, *Life of Lucullus*, XI.1.45, Loeb Classical Library edition, 1914, https://penelope.uchicago.edu/Thayer/E/Roman/Texts/Plutarch/Lives/Lucullus*.html.

104 See 'How Is China Feeding Its Population of 1.4 Billion?', Center for Strategic and International Studies, 2017, https://chinapower.csis.org/china-food-security/.

105 See Daniela Sirtori, 'China Has Bought 37% of Next Year's Corn Imports Just from the U.S.', Bloomberg, 19 May 2021, https://www.bloomberg.com/news/articles/2021-05-19/china-has-bought-37-of-next-year-s-corn-imports-just-from-u-s; and Cissy Zhou, 'China Food Security: Why the Nation's "Food Crisis" Is More of a Livestock Feed Challenge', *South China Morning Post*, 27 April 2021,

https://www.scmp.com/economy/
china-economy/article/3131211/china-
food-security-why-nations-food-crisis-
more-livestock.

106 On China's shrinking proportion of
arable land, and its desperate efforts
to reverse desertification, see 'China's
Desert-taming "Green Great Wall"
Is Not as Great as it Sounds', *The
Economist*, 18 May 2019, https://www.
economist.com/china/2019/05/18/
chinas-desert-taming-green-great-
wall-is-not-as-great-as-it-sounds;
and Aiqi Chen et al., 'A Study on
the Arable Land Demand for Food
Security in China', *Sustainability*, vol.
11, no. 17, 2019, pp. 1–15.

107 See 'How Does Water Security Affect
China's Development?', Center for
Strategic and International Studies,
2020, https://chinapower.csis.org/
china-water-security/.

108 See Liu Mingtai and Zhou Hiuying,
'Effective Measures Adopted
to Protect Black Soil', *China
Daily*, 5 May 2021, https://www.
chinadaily.com.cn/a/202105/05/
WS6091d696a31024ad0babbf86_3.
html; 'President Xi Jinping Urges
the Protection of Black Soil', CGTN,
24 July 2020, https://news.cgtn.
com/news/2020-07-23/President-Xi-
Jinping-urges-to-protect-black-soil-
-SlW5ugkxeU/index.html; and Bella
Huang and Amy Quin, 'Xi Declares
War on Food Waste and China
Races to Tighten Its Belt', *New York
Times*, 21 August 2020, https://www.
nytimes.com/2020/08/21/world/asia/
china-food-waste-xi.html.

109 See Valerie Tan, 'Food Security Rises
as a Concern for China's Leadership',
Mercator Institute for China Studies,
2020, https://merics.org/en/analysis/
food-security-rises-concern-chinas-
leadership. An estimated 13m people
died during the Incredible Famine of
1876–9. On the Great Leap Forward
and the atrocious levels of misery and
starvation it engendered, see Kimberly

Ens Manning and Felix Wemheuer
(eds), *Eating Bitterness: New Perspectives
on China's Great Leap Forward and
Famine* (Vancouver: University of
British Columbia Press, 2011).

110 Nicholas Eberstadt, Derek Scissors
and Evan Abramsky, 'America Is
Petroleum-independent, for Now',
National Review, 18 March 2021,
https://www.nationalreview.com/
magazine/2021/04/05/america-is-
petroleum-independent-for-now/.

111 *Ibid.*

112 See 'In Fast-aging China, Elder Care
Costs Loom Large', VOA News, 23
May 2021, https://www.voanews.
com/a/east-asia-pacific_voa-news-
china_fast-aging-china-elder-care-
costs-loom-large/6206123.html.

113 See Laura Silver and Christine
Huang, 'Key Facts About China's
Declining Population', Pew Research
Center, 5 December 2022, https://
www.pewresearch.org/short-
reads/2022/12/05/key-facts-about-
chinas-declining-population/.

114 See Lily Kuo, 'China's Military Worries
that Its Only-child Recruits Are
"Wimps"', Quartz, 6 February 2014,
https://qz.com/174402/chinas-military-
worries-that-its-one-child-recruits-are-
wimps/; and Minnie Chan, 'Soldiers
of the One-child Era: Are They Too
Weak to Fulfill Beijing's Military
Ambitions?', *South China Morning
Post*, 5 February 2014, https://www.
scmp.com/news/china/article/1421451/
soldiers-one-child-era-are-they-too-
weak-fulfill-beijings-military.

115 Nicholas Eberstadt and Ashton
Verdery, 'China's Shrinking
Families: The Demographic
Trend that Could Curtail Beijing's
Ambitions', *Foreign Affairs*, 7 April
2021, https://www.foreignaffairs.
com/articles/china/2021-04-07/
chinas-shrinking-families.

116 Indeed, since the end of the
Cold War, 'the overall American
population and its number of

working-age people (between the ages of 20 and 64) have grown more rapidly than those of other developed countries'. See Nicholas Eberstadt, 'With Great Demographics Comes Great Power: Why Population Will Drive Geopolitics', *Foreign Affairs*, July/August 2019, https://www.foreignaffairs.com/articles/world/2019-06-11/great-demographics-comes-great-power; and Hal Brands, 'America's Big Advantage over China and Russia: Demographics', Bloomberg, 24 March 2019, https://www.bloomberg.com/opinion/articles/2019-03-24/america-s-big-advantage-over-china-and-russia-demographics.

[117] Rana Foroohar, 'Ageing Populations: A Midlife Crisis Takes Shape in the US', *Financial Times*, 16 May 2012, https://www.ft.com/content/a8431f77-653e-4091-856b-dd58a5867b40.

[118] Daniel J. Graeber, 'US Population Grew 0.4% amid Increases in Births, Migration', United Press International, 22 December 2022, https://www.upi.com/Top_News/US/2022/12/22/population-census-lifespan-covid19-birth-migration/3721671731358/; and United States Census Bureau, 'Growth in U.S. Population Shows Early Indication of Recovery amid COVID-19 Pandemic', 22 December 2022, https://www.census.gov/newsroom/press-releases/2022/2022-population-estimates.html.

[119] See Nicholas Eberstadt, 'America Hasn't Lost Its Demographic Advantage: Its Rivals Are in Much Worse Shape', *Foreign Affairs*, 24 May 2021, https://www.foreignaffairs.com/articles/united-states/2021-05-24/america-hasnt-lost-its-demographic-advantage.

[120] Krepinevich, 'Protracted Great-power War: A Preliminary Assessment', p. 40.

[121] See Edward Segal, '7 Crisis Management Lessons from Colonial Pipeline's Response to Cyber Attack', *Forbes*, 8 May 2021, https://www.forbes.com/sites/edwardsegal/2021/05/08/colonial-pipeline-cyber-attack-is-providing-crisis-management-lessons-in-real-time/?sh=308e27123d82.

[122] See Benjamin Mueller and Eleanor Lutz, 'U.S. Has Far Higher Covid Death Rate than Other Wealthy Countries', *New York Times*, 1 February, 2022, https://www.nytimes.com/interactive/2022/02/01/science/covid-deaths-united-states.html.

[123] See Ana Swanson, 'Coronavirus Spurs U.S. Efforts to End China's Chokehold on Drugs', *New York Times*, 11 March 2020, https://www.nytimes.com/2020/03/11/business/economy/coronavirus-china-trump-drugs.html.

[124] See Office of Senator Tina Smith, US Senator for Minnesota, 'Sens. Smith, Cotton and Reps. Craig, Mullin Introduce Bipartisan Legislation to Boost U.S. Pharmaceutical Manufacturing', 5 April 2022, https://www.smith.senate.gov/sens-smith-cotton-and-reps-craig-mullin-introduce-bipartisan-legislation-to-boost-u-s-pharmaceutical-manufacturing/. The 2022 America Competes Act also committed to increasing the domestic drug-manufacturing base and improve pharmaceutical production.

[125] Sydney Lupkin, 'Defense Production Act Speeds Up Vaccine Production', NPR, 13 March 2021, https://www.npr.org/sections/health-shots/2021/03/13/976531488/defense-production-act-speeds-up-vaccine-production.

[126] For an interesting academic examination of this phenomenon, see Yuval Feinstein, 'Rallying Around the President: When and Why Do Americans Close Ranks Behind Their Presidents During International Crisis and War?', *Social Science History*, vol. 40, no. 2, 2016, pp. 305–38.

127 See James T. Areddy, 'More Americans View China as a Threat, Poll Finds', *Wall Street Journal*, 28 April 2022; and Benjy Salrin and Sahil Kapur, 'Why China May Be the Last Bipartisan Issue Left in Washington', NBC News, 21 March 2021, https://www.nbcnews.com/politics/congress/why-china-may-be-last-bipartisan-issue-left-washington-n1261407. For a deeper discussion on the potentially disciplining effects of peer competition with China for US policymaking and grand strategy, see Iskander Rehman, 'Metus Hostilis: Sallust, American Grand Strategy, and the Disciplining Effects of Peer Competition with China', War on the Rocks, 3 May 2021, https://warontherocks.com/2021/05/metus-hostilis-sallust-american-grand-strategy-and-the-disciplining-effects-of-peer-competition-with-china/.

128 For a broader discussion of the numbing, anesthetising aspect of life under authoritarian rule, see Iskander Rehman, 'Thrones Wreathed in Shadow: Tacitus and the Psychology of Authoritarianism', War on the Rocks, 1 July 2020, https://warontherocks.com/2020/07/thrones-wreathed-in-shadow-tacitus-and-the-psychology-of-authoritarianism/. See also Max Fisher, 'China's Bystander Problem', *Washington Post*, 24 October 2013, https://www.washingtonpost.com/news/worldviews/wp/2013/10/24/chinas-bystander-problem-another-death-after-crowd-ignores-woman-in-peril/.

129 See Chris Buckley, Alexandra Stevenson and Keith Bradsher, 'From Zero COVID to No Plan: Behind China's Pandemic U-Turn', *New York Times*, 21 December 2022, https://www.nytimes.com/2022/12/19/world/asia/china-zero-covid-xi-jinping.html; and Elaine Chong, '"The Protests Awakened Us": Student Activists in China Speak Out – While the Government Relents', *Rolling Stone*, 11 December 2022, https://www.rollingstone.com/politics/politics-features/the-protests-awakened-us-student-activists-in-china-speak-out-1234644947/.

130 See Michael Martina and David Brunnstrom, 'China's Xi Unwilling to Accept Western Vaccines, U.S. Official Says', Reuters, 4 December 2022, https://www.reuters.com/world/china/chinas-xi-unwilling-accept-vaccines-despite-threat-protests-us-intel-2022-12-04/; and 'China's Failed Vaccine Nationalism', *Wall Street Journal*, 29 November 2022.

131 Sydney J. Freedberg Jr, 'WW II on Speed: Joint Staff Fears Long War', Breaking Defense, 11 January 2017, https://breakingdefense.com/2017/01/ww-ii-on-speed-joint-staff-fears-long-war/. It is estimated that the US merchant fleet currently has fewer than 80 commercial ships in international service, while China can boast more than 5,500. See Xiaoshan Xue, 'As China Expands Its Fleets, US Analysts Call for Catch-up Efforts', Voice of America, 13 September 2022, https://www.voanews.com/a/as-china-expands-its-fleets-us-analysts-call-for-catch-up-efforts-/6746352.html.

132 See 'Does China Pose a Threat to Global Rare Earth Supply Chains?', Center for Strategic and International Studies, 2021, https://chinapower.csis.org/china-rare-earths/.

133 See Doug Cameron and Gordon Lubold, 'U.S. Efforts to Arm Ukraine Shed Light on Limited Production Lines', *Wall Street Journal*, 28 April 2022, https://www.wsj.com/articles/u-s-efforts-to-arm-ukraine-shine-light-on-limited-production-lines-11651143601. On the return of 'industrial warfare' and the West's collective unpreparedness, see Alex Vershinin, 'The Return of Industrial Warfare', Royal United Services Institute, 17 June 2022, https://www.rusi.org/

explore-our-research/publications/
commentary/return-industrial-
warfare; and Steven Erlanger and
Lara Jakes, 'US and NATO Scramble
to Arm Ukraine and Refill Their
Own Stockpiles', *New York Times*, 29
November 2022, https://www.nytimes.
com/2022/11/26/world/europe/nato-
weapons-shortage-ukraine.html.

134 See 'Japan's Defense Ministry
Haunted by Ammo and Parts
Shortage', *Japan Times*, 1 November
2022, https://www.japantimes.co.jp/
news/2022/11/01/national/japan-
sdf-defense-ministry-shortages/;
and Elise Vincent, 'Macron Says
France Must Enter "War Economy"',
Announcing Military Budget
Re-evaluation', *Le Monde*, 14 June
2022, https://www.lemonde.fr/en/
france/article/2022/06/14/macron-
says-france-must-enter-war-economy-
announcing-military-budget-re-
evaluation_5986750_7.html.

135 Mykhaylo Zabrodskyi et al.,
'Preliminary Lessons in Conventional
Warfighting from Russia's Invasion
of Ukraine: February–July 2022',
Royal United Services Institute, 30
November 2022, https://rusi.org/
explore-our-research/publications/
special-resources/preliminary-lessons-
conventional-warfighting-russias-
invasion-ukraine-february-july-2022.
For a superlative analysis of the battle
for the Donbas – and the importance of
artillery therein – see Michael Kofman
and Rob Lee, 'How the Battle for the
Donbas Shaped Ukraine's Success',
Foreign Policy Research Institute, 23
December 2022, https://www.fpri.org/
article/2022/12/how-the-battle-for-the-
donbas-shaped-ukraines-success/.

136 On this, see Mark F. Cancian,
'Rebuilding U.S. Inventories: Six
Critical Systems', Center for Strategic
and International Studies, 9 January
2023, https://www.csis.org/analysis/
rebuilding-us-inventories-six-critical-
systems; and Dan Parson, 'Ukraine

Situation Report: Concerns Continue to
Loom over U.S. Weapons Stocks', The
Drive, 17 November 2022, https://www.
thedrive.com/the-war-zone/ukraine-
situation-report-concerns-continue-to-
loom-over-u-s-weapons-stocks.

137 See Mark F. Cancian et al., 'Industrial
Mobilization: Assessing Surge
Capabilities, Wartime Risk, and
System Brittleness', Center for
Strategic and International Studies,
January 2021, p. 2, https://csis-
website-prod.s3.amazonaws.com/
s3fs-public/publication/210108_
Cancian_Industrial_Mobilization.
pdf. See also US Department of
Defense, 'Industrial Capabilities
Report to Congress', 2018, https://
www.airandspaceforces.com/PDF/
DocumentFile/Documents/2019/
DOD-Annual-Industrial-Capabilities-
Report-to-Congress-for-FY-2018.pdf.

138 Richard Overy, *Blood and Ruins: The
Last Imperial War, 1931–1945* (New
York: Viking, 2021), p. 528.

139 *Ibid.*, p. 529.

140 *Ibid.*, p. 541.

141 See Andrew Stettner, 'The Great
Manufacturing Comeback
Could Save America', Business
Insider, 21 July 2022, https://
www.businessinsider.com/how-
manufacturing-factories-save-
america-economy-future-crappy-
service-jobs-2022-7.

142 *Ibid.*

143 US Department of Defense, 'Small
Business Strategy', January 2023,
https://media.defense.gov/2023/
Jan/26/2003150429/-1/-1/0/SMALL-
BUSINESS-STRATEGY.PDF.

144 See Mark Duggan and Rodrigo
Carril, 'The Impact of Industry
Consolidation on Government
Procurement: Evidence from DOD
Contracting', Stanford Institute for
Economic Policy Research, July
2018, https://siepr.stanford.edu/
publications/working-paper/impact-
industry-consolidation-government-

procurement-evidence-dod. As one recent DOD report notes, 'additional risks beyond pricing come with consolidation. Growing concentration can reduce the availability of key supplies and equipment, diminish vendors' incentives for innovation and performance in government contracts, and lead to supply chain vulnerabilities'. See Office of the Under Secretary of Defense for Acquisition and Sustainment, 'Department of Defense Report: State of Competition Within the Industrial Base', February 2022, pp. 5–6, https://media.defense.gov/2022/Feb/15/2002939087/-1/-1/1/STATE-OF-COMPETITION-WITHIN-THE-DEFENSE-INDUSTRIAL-BASE.PDF.

145 National Defense Industrial Association, 'Vital Signs 2023: Posturing the Defense Industrial Base for Great Power Competition', 2023, p. 13, https://www.ndia.org/policy/publications/vital-signs.

146 For a good recent overview of these challenges, see Eric Lipton, 'From Rockets to Ball Bearings: Pentagon Struggles to Feed War Machine', *New York Times*, 24 March 2023, https://www.nytimes.com/2023/03/24/us/politics/military-weapons-ukraine-war.html.

147 Sam LaGrone, 'Chinese Fleet Expansion Pushing U.S. Navy to Catch Up on Maintenance', USNI News, 20 September 2022, https://news.usni.org/2022/09/20/chinese-fleet-expansion-pushing-u-s-navy-to-catch-up-on-maintenance-as-backlogs-persist. For an excellent overview of the myriad crises currently affecting the US Navy, see Christopher Dougherty, 'Gradually and Then Suddenly: Explaining the Navy's Strategic Bankruptcy', War on the Rocks, 30 June 2021, https://warontherocks.com/2021/06/gradually-and-then-suddenly-explaining-the-navys-strategic-bankruptcy/.

148 Over the past 50 years, more than 14 battleship-producing shipyards have closed, while only one new shipyard has opened, leaving only seven Navy shipyards owned by four prime contractors. See United States Government Accountability Office, 'Defense Industrial Base: DOD Should Take Actions to Strengthen Its Risk Mitigation Approach', July 2022, https://s3.documentcloud.org/documents/22082094/defense-industrial-base-dod-should-take-actions-to-strengthen-its-risk-mitigation-approach-july-7-2022.pdf.

149 Megan Eckstein, 'US Navy Avoided a 2022 "Trough" in Submarine Fleet Size, but Industry Challenges Threaten Future Growth', Defense News, 3 January 2022, https://www.defensenews.com/naval/2022/01/03/us-navy-avoided-a-2022-trough-in-submarine-fleet-size-but-industry-challenges-threaten-future-growth/; and Anthony Capaccio, 'New US Nuclear-missile Submarines Hobbled by Billions in Growing Costs and Delays', Bloomberg, 8 June 2022, https://www.bloomberg.com/news/articles/2022-06-08/new-us-submarines-hobbled-by-billions-in-added-costs-and-delays.

150 See Ji Siqi, 'China Shipping: From Its Monopoly on Containers, to Its Critical Role in the Global Supply Chain', *South China Morning Post*, 10 November 2021, https://www.scmp.com/economy/global-economy/article/3155405/china-shipping-its-monopoly-containers-its-critical-role; and Commissioner Carl W. Bentzel, 'Assessment of P.R.C. Control of Container and Intermodal Chassis Manufacturing: Final Report', US Federal Maritime Trade Commission, March 2022, https://www.fmc.gov/wp-content/uploads/2022/03/ContainerandChassisManufacturingFinalReport.pdf. It is worth noting, in passing, that there is no universally accepted – or wholly

satisfactory – methodology for comparing the relative size of two navies. Commonly accepted approaches include not only total crewed-hull numbers, but also total full-load displacement of crewed hulls, or total number of missile tubes. When employing these two alternative metrics (overall tonnage and missile load-out), the US Navy can still boast a margin of superiority – albeit a diminishing one – over its fast-growing Chinese rival. See David Axe, 'Yes, the Chinese Navy Has More Ships than the U.S. Navy. But It's Got Far Fewer Missiles', Forbes, 10 November 2021, https://www.forbes.com/sites/davidaxe/2021/11/10/yes-the-chinese-navy-has-more-ships-than-the-us-navy-but-its-got-far-fewer-missiles/?sh=7e361bc761b6.

151 See Ronald O'Rourke, 'China Naval Modernization: Implications for U.S. Navy Capabilities – Background and Issues for Congress', Congressional Research Service, 2022, https://crsreports.congress.gov/product/pdf/RL/RL33153/265; Jack Bianchi et al., 'China's Choices: A New Tool for Assessing the PLA's Modernization', Center for Strategic and Budgetary Assessments, 14 July 2022, https://csbaonline.org/research/publications/chinas-choices-a-new-tool-for-assessing-the-plas-modernization; and US Department of Defense, 'Military and Security Developments Involving the People's Republic of China: Annual Report to Congress', 2022, p. 52

152 See US Navy, Naval Vessel Register, 'Ship Battle Forces', https://www.nvr.navy.mil/NVRSHIPS/SHIPBATTLEFORCE.HTML. For an overview of the US Navy's oft-fluctuating force level and shipbuilding plans, along with some of the vigorous debates these competing ambitions have engendered in recent years, see Congressional Research Service, 'Navy Force Structure and Shipbuilding Plans: Background and

Issues for Congress', 19 April 2023, https://sgp.fas.org/crs/weapons/RL32665.pdf; Congressional Budget Office, 'An Analysis of the Navy's Fiscal Year 2023 Shipbuilding Plan', November 2022, https://www.cbo.gov/publication/58745; and Lara Seligman, Lee Hudson and Paul McLeary, 'Inside the Pentagon Slugfest over the Future of the Fleet', Politico, 24 July 2022, https://www.politico.com/news/2022/07/24/pentagon-slugfest-navy-fleet-00047551.

153 See Paul McLeary, 'In War, Chinese Shipyards Could Outpace US in Replacing Losses; Marine Commandant', Breaking Defense, 17 June 2020; and Everett Pyatt, 'China Will Only Benefit from the US Navy's Shipbuilding Budget', Defense News, 4 June 2021, https://www.defensenews.com/opinion/commentary/2021/06/04/china-will-only-benefit-from-the-us-navys-shipbuilding-budget/.

154 Statement of Frederick J. Stefany, Assistant Secretary of the Navy (Research, Development and Acquisition), Acting and Vice Admiral Scott Conn, Deputy Chief of Naval Operations, Warfighting Requirements and Capabilities (OPNAV N9), and Lieutenant General Karsten S. Heckl, Deputy Commandant, Combat Development and Integration Commanding General, Marine Corps Combat Development Command, Before the Subcommittee on Seapower of the Senate Armed Services Committee on Department of the Navy Fiscal Year 2024 Budget Request for Seapower, 28 March 2023, https://www.armed-services.senate.gov/imo/media/doc/HS-28-Mar-2023-SASC-Seapower-Hearing%20on%20Shipbuilding%20Aviation%20Weapons%20US....pdf.

155 For an overview of the US Navy's uncrewed ambitions and desired 'hybrid' force-structure end state,

see US Department of the Navy, 'Unmanned Campaign Framework', 16 March 2021, https://www.navy. mil/Portals/1/Strategic/20210315%20 Unmanned%20Campaign_ Final_LowRes.pdf?ver=LtCZ-BPlWki6vCBTdgtDMA%3D%3D.

156 See Oishee Majumdar, 'China Looks to Bolster PLA's Logistics as Its Unmanned Systems Market Swells', *Janes Defence Weekly*, 29 April 2022, https://www.janes. com/defence-news/news-detail/ china-looks-to-bolster-plas-logistics-as-its-unmanned-systems-market-swells; Kristin Huang, 'China Showcases Never Before Seen Range of Unmanned Maritime Vehicles at Zhuhai Air Show', *South China Morning Post*, 13 November 2022, https://www.scmp.com/news/ china/military/article/3199399/ china-showcases-never-seen-range-unmanned-maritime-vehicles-zhuhai-air-show; and Ryan Fedasiuk, 'Leviathan Wakes: China's Growing Fleet of Autonomous Undersea Vehicles', CIMSEC, 17 August 2021, https://cimsec.org/leviathan-wakes-chinas-growing-fleet-of-autonomous-undersea-vehicles/.

157 See 'Mid-decade Challenges to National Competitiveness', Special Competitive Studies Project, September 2022, https://www.scsp.ai/ wp-content/uploads/2022/09/SCSP-Mid-Decade-Challenges-to-National-Competitiveness.pdf; and Zaheena Rasheed, 'How China Became the World's Leading Exporter of Combat Drones', Al Jazeera, 24 January 2023, https://www.aljazeera.com/ news/2023/1/24/how-china-became-the-worlds-leading-exporter-of-combat-drones.

158 See Sam LaGrone, 'Navy Wants 100 Unmanned Ships Monitoring Middle East Waters by Next Year', USNI News, 12 October 2022, https://news. usni.org/2022/10/11/navy-wants-100-unmanned-ships-monitoring-middle-east-waters-by-next-year; and Sam Dagher, 'US Navy Planning More "Robots at Sea" in Middle East to Combat Iran', Bloomberg, 5 May, 2023, https://www.bloomberg.com/ news/articles/2023-05-05/us-planning-more-robots-at-sea-in-middle-east-to-combat-iran#xj4y7vzkg.

159 Figures derived from US Department of Defense, 'Military and Security Developments Involving the People's Republic of China: Annual Report to Congress 2022'; and IISS, *The Military Balance* (Abingdon: Routledge for the IISS, 2023). See also Lt-Gen. Joseph Guastella et al., 'Accelerating 5th Generation Airpower: Bringing Capability and Capacity to the Merge', Mitchell Institute for Aerospace Studies Policy Paper, vol. 43, June 2023, p. 30, https://mitchellaerospacepower. org/wp-content/uploads/2023/06/ Accelerating_Fifth_Generation_ Airpower_Policy_Paper_43-FINAL.pdf.

160 See Stephen Losey, 'Fighter Fleet Is Strained – and Bill Is Coming Due, ACC Chief Says', Defense News, 23 September 2022, https://www. defensenews.com/air/2022/09/23/ fighter-fleet-is-strained-and-bill-is-coming-due-acc-chief-says/; and Dave Deptula, 'U.S. Cuts Pacific Airpower Presence as China's Military Grows', *Forbes*, 1 November 2022, https://www.forbes.com/sites/ davedeptula/2022/11/01/us-cuts-pacific-airpower-presence-as-chinas-military-grows/?sh=6f038b248bba. As of late 2022, the USAF had 2,123 tactical combat aircraft and 141 bombers in its inventory, in addition to around 140 manned intelligence, surveillance and reconnaissance (ISR); command, control and communications (C3), electronic warfare (EW) and electronic intelligence (ELINT) aircraft, along with hundreds of tankers, transports, special operations forces

(SOF) aircraft, unmanned aerial vehicles (UAVs), helicopters, etc. See IISS, *The Military Balance 2023*; and '2023 USAF & USSF Almanac: Equipment: Aircraft Total Active Inventory (TAI)', *Air & Space Forces Magazine*, 22 June 2023, https://www.airandspaceforces.com/article/2023-usaf-ussf-almanac-equipment/.

161 See Lt-Gen. Duke Z. Richardson, USAF, Lt-Gen. David S. Nahom, USAF and Lt-Gen. Joseph T. Guastella, USAF, 'Air Force, Force Structure and Modernization Programs', presentation to the Senate Armed Services Committee', 22 June 2022, p. 14, https://www.armed-services.senate.gov/imo/media/doc/SASC-AL%20Written%20Testimony_FINAL%20CLEARED%20(2).pdf; and Mark F. Cancian, 'U.S. Military Forces in FY 2022: Air Force', Center for Strategic and International Studies, 30 November, 2021, https://www.csis.org/analysis/us-military-forces-fy-2022-air-force.

162 See IISS, *The Military Balance 2023*; US Air Force, 'Statistical Digest, Fiscal Year 1991', https://media.defense.gov/2011/Apr/19/2001330028/-1/-1/0/AFD-110419-007.pdf; '2023 USAF & USSF Almanac: Equipment: Aircraft Total Active Inventory (TAI)'; and US Department of the Air Force, 'Fiscal Year 2024 Budget Overview', p. 43, https://www.saffm.hq.af.mil/Portals/84/documents/FY24/Budget/FY24%20Budget%20Overview%20Book.pdf?ver=JjFXW89XqB_YsIGx1wx4IA%3d%3d. See also David A. Deptula and Mark A. Gunziger, 'Decades of Air Force Underfunding Threaten America's Ability to Win', Mitchell Institute for Aerospace Studies, September 2022, https://mitchellaerospacepower.org/wp-content/uploads/2022/09/Decades_-of_Air_Force_Underfunding_-Policy_Paper_37-Final.pdf.

163 See Justin Katz, 'Delayed Again, Navy Won't Resolve Strike Fighter Shortfall Until 2031: Lawmaker', Breaking Defense, 27 April 2022, https://breakingdefense.com/2022/04/delayed-again-navy-wont-resolve-strike-fighter-shortfall-until-2031-lawmaker/.

164 Christopher Dougherty, 'Buying Time: Logistics for a New American Way of War', 13 April 2023, Center for a New American Security, https://www.cnas.org/publications/reports/buying-time.

165 See 'Statement of General Jacqueline D. Van Ovost, United States Air Force, Commander, United States Transportation Command, Before the House Armed Services Committee on the State of the Command', 28 March 2023, p. 14, https://armedservices.house.gov/sites/republicans.armedservices.house.gov/files/General%20Van%20Ovost%20Witness%20Statement.pdf.

166 See John Grady, 'TRANSCOM Commander: American Shipyards Need Revitalization to Help Modernize Military Sealift Command', USNI News, 4 February 2022, https://news.usni.org/2022/02/04/transcom-commander-american-shipyards-need-revitalization-to-help-modernize-military-sealift-command.

167 See Tyler Rogoway, 'Vital Logistics Ships Will Be Without Critical U.S. Navy Escorts in a Major Conflict', The Drive, 1 December 2019, https://www.thedrive.com/the-war-zone/24155/vital-logistics-ships-will-be-without-critical-u-s-navy-escorts-in-a-major-conflict; and David B. Larter, '"You're on Your Own": US Sealift Can't Count on Navy Escorts in the Next Big War', Defense News, 10 October 2018, https://www.defensenews.com/naval/2018/10/10/youre-on-your-own-us-sealift-cant-count-on-us-navy-escorts-in-the-next-big-war-forcing-changes/?utm_medium=social&utm_

campaign=Socialflow+DFN&utm_source=twitter.com.

168 Anushu Siripurapu and Noah Berman, 'Is Industrial Policy Making a Comeback?', Council on Foreign Relations, 18 November 2022, https://www.cfr.org/backgrounder/industrial-policy-making-comeback; and 'Special Report: The New Interventionism: Many Countries Are Seeing a Revival of Industrial Policy', *The Economist*, 10 January 2022.

169 This effort has been undertaken under both the Trump and Biden administrations, further underscoring the cross-partisan nature of the threat perception. See, for example, The White House, 'Executive Order on Securing Information and Communications Technology and Services Supply Chain', 15 May 2019, https://trumpwhitehouse.archives.gov/presidential-actions/executive-order-securing-information-communications-technology-services-supply-chain/; and The White House, 'Fact Sheet: Securing a Made in America Supply Chain for Critical Minerals', February 2022, https://www.whitehouse.gov/briefing-room/statements-releases/2022/02/22/fact-sheet-securing-a-made-in-america-supply-chain-for-critical-minerals/. The term 'friendshoring' refers to the attempt to relocate critical supply chains to more friendly, or less hostile, nations. See Sarah Kessler, 'What Is "Friendshoring"?', *New York Times*, 18 November 2022, https://www.nytimes.com/2022/11/18/business/friendshoring-jargon-business.html.

170 Demetri Sevastopulo and Sam Fleming, 'Netherlands and Japan Join US in Restricting Chip Exports to China', *Financial Times*, 27 January 2023, https://www.ft.com/content/baa27f42-0557-4377-839b-a4f4524cfa20.

171 Gabriel Dominguez, 'Potentially Divided U.S. Congress to Remain United on at Least One Issue: China', *Japan Times*, 10 November 2022, https://www.japantimes.co.jp/news/2022/11/10/world/politics-diplomacy-world/china-policy-us-new-congress/.

172 For a good overview of the Clawback Clause, see 'President Biden Signs CHIPS and Science Act into Law', White and Case, 12 August 2022, https://www.whitecase.com/insight-alert/president-biden-signs-chips-and-science-act-law.

173 See Ana Swanson, 'Biden Administration Clamps Down on China's Access to Chip Technology', *New York Times*, 7 October 2022, https://www.nytimes.com/2022/10/07/business/economy/biden-chip-technology.html.

174 Iori Kawate and Shoya Okinaga, 'China Limits Exports of Chipmaking Metals in Trade Spat with U.S.', *Nikkei Asia*, 4 July 2023, https://asia.nikkei.com/Business/Tech/Semiconductors/China-limits-exports-of-chipmaking-metals-in-trade-spat-with-U.S.

175 The White House, 'Executive Order (14105) on Addressing United States Investments in Certain National Security Technologies and Products in Countries of Concern', 9 August 2023, https://www.whitehouse.gov/briefing-room/presidential-actions/2023/08/09/executive-order-on-addressing-united-states-investments-in-certain-national-security-technologies-and-products-in-countries-of-concern/. For 'technologies critical to the next generation of military innovation', see US Department of the Treasury, 'Press Release: Treasury Seeks Public Comment on Implementation of Executive Order Addressing U.S. Investments in Certain National Security Technologies and Products in Countries of Concern', 9 August 2023, https://home.treasury.gov/news/press-releases/jy1686.

176 See Executive Order (14105) on Addressing United States Investments in Certain National Security Technologies and Products in Countries of Concern.

177 See Gordon Lubold, Doug Cameron and Nancy A. Youssef, 'U.S. Effort to Arm Taiwan Faces New Challenge with Ukraine Conflict', *Wall Street Journal*, 17 November 2022, https://www.wsj.com/articles/u-s-effort-to-arm-taiwan-faces-new-challenge-with-ukraine-conflict-11669559116.

178 See Bill Greenwalt, 'FTC Activism and Ukraine Signal a New Era for the US Defense Industrial Base', Breaking Defense, 10 August 2022, https://breakingdefense.com/2022/08/ftc-activism-and-ukraine-signal-a-new-era-for-the-us-defense-industrial-base/; and Doug Cameron, 'Lagging Arms Production Makes Pentagon Wary of Further Industry Consolidation', *Wall Street Journal*, 3 January 2023, https://www.wsj.com/articles/lagging-arms-production-makes-pentagon-wary-of-further-industry-consolidation-11672754128.

179 See David Vergun, 'Defense Official Speaks on Supply Chain Investments', DOD News, 7 September 2022, https://www.defense.gov/News/News-Stories/Article/Article/3151356/defense-official-speaks-on-supply-chain-investments/. It is worth drawing attention, here in passing, to the critical role played by Congress on the issue of multi-year munitions contracting, in the form of the emergency munitions provision of the National Defense Authorizations Act (NDAA) for Fiscal Year 2023. See Bryant Harris, 'Congress Supersizes Munitions Production with Emergency Authorities', Defense News, 13 December 2022, https://www.defensenews.com/congress/budget/2022/12/13/congress-supersizes-munitions-production-with-emergency-authorities/.

180 See the excellent and comprehensive report, Bryan Clark, Timothy A. Walton and Adam Lemon, 'Strengthening the U.S. Defense Maritime Industrial Base: A Plan to Improve Maritime Industry's Contribution to National Security', Center for Strategic and Budgetary Assessments, 12 February 2020, https://csbaonline.org/research/publications/strengthening-the-u.s-defense-maritime-industrial-base-a-plan-to-improve-maritime-industrys-contribution-to-national-security.

181 See US Department of Transportation Maritime Administration, 'Having a Reliable Logistics Systems Wins Wars for the Nation', 2022, https://www.maritime.dot.gov/sites/marad.dot.gov/files/2022-02/MARAD_MSPVISA_Pamphlet_Web.pdf.

182 See David B. Larter, 'The US Military Ran the Largest Stress Test of Its Sealift Fleet in Years. It's in Big Trouble', Defense News, 31 December 2019, https://www.defensenews.com/naval/2019/12/31/the-us-military-ran-the-largest-stress-test-of-its-sealift-fleet-in-years-its-in-big-trouble/; and Jeremy Greenwood and Emily Miletello, 'To Expand the Navy Isn't Enough: We Need a Bigger Commercial Fleet', Brookings Institution, 4 November 2021, https://www.brookings.edu/blog/order-from-chaos/2021/11/04/to-expand-the-navy-isnt-enough-we-need-a-bigger-commercial-fleet/.

183 The Shipyard Act Bill, introduced in the 117th Congress (2021–22) by Senator Roger Wicker of Mississippi, was co-sponsored by 17 other senators (one Independent, nine Democrats and seven fellow Republicans). For more details on the bill, see 'S.1441 – Shipyard Act', 117th Congress 2021–2022, https://www.congress.gov/bill/117th-congress/senate-bill/1441?r=100&s=1.

184 See, for instance, the various recommendations nested in the recently updated doctrinal

publication of the US Marine Corps on logistics. United States Marine Corps Headquarters, 'MCDP 4: Logistics', 21 March 2023, https://www.marines.mil/News/Publications/MCPEL/Electronic-Library-Display/Article/899840/mcdp-4/.

185 See, for example, Kyle Mizoami, 'The Navy Is Using 3D Printers to Turn Warships into Weapons Factories', *Popular Mechanics*, 12 July 2022, https://www.popularmechanics.com/military/a40577952/navy-3d-printing-spares-drone-parts/.

186 See Sam LaGrone, 'Unmanned Supply Drones, Forward Basing Key to Marines' New Logistics Plan', USNI News, 24 February 2023, https://news.usni.org/2023/02/23/unmanned-supply-drones-forward-basing-key-to-marines-new-logistics-plan; and Inder Singh Bisht, 'US Navy Demonstrates Unmanned Cargo Delivery to Moving Ship', Defense Post, 7 December 2022, https://www.thedefensepost.com/2022/12/27/us-navy-unmanned-cargo-delivery/.

187 Larry M. Wortzel, 'Military Mobilization in Communist China', Association of the United States Army Land Warfare Paper 136, December 2020, https://www.ausa.org/publications/military-mobilization-communist-china. See also Larry Wortzel, 'The Limitations of Military–Civil Mobilization: Problems with Funding and Clashing Interests in Industry-based PLA Reserve Units', *China Brief*, vol. 19, no. 18, 8 October 2019, pp. 13–24.

188 For 'architecture for whole-of nation mobilization', see Elsa B. Kania and Emma Moore, 'The US Is Unprepared to Mobilize for Great Power Conflict', Defense One, 21 July 2019, https://www.defenseone.com/ideas/2019/07/us-unprepared-mobilize-great-power-conflict/158560/. On the issue of competitive mobilisation, see also Robert Haddick, 'Competitive Mobilization: How Would We Fare Against China?', War on the Rocks, 15 March 2016, https://warontherocks.com/2016/03/competitive-mobilization-how-would-we-fare-against-china/.

189 See Thomas Novelly, 'Even More Young Americans Are Unfit to Serve, a New Study Finds. Here's Why', Military.com, 28 September 2022, https://www.military.com/daily-news/2022/09/28/new-pentagon-study-shows-77-of-young-americans-are-ineligible-military-service.html; and 'America's Army Has Launched a Scheme to Slim Down Its Recruits', *The Economist*, 12 January 2023.

190 See Stef W. Kight, 'Study: Immigrants and Their Kids Founded 45% of Fortune 500 Companies', Axios, 22 July 2019, https://www.axios.com/2019/07/22/immigrants-founders-fortune-500-companies.

191 See William R. Kerr, 'Global Talent and U.S. Immigration Policy', Harvard Business School Working Paper 20-107, 2020, https://www.hbs.edu/ris/Publication%20Files/20-107_0967f1ab-1d23-4d54-b5a1-c884234d9b31.pdf. On the percentage of college-educated migrants, see the detailed analysis, looking primarily at 1990–2010, in Sari Pekkala Kerr et al., 'Global Talent Flows', *Journal of Economic Perspectives*, vol. 30, no. 4, 2016, pp. 83–106. On Nobel Prize-winning immigrants in the US, see 'Immigrants and Nobel Prizes 1901–2021', National Foundation for American Policy, 2021, https://nfap.com/wp-content/uploads/2021/10/Immigrants-and-Nobel-Prizes-1901-to-2021.NFAP-Policy-Brief.October-2021.pdf; and William R. Kerr, *The Gift of Global Talent: How Migration Shapes Business, Economy and Society* (Stanford, CA: Stanford University Press, 2018), pp. 22–4, which analyses Nobel Prize recipient data from the prize's creation to 2016.

192 See '2022 Silicon Valley Index', https://jointventure.org/download-the-2022-index.

193 Drew Desilver, 'U.S. Students' Academic Achievement Still Lags That of Their Peers in Many Other Countries', Pew Research Center, 15 February 2017, https://www.pewresearch.org/fact-tank/2017/02/15/u-s-students-internationally-math-science/.

194 Remco Zwetsloot et al., 'China Is Fast Outpacing U.S. STEM PhD Growth', Center for Security and Emerging Technology, August 2021, https://cset.georgetown.edu/publication/china-is-fast-outpacing-u-s-stem-phd-growth/.

195 National Security Commission on Artificial Intelligence, 'Final Report', March 2021, https://www.nscai.gov/wp-content/uploads/2021/03/Full-Report-Digital-1.pdf, p. 368.

196 US Department of Defense, 'Industrial Capabilities Report to Congress: Fiscal Year 2020', January 2021, https://media.defense.gov/2021/Jan/14/2002565311/-1/-1/0/FY20-INDUSTRIAL-CAPABILITIES-REPORT.PDF.

197 For a broader discussion of this issue, see Iskander Rehman, 'Battling for the Best and Brightest: Immigration, Great Power Rivalry, and the History of Talent Importation', Engelsberg Ideas, 12 May 2022, https://engelsbergideas.com/essays/battling-for-the-best-and-brightest-immigration-great-power-rivalry-and-the-history-of-talent-importation/.

198 See Lindsey W. Ford and James Goldgeier, 'Retooling America's Alliances to Manage the China Challenge', Brookings Institution, 25 January 2021, https://www.brookings.edu/articles/retooling-americas-alliances-to-manage-the-china-challenge/.

199 See Japanese Prime Minister Kishida Fumio's comments on the broader ramifications of Russia's invasion of Ukraine in Josh Rogin, 'Japan's Prime Minister Warns of a Historic – and Dangerous – Moment in Asia', *Washington Post*, 11 January 2023, https://www.washingtonpost.com/opinions/2023/01/11/japan-prime-minister-rearmament-china-north-korea/; and 'In Rare Stand, South Korea, Singapore Unveil Sanctions on Russia', Al Jazeera, 28 February 2022, https://www.aljazeera.com/economy/2022/2/28/in-rare-stand-south-korea-singapore-unveil-sanctions-on-russia.

200 Jason Horowitz and Catherine Porter, 'Even as Challenges Mount, Europeans Stick by Ukraine', *New York Times*, 7 November 2022, https://www.nytimes.com/2022/11/07/world/europe/europe-ukraine-war-support.html.

201 See the detailed findings in Laura Silver, Christine Huang and Laura Clancy, 'How Global Public Opinion of China Has Shifted in the Xi Era', Pew Research Center, 28 September 2022, https://www.pewresearch.org/global/2022/09/28/how-global-public-opinion-of-china-has-shifted-in-the-xi-era/.

202 See Zhen Han and Mihaela Papa, 'Alliances in Chinese International Relations: Are They Ending or Rejuvenating?', *Asian Security*, vol. 17, no. 2, 2020, pp. 158–77; and Lindsey Ford, 'Network Power: China's Effort to Reshape Asia's Regional Security Architecture', Brookings Institution, September 2020, https://www.brookings.edu/wp-content/uploads/2020/09/FP_20200914_china_network_power_ford.pdf. On China's perception of the encircling threat posed by the US alliance system in Asia, see Adam P. Liff, 'China and the US Alliance System', *The China Quarterly*, vol. 233, 2018, pp. 137–65. On the Xi-era concept of a 'new type of security partnership', more flexible and transactional than traditional alliances, see Alice Ekman, 'China's "New Type

of Security Partnership" in Asia and Beyond: A Challenge to the Alliance System and "Indo-Pacific" Strategy', Elcano Royal Institute, 26 March 2019, https://www.realinstitutoelcano.org/en/analyses/chinas-new-type-of-security-partnership-in-asia-and-beyond-a-challenge-to-the-alliance-system-and-the-indo-pacific-strategy/.

203 See Emma Helfrich and Tyler Rogoway, 'U.S. Building Advanced Over-the-horizon Radar on Palau', The Drive, 30 December 2022, https://www.thedrive.com/the-war-zone/u-s-building-advanced-over-the-horizon-radar-on-palau; and 'U.S. Military Poised to Return to Subic Bay, Counter China's Presence', Kyodo News, 24 November 2022, https://english.kyodonews.net/news/2022/11/34dad3ba3fae-us-military-poised-to-return-to-subic-bay-counter-chinas-presence.html.

204 On the China–Russia relationship, see Artyom Lukin, 'The Russia–China Entente and Its Future', *International Politics*, vol. 58, 2021, pp. 363–80; Stephen Blank, 'The Un-holy Russo-Chinese Alliance', *Defense and Security Analysis*, vol. 36, no. 3, 2020, pp. 249–74; and Alexander Korolev, 'On the Verge of an Alliance: Contemporary China–Russia Military Cooperation', *Asian Security*, vol. 15, no. 3, 2019, pp. 233–52.

205 See Cortney Weinbaum et al., 'Assessing Systemic Strengths and Vulnerabilities of China's Defense Industrial Base', RAND Corporation, 2022, https://www.rand.org/pubs/research_reports/RRA930-1.html. See also Andrew S. Erickson and Gabriel B. Collins, 'Putin's Ukraine Invasion: Turbocharging Sino-Russian Collaboration in Energy, Maritime Security and Beyond?', *Naval War College Review*, vol. 75, no. 4, 2022, pp. 91–125.

206 Erickson and Collins, 'Putin's Ukraine Invasion: Turbocharging Sino-Russian Collaboration in Energy, Maritime Security and Beyond?', p. 109.

207 Russia, as the world's largest wheat exporter, has already emerged as a major supplier of grain to China. See 'China Lifts Restrictions on Imports of Russian Wheat, Barley', Reuters, 4 February 2022, https://www.reuters.com/article/russia-china-grains-idAFL1N2UF10Y. See also 'Russia Becomes China's Top Oil Supplier amid Ukraine War Sanctions', *Guardian*, 20 June 2022, https://www.theguardian.com/business/2022/jun/20/russia-becomes-chinas-top-oil-supplier-amid-ukraine war sanctions.

208 For 'Eurasian nightmare', see Hal Brands, 'The Eurasian Nightmare: Chinese–Russian Convergence and the Future of American Order', *Foreign Affairs*, 25 February 2022, https://www.foreignaffairs.com/articles/china/2022-02-25/eurasian-nightmare. On the emergence of Chinese and Russian 'fortress economics' and its future consequences, see David Lubin, 'Huge Impact of Fortress Economics', Chatham House, 2 February 2022, https://www.chathamhouse.org/2022/02/huge-impact-fortress-economics-russia-and-china. For Mackinder's famous ruminations on the Eurasian 'pivot area' and 'world island', see H.J. Mackinder, 'The Geographical Pivot of History', *The Geographical Journal*, vol. 23, no. 4, 1904, pp. 421–37.

209 On the Macedon–Carthage alliance, see Pedro Barcelo, 'Punic Politics, Economy, and Alliances, 218–201', in Dexter Hoyos (ed.), *A Companion to the Punic Wars* (Oxford: Wiley-Blackwell, 2010), ch. 20.

210 See Sushant Singh, 'The Challenge of a Two-front War: India's China–Pakistan Dilemma', Stimson Center, 19 April 2021, https://www.stimson.org/2021/the-challenge-of-a-two-front-war-indias-china-pakistan-dilemma/.

211 Patrick Wintour, 'Recall of
Ambassadors Indicates Extent of
Aukus Anger in France', *Guardian*,
18 September 2021, https://www.
theguardian.com/world/2021/sep/18/
french-recall-of-ambassadors-indicates-
extent-of-anger-over-aukus-rift.

212 For detailed recommendations on
how to better integrate allies into
the United States' evolving defence
strategy and concepts of operation,
see Stacie L. Pettyjohn and Becca
Wasser, 'No.1 in Team: Integrated
Deterrence with Allies and Partners',
Center for a New American Security,
14 December 2022, https://www.
cnas.org/press/press-release/new-
cnas-report-no-i-in-team-integrated-
deterrence-with-allies-and-partners;
and Todd Harrison and Christopher
Reid, 'Battle Networks and the
Future Force, Part 3: The Role of
Allies and Partners', Center for
Strategic and International Studies,
2022, https://www.csis.org/analysis/
battle-networks-and-future-force-1.

213 See John A. Tirpak, 'US and Partners
Now Moving Toward Interchangeable
– Not Just Interoperable – Weapons',
Air and Space Forces Magazine, 30
September 2022, https://www.
airandspaceforces.com/us-and-
partners-now-moving-toward-
interchangeable-not-just-interoperable-
weapons/; and 'U.S. Considering Joint
Weapons Production with Taiwan',
Reuters, 19 October 2022, https://
www.reuters.com/world/asia-pacific/
us-government-considering-joint-
production-weapons-with-taiwan-
nikkei-2022-10-19/. The Naval
Strike Missile, jointly produced by
Kongsberg and Raytheon, provides
one particularly positive example
of allied weapon co-production. See
Megan Eckstein, 'Kongsberg, Raytheon
Ready to Keep Up as Naval Strike
Missile Demand Grows', Defense
News, 27 October 2021, https://www.
defensenews.com/naval/2021/10/27/
kongsberg-raytheon-ready-to-keep-up-
as-naval-strike-missile-demand-grows/.

214 See Australian Government,
Department of Foreign Affairs
and Trade, 'Joint Statement on
Australia–United States Ministerial
Consultations (AUSMIN) 2023', 29
July 2023, https://www.dfat.gov.
au/news/news/joint-statement-
australia-united-states-ministerial-
consultations-ausmin-2023.

215 See Dougherty, 'Buying Time:
Logistics for a New American Way
of War'; and Lt. Katherine Serrano,
'U.S., Japan, Australia Integrate
Allied Logistics During Trilateral
Operations', PACOM News, 21
November 2022, https://www.pacom.
mil/Media/News/News-Article-View/
Article/3225183/us-japan-australia-
integrate-allied-logistics-during-tri-
lateral-operations/.

216 As General Charles Flynn and Lt-Col.
Sarah Starr candidly observe, 'and
should conflict come, the presence
built by rotational forces building
interior lines may make all the
difference. A country that does not
already host U.S. forces may not,
for example, agree to U.S. requests
to launch missiles or aircraft from
within its borders. … But ally and
partner decision-making changes
if the U.S. already has forces on the
ground – say, for an exercise.' General
Charles Flynn and Lt-Col. Sarah
Starr, 'Interior Lines Will Make Land
Power the Asymmetric Advantage
in the Indo-Pacific', Defense One, 15
March 2023, https://www.defenseone.
com/ideas/2023/03/interior-lines-
will-make-land-power-asymmetric-
advantage-indo-pacific/384002/.

217 The three largest shipbuilding
nations in the world in 2022, based
on deliveries in millions of gross
tons, were China (36.7), South
Korea (23.7) and Japan (15.6). See
'Largest Shipbuilding Nations in
2022, Based on Deliveries', Statista,

7 June 2023, https://www.statista.
com/statistics/263895/shipbuilding-
nations-worldwide-by-cgt/.

218 See Lt. Jeong Soo Kim, 'Use Allies in
Shipyard Modernization', US Naval
Institute, *Proceedings*, vol. 149, no.
5, May 2023, https://www.usni.org/
magazines/proceedings/2023/may/use-
allies-shipyard-modernization; and
Rahm Emanuel, 'Japan Is Ready and
Able to Maintain U.S. Naval Vessels',
Wall Street Journal, 11 July 2023, https://
www.wsj.com/articles/japan-able-
maintain-america-naval-vessels-repair-
shipyards-pacific-e2bfd39b.

219 For some useful background on
the US Navy's frequent practice
of engaging in long-term leases of
foreign cargo vessels, see Ronald O'
Rourke, 'DOD Leases of Foreign-built
Ships: Background for Congress',
Congressional Research Service, 18
January 2011, https://apps.dtic.mil/sti/
pdfs/AD1171867.pdf.

220 On the urgent need to promote
a new US-led free-trade agenda
in Asia, see 'Biden's No-show on
Trade Deals Risks Isolating Friend
in Asia', Bloomberg, 11 May 2022,
https://www.bloomberg.com/news/
articles/2022-05-11/biden-s-fear-of-
free-trade-deals-risks-isolating-friends-
in-asia#xj4y7vzkg; and Bob Davis,
'Biden Promised to Confront China.
First He Has to Confront America's
Bizarre Trade Politics', Politico, 31
January 2022, https://www.politico.
com/news/magazine/2022/01/31/
biden-china-trade-politics-00003379.

221 See Victor Cha, 'Seeking a "Win–
Win" Solution on the Inflation
Reduction Act for Korea', Center for
Strategic and International Studies,
6 December 2022, https://www.
csis.org/analysis/seeking-win-win-
solution-inflation-reduction-act-korea;
and Olivier Knox and Caroline
Anders, 'Europe's Not Happy with
Biden's Inflation Reduction Act',
Washington Post, 17 January 2023,
https://www.washingtonpost.
com/politics/2023/01/17/europe-
not-happy-with-bidens-inflation-
reduction-act/?utm_source=rss&utm_
medium=referral&utm_
campaign=wp_homepage.

Conclusion

1 See 'China's Xi Tells Putin of
"Changes Not Seen for 100 Years"', Al
Jazeera, 22 March 2023, https://www.
aljazeera.com/news/2023/3/22/xi-tells-
putin-of-changes-not-seen-for-100.

2 Both in his correspondence with
Truman, and in his comments to
congressional leaders. See Robert L.
Beisner, *Dean Acheson: A Life in the
Cold War* (Oxford: Oxford University
Press, 2006), p. 56.

3 See 'America's Economic
Outperformance Is a Marvel to
Behold', *The Economist*, 13 April 2023.

INDEX

Six *Adelphi* numbers are published each year by Routledge Journals, an imprint of Taylor & Francis, 4 Park Square, Milton Park, Abingdon, Oxfordshire OX14 4RN, UK.

A subscription to the institution print edition, ISSN 1944-5571, includes free access for any number of concurrent users across a local area network to the online edition, ISSN 1944-558X. Taylor & Francis has a flexible approach to subscriptions enabling us to match individual libraries' requirements. This journal is available via a traditional institutional subscription (either print with free online access, or online-only at a discount) or as part of our libraries, subject collections or archives. For more information on our sales packages please visit www.tandfonline.com/page/librarians.

2023 Annual *Adelphi* Subscription Rates			
Institution	£973	US$1,707	€1,439
Individual	£333	US$571	€457
Online only	£827	US$1,451	€1,223

Dollar rates apply to subscribers outside Europe. Euro rates apply to all subscribers in Europe except the UK and the Republic of Ireland where the pound sterling price applies. All subscriptions are payable in advance and all rates include postage. Journals are sent by air to the USA, Canada, Mexico, India, Japan and Australasia. Subscriptions are entered on an annual basis, i.e., January to December. Payment may be made by sterling cheque, dollar cheque, international money order, National Giro, or credit card (Amex, Visa, Mastercard).

For a complete and up-to-date guide to Taylor & Francis journals and books publishing programmes, and details of advertising in our journals, visit our website: **http://www.tandfonline.com.**

Ordering information:
USA/Canada: Taylor & Francis Inc., Journals Department, 530 Walnut Street, Suite 850, Philadelphia, PA 19106, USA. **UK/Europe/Rest of World:** Routledge Journals, T&F Customer Services, T&F Informa UK Ltd., Sheepen Place, Colchester, Essex, CO3 3LP, UK.

Advertising enquiries to:
USA/Canada: The Advertising Manager, Taylor & Francis Inc., 530 Walnut Street, Suite 850, Philadelphia, PA 19106, USA. Tel: +1 (800) 354 1420. Fax: +1 (215) 207 0050. **UK/Europe/Rest of World**: The Advertising Manager, Routledge Journals, Taylor & Francis, 4 Park Square, Milton Park, Abingdon, Oxfordshire OX14 4RN, UK. Tel: +44 (0) 20 7017 6000. Fax: +44 (0) 20 7017 6336.